GANGS (
THE MAKING C

Off the brand management and marketing wagon, Jigna Kothari turned entrepreneur with Natraj Creations/the WORD to provide qualitative research and niche-writing services where her credits include working on *The Making of Om Shanti Om* and *Still Reading Khan*. In 2012, she co-authored *Mother Maiden Mistress: Women in Hindi Cinema 1950 to 2010*, with Bhawana Somaaya and Supriya Madangarli and despite being left a whole lot wiser decided to go ahead and write this book.

*

After fifteen years as a writer in print media, with stints at *Mid-Day* and *Hindustan Times*, Supriya Madangarli has spent the past eight years researching and writing for the WORD where her projects included *The Making of Om Shanti Om* and *Still Reading Khan*. Her area of interest is gender and film studies, specifically when the two converge. She is the co-author of *Mother Maiden Mistress: Women in Hindi Cinema 1950 to 2010*, with Bhawana Somaaya and Jigna Kothari.

Praise for *Gangs of Wasseypur*

'*Gangs of Wasseypur* is a sprawling, exuberant, ferociously ambitious piece of film making, which hits most of its marks. A savagely uncompromising cracker of a tale. Anurag Kashyap, the storyteller whose skills are on full display in this film, is back' – Shubhra Gupta, *Indian Express*

'Robust storytelling, crackling performances and thick textures. It's an irresistible cocktail' – Sanjukta Sharma, livemint.com

'Though it runs over five hours, there's never a dull moment in this Indian gangland epic by one of India's hottest indie directors, Anurag Kashyap. Oozing visual style, laced with tight and often blackly comic dialogue, bolstered by tasty performances and a driving neo-Bollywood soundtrack, this Tarantino-tinged Bihari take on *The Godfather* has what it takes to cross over from the Indian domestic and Diaspora markets to reach out to action-loving, gore-tolerant theatrical and auxiliary genre audiences worldwide' – Lee Marshall, *Screen Daily*

'A dizzying explosion of an Indian gangster film, whose epic structure and colourful, immoral killers capture the imagination for over five hours. An extraordinary ride through Bollywood's spectacular, over-the-top film-making, *Gangs of Wasseypur* puts Tarantino in a corner with its cool command of cinematically inspired and referenced violence, ironic characters and breathless pace' – From Cannes 65, Directors' Fortnight, 2012

Gangs of Wasseypur

The Making of a Modern Classic

Jigna Kothari
Supriya Madangarli

HarperCollins *Publishers* India

First published in India by
HarperCollins *Publishers* in 2013

4th Floor, Tower A, Building No. 10, Phase II,
DLF Cyber City, Gurugram, Haryana -122002
www.harpercollins.co.in

10 9

P-ISBN: 978-93-5029-621-9
E-ISBN: 978-93-5029-407-9

Typeset in 10/13 Adobe Garamond at
SŪRYA

Printed and bound at
MicroPrints India, New Delhi

For our families

Contents

Cast of Characters

Character's name in film	*Based on*	*Relationship*
Shahid Khan	Mukhtar Khan	
Sardar Khan	Shafi Khan	Son of Mukhtar Khan
Nagma Khan	Najma Khan	Wife of Shafi Khan
Danish Khan	Shamim Khan	Son of Shafi Khan and Najma Khan; Shama Parveen's husband
Shama Parveen	Shama Parveen	Wife of Shamim Khan
Faizal Khan	Fahim Khan	Son of Shafi Khan and Najma Khan; Rehana's husband
Mohsina	Rehana	Wife of Fahim Khan
Fazlu	Fazlu	Friend-turned-traitor
Guddu	Tunnu	Right-hand man
Perpendicular	Chottna Khan	Son of Shafi Khan and Najma Khan
Sano Khan	Not shown in the film	Son of Shafi Khan and Najma Khan
Durga	Durga	Shafi Khan's second wife
Definite	Based on Gopi Khan	Definite is fictionalized as Sardar Khan and Durga's son
Tangent	Arif	Perpendicular's friend

Character's name in film	*Based on*	*Relationship*
Qamar Makhdoomi	Qamar Makhdoomi	Fictionalized as guardian to Durga
Nasir Khan	Fictional	Right-hand man of Shahid Khan
Asgar	Fictional	Right-hand man of Sardar Khan
Sultana Daku/ Sharif Qureshi	Fictional	Fictionalized as grandfather of Badoor Qureshi and related to Sultan
Ehsan Qureshi	Fictional	Associate to Ramadhir Singh
Sultan	Sultan	Relationship to Badoor Quereshi and Shama Parveen is fictionalized.
Badoor Quershi	Fictional	Grandson of Sultana Daku
Ramadhir Singh	Suryadeo Singh + B.P. Sinha	Politician
J.P. Singh	Rajeev Ranjan Singh	Suryadeo Singh's Son
S.P. Sinha	B.P. Sinha (partly)	BCCL official
C.S.	Chandrashekhar (former Prime Minister)	Suryadeo Singh's mentor/supporter
Shamshad Alam	Saabir Alam	Friend to Fahim Khan, later rival
Iqlakh	Fictional	Betrays Faizal Khan

Additional key fictional characters

• **Qasim:** He shot at Nagma and Asgar. He was killed by Definite and others.

• **Mangat:** Trader dealing with Shamshad and Nawab.

• **Laxman:** Pehelwan who is killed by Sardar.

• **Saggir:** He shot at Sardar. Khalid, Sultan and fourth man helped him in the shootout. Saggir is killed by Danish.

• **Nawed:** Faizal kills him when he challenges Faizal's instant leadership position.

• **Khalid:** He also shot at Sardar. His head was shaved by Fazial and later killed.

• **Yadav Ji:** He killed Shahid Khan and Faizal Khan kills him.

Foreword

Anurag Kashyap

Before *Gangs of Wasseypur* I had never worked on a film that was conceived by someone else. It was in May 2009 that I met Sachin Ladia and Akhilesh Jaiswal. *The Skeleton Woman*, a play co-written by Kalki which I produced, was being performed at Prithvi Theatre. Rucha Pathak and Vikas Bahl from UTV and Irrfan Khan were with me. I had stepped out for a smoke when Sachin walked up to me and asked me to read the treatment. It was about ten pages long. I started reading it and liked it. Zeishan's elaboration of the treatment would not have caught my attention had he not begun to tell me stories from the past and present of Wasseypur. Endless stories, tales and legends.

After *Satya* and *Black Friday* I had decided never to make a gangster film again. But then I had not yet seen *Subramaniapuram* and *Paruthiveeran*. Watching these movies, in this new language of cinema from Chennai, I wanted to go to my roots, explore them. Then I found Wasseypur and its stories. I began to think of this as a definitive gangster movie, in the sense that it explores the whole story of the mafia. I decided to make the film and it became a 240-page screenplay, which would approximate a six and a half hour movie. And then I got it funded. It got edited to five and a half hours, beginning in 1940 and ending in 2004. It also became a personal journey – going back to where I grew up, shooting in the same house in which I spent my childhood, having my uncles and aunts in the songs, casting my two best friends from my young days ... it was like going back to the world that created me.

We spent a lot of time researching for the script but I just couldn't bring myself to actually sit down and write it. Zeishan was desperate for it to start and Aditya (Perpendicular) was already one year into playing with a blade in his mouth when I went for a break to Spain. Kalki was shooting *Zindagi Na Milegi Dobara.* That's when I got into a zone to write it. I had carried this film in my mind for nearly two years; it took me five days to write the script. I wrote it in Madrid and lost the script on my way back. The airline misplaced my bag. I stayed at the airport for two days to find it. It was the only copy I had. I still write on paper, with pen.

That's how the journey of *Wasseypur* started. It changed many hands as it went from UTV to Viacom. It also caused me to call off the nine-film deal with UTV. It became the reason why we started Phantom with Vikram (Vikramaditya Motwane, director), Madhu (Madhu Mantena, producer) and Vikas (Vikas Bahl) – to make movies the way we want to, produce films we believe in and be able to back the projects all the way. This year AKFPL and Phantom had four films at Cannes.

We had no idea what the film would become and still

cannot understand the craze around it. There were so many discussions taking place about it. Somebody said it is a left-wing film, others said it is a right-wing film. It has also been said that RSS funded the film. There has been a lot of discussion around *Wasseypur* by sociologists, anthropologists and other academicians. This country is obsessed with cinema. But this is one film we had most fun making and hopefully that came across on screen.

It wouldn't have been the same without Rajeev Ravi, Kunal, Wasiq, Sneha, GV and my sister Anubhuti. And Sohail, whom we lost in a tragic accident.

The idea of this book was born when I shared a rough cut of the film with Supriya and Jigna. I never showed it to them with the expectation that a book would come out of it. But as we got talking I told them how I had to change many names and incidents in the film to avoid any kind of censorship. And they called back after two days saying they would like to do a book on it.

A book!

Since a book can have more details, less censorship and can be fearless...

Mumbai
August 2013

Flashback…

Jigna Kothari and Supriya Madangarli

'After the last interview was done, we asked, "Why did you agree to us writing the book?"

"Because you wanted to write it…" Anurag said simply.'

A doped-up man walks aimlessly through the streets and into his brother's funeral, his stoned eyes watching his mother berate him. Later, the same man slashes away at another's throat. 'You need to see this too,' says Anurag Kashyap as he fast forwards to a hilarious chase sequence after a remarkably inept murder attempt. As we watch, Kashyap peppers the scenes with titbits about Wasseypur and its mafia and about the film. It's all over but the editing, he says.

We walk out of the room and into the world, and instead of our usual practice of dissecting the responses post-interview (about contemporary Hindi cinema), we mull over Wasseypur. As the lift descends into the real world, we speak in half-sentences, each in our own thoughts. Though all we had was a glimpse of a five-and-a-half-hour film, *Wasseypur* has us in its grip. We were pretty much doomed the minute Faizal walked into the funeral to the tune of a 1980s Hindi film song wailing from a mike – the poignancy of the scene accentuated by the absurdity of the live performance. By the time the lift dumps us on the ground floor, it's pretty clear that we are hooked plain and simple and with our itch to chronicle, to know how and why, who and which and where, we turn towards each other and say, 'A book.'

A day later, with an exuberant 'okay' from our editor, we dash off a seemingly routine thank-you note with a hopeful postscript. 'Don't you think that this film deserves a book of its own?' it reads. Anurag replies promptly, 'Yaar ... mujhe nahi pata ... tumhe kuch karna hai to kar lo.' That's all we needed to know. There is a flurry of formalities and permissions, and once the dust has settled, we are left holding an armful of material to read through – a colourful, no-holds-barred rendering of past and present lives of Wasseypur by Zeishan Quadri and two screenplays with the heading 'Version 17 – Gangs of Wasseypur'.

We place story and screenplay side by side and work out where fact ends and fiction begins. That is Act I. Act II begins with interviews. Kashyap has directed his crew to help us (Keep mine for last, he says) and they open up, disarmingly honest and expansive.

We haunt the production offices at Aaram Nagar; we talk to the first-time writers, the soft-spoken Akhilesh and Zeishan, a bundle of nervous energy. Anubhuti Kashyap, with her remarkable memory and crisp narrative, and Neeraj Ghaywan, his passion pouring through his words, recreate the timeline and structure of the production schedule. For Zeishan, Akhilesh and Neeraj it is a turning point in their career, they bring with them the freshness of first-timers. Shlok, the second unit director, and his right-hand man, Vicky, help us get a sense of their adventures off-screen.

The excitement is palpable within and outside Anurag Kashyap's editing office. In every interview we find a sense of achievement, a delight which spills over as they talk. Piyush Mishra plays Mark Antony, burying and praising Anurag with equal passion. Nawazuddin dissects Faizal Khan – this is where I got it wrong; this is how we put it right. At one point, Kashyap joins us and we fall silent. He grins, says, 'Nawaz bhai, jo bolna hai bolo mujko gali dena hai to do, no problem.' Still silence. So Anurag attempts to get up and is pulled down by a collective 'No'. Manoj Bajpai is precise and deft; while Richa Chadda seems innocent of the fact that she has remarkable talent. Dhulia is relieved that the experience is over, and despite feeling that the film is not stylistic, marvels at Kashyap's courage.

In the midst of the interviews, we get a chance to watch the films in their raw glory – without CG and FX, and without the soundtrack. There's a little more editing to be done too, we are informed. We watch the films a second time with Kashyap and it's a delightful experience as each scene comes alive with comments on how it was done; the mystery unfolding shot by shot. Everyone we speak to provides context and subtext – an insight into what they started with, what changed, why it changed and what they feel about it now.

The tough part of writing this book (apart from getting interview dates from an extremely busy Kashyap who is doubling up as a travelling salesman for the film) is the realization that we were never on location during the shoot, let alone being there when the idea of the film struck the writers and the director. But we realize that being outsiders has its advantages. It offers perspectives denied to those who are in the thick of the action.

We decide to write the book in the chronological format of how the film was done – from the time the writers met Kashyap and nervously put forward their idea of a mafia film, to Kashyap penning the script a long way away from home, to the crew hunting down the cast, through the chaotic scheduling and shooting of the film, and finally to the editing room and the creation of the soundtrack.

One evening, listening to Anurag describing a real-life person on which a particular character is based, we tell him, 'Just to let you know, we will be putting his real name in the book.'

'Do that,' he replies, 'cinema has certain limitations. You are writing a book. This needs to be documented in some form. The honesty, the reality should come out.'

We hope we have achieved this in our narration. It is to maintain this honesty, to make the book an authentic rendition of the making of *Gangs of Wasseypur* that we have retained in our content the original voices of those who spoke to us. We kept our interpretation of the film to the questions we asked and let the answers tell the story in their words.

The rest is history.

1

Three Streets and a Saga

'Now, okay this is how it is ... Ek banda hai, who has knowledge and has struggled, has a real grip over cinema and he becomes Anurag Kashyap. And everybody knows him. Then there is this other guy, not much knowledge or struggle but he becomes Fahim Khan and everybody knows him too. The fact is in Wasseypur there is a Fahim Khan born every day. Everybody is a Fahim Khan there. Everybody is a boss. Even Fahim Khan thinks twice before lifting a finger. This is Wasseypur, sab dabangg hai yahan.'

– Syed Zeishan Quadri,
writer and actor

One cannot locate Wasseypur on a Dhanbad town map, neither in the Dhanbad district authority map, nor the one from the Dhanbad Municipal Corporation. Riddled with small alleys and by-lanes that are said to be a boon to criminals who could lose their pursuers in the maze, Wasseypur is divided into nineteen-odd mohallas, and occupies just two to three streets in the urban area of Dhanbad.

Named after a local zamindar M.A. Javed's younger

brother, Wassey mian, in 1964, Wasseypur came into being with the merging of the two gram panchayats of Matkuriya and Vishnupur.[1] From a population of around 2000, it has grown to become home to nearly two lakh people, expanding its boundaries till the outskirts of the Dhanbad railway station. The residents, vocal about their displeasure over the portrayal of their home in *Gangs of Wasseypur*, insist that crime is a thing of the past. Doctors, engineers, and IAS officers are born here every day, and not gangsters, they aver.

It is, however, an area steeped in legends. Notorious outlaw Sultana Daku allegedly took asylum here and the tales of his exploits against the British have been told over generations in almost every other village in northern India. Today, Wasseypur is infamous for gunrunning, sharp shooters, gang wars, where as the lore goes even a family that could ill afford two meals a day would own a gun.

'Class, caste, religion does not matter, you could be a millionaire or a bum on the street with nary a rupee in your pocket,' says Syed Zeishan Quadri, writer and actor of *Gangs of Wasseypur*. 'How you are judged is whether you are *dabangg*.' The word dabangg, according to the dictionaries, translates as bold, authoritarian, powerful, or fearless. The translations, however, lack the swagger in the usage of the term here. It deems power as a birthright and conveys a casual irreverence for life – one's own and

---

[1]As quoted in newspapers, and from Zeishan Quadri's research material

one's enemy's. In fact, a popular saying in Wasseypur goes: *Ek hi jaan hai, yah to Allah lega, yah mohalla* (You have one life, you will lose it either to God or your neighbourhood). 'It's not whether you are a Hindu or Muslim. That you are beautiful and I am ugly. That you have ten cars and I have none. This doesn't matter. I am walking on the road in a half-pant. Not even ten paise in my pocket, but I am king. The fight arises out of the fact that I am dabangg, that's where the conflict originates,' says Zeishan.

Along with dabangg goes the word '*varchasv*'. Noun: Domination. Transitive Verb: To Dominate. Adjective: Absolute Power. Varchasv, as in domination, is about having the power 'to rule, have dominion over'.

Though being dabangg could be democratic as claimed by Zeishan, the question of varchasv was pretty much demarcated in Wasseypur and Dhanbad along class/caste lines. In Wasseypur, local gangs of Pathans and Qureshis fought turf wars over illegal trading of iron-scrap or rangdari (extortion), wielding the gun as the source of their power. Their world revolved around Wasseypur. Across the railway line in Dhanbad is the Rajput-dominated coal mafia, a.k.a. the Singh Mansion, home to erstwhile MLA, the late Suraj Deo Singh[2] and his ilk. They have held sway over the grafts and scams of coal mines, with a political power base that rose from the ground up to an entity none other than a former prime

---

[2]In reference material, the name has been spelt Surajdeo and Suraj Deo Singh. The latter has been used here.

minister of the country. Street stories and unofficial records have it that the Singh Mansion – which seems to have become a collective noun for the Rajput coal mafia – has interfered with, influenced and used Wasseypur gangs whenever necessary.

One of the mohallas of Wasseypur is Qamar Makhdoomi Road, named after a man who was much respected as a mukhiya. The road where, according to Zeishan, '*jo dabangg hai wohi reh sakta hai, baaki koyi nahi reh sakta*' (where only a dabangg can survive), is also home to Fahim Khan and Saabir Alam, two of the pre-eminent names in its history of violence. Fahim Khan, who allegedly inherited his father's Shafi Khan's mantle of rangdari and iron-scrap trading, established his turf in the locality after a bloody battle that destroyed his rival, Sultan of the Naya Bazaar (situated close to Wasseypur) gang.

The story of Fahim Khan and Saabir Alam is a friends-turn-foes story.

After dabbling in the cloth trade and transport business, Saabir Alam decides to venture into buying and selling of iron scrap. Since one cannot do business in this unorganized sector without the approval of 'market leader' Fahim Khan, he is approached for his blessings. Saabir Alam cultivates Fahim Khan's friendship by setting up a youth association and installing Khan at its helm. Things go sour when Fahim Khan apparently wants prasad, a share in the profits, in return for his blessing. Saabir Alam and his friend Munna lay a trap for Fahim Khan and get him arrested for extortion.

On 12 May 2001, the offices of Saabir Alam and his business partner are bombed by a masked youth. The youth, it is said, is Gopi Khan, soon to be an important player in the Wasseypur gang wars. The retaliation by Saabir's gang is brutal. In an attack on Fahim Khan's house, its sole occupant, Shama Parveen, widow of Fahim Khan's elder brother Shamim Khan, is shot in the head. The ensuing warfare has since claimed the lives of many members of each gang, including that of Fahim Khan's mother Najma Khatoon.

December 2004. A key episode in the prime-time television saga *Kyon ki Saas Bhi Kabhi Bahu Thi* keeps most residents of Qamar Makhdoomi Road glued to their television sets. The rest are asleep when bursts of gunfire shatter the stillness. In one of the houses, a mere hundred yards from Fahim Khan's, is a young man who sleeps through the roar of AK-47s. The morning brings him the news.

Fahim Khan ke ghar par goli chali thi … AK 47.

Oh? Who was it?

Saabir Alam's people.

And Fahim Khan?

He is in the hospital, broke his foot.

The young man is Zeishan Quadri. Six years later he is back in Wasseypur, researching what exactly happened that night.

The attack on Fahim Khan's house could very well have walked out of an Anurag Kashyap script.

There were four of them that night, Zeishan learns. One was said to be Saabir Alam's servant Sultan; the other a known shooter from Bihar, Tabrez alias Tabbu, and his two companions. The firing is relentless – the guard at the door is killed immediately. As the shooters clamber up the stairs, they are stopped at the door by a huge iron lock which not even an AK-47 magazine is able to break. The shooters sieve the door with bullets and stick the muzzles of the guns into holes and keep shooting, hoping the bullets will find the targets inside. When they run out of bullets, they listen – to an absence of sound from within the walls. No voices, no noises. Nothing.

Assuming that Fahim Khan is dead, they make their getaway in the Maruti van in which they had come. What they do not know is that a lungi-clad Fahim Khan had heard the gunfire from his office, run to the roof and jumped onto the terrace of the house next door, thus breaking his foot. What follows is a series of misadventures. Barely has the Maruti van carrying the assailants turned into the main street than it runs into a local police jeep on a routine patrol. The shooters panic and fire at the jeep which promptly pursues them, despite the driver and the cop in the front being injured. The van breaks down and the shooters decide to make it on foot, but not before shooting dead Saabir Alam's servant Sultan, who is in the throes of a panic attack and hence could be a weak link. Strangers to the area, they run helter-skelter and bang into a colony of shepherds who, seeing the men with guns, think they are being attacked by dacoits. The three jump into a huge mound of dried cow dung to hide from the police and the villagers. The villagers surround them, creating an impromptu manure prison till the police arrive. The night ends tragically for the valiant constable driving the jeep. He dies in the hospital.

The next morning the news spreads through Wasseypur. Residents discuss the event with nonchalant interest, the street shrugs at the violence. It is just another episode in the ongoing warfare between the two powerful gangs of Wasseypur. Another story in the lore that Zeishan has listened to and experienced while growing up in the most dabangg area of Wasseypur.

*

It is late at night in an apartment in Versova, Andheri, Mumbai. After a viewing of Fernando Meirelles's and Kátia Lund's Brazilian 'crime' drama, *City of God*, Zeishan tells his friends Sachin Ladia and Akhilesh, 'If that's how real your cinema is, you should look at Wasseypur.'

Born and brought up in an upper-middle-class family, Zeishan's journey from Wasseypur to Mumbai begins when he abandons a vague idea of a management school, a plan that his father likes very much, and decides to pursue an acting career in films. He has no clue of how films work. He likes to dance, to watch plays but that is the extent of his involvement with the creative arts. He has dabbled in writing – the usual poems in journals that young minds turn to. He is, however, under no illusion of becoming a star overnight. 'Didn't know what was Bollywood or Bombay but hero banna hai. I had seen enough of real life so I knew this would take time. I decided that if I don't become a hero in six months, I would come back home. I just didn't want to regret not going,' says Zeishan.

In Mumbai, Zeishan meets an old friend, Sachin Ladia, who has been in the city for the past two years and is struggling to get a foothold in Hindi film industry. Still clueless about film-making, what a cinematographer does or what a casting director is, Zeishan goes through the steps: creates a portfolio, goes for auditions, and meets casting directors. With nothing much happening, he spends his time at home watching the movies that Sachin leaves for him daily before he goes to work.

In the evenings, Sachin's friend Akhilesh comes over and the three discuss the movies Zeishan has seen during the day. Akhilesh is from Bhopal. He came to the city after his twelfth standard, on the pretext of getting a bachelor's degree in mass media. 'I dropped out of college after one year; it was not working out. In 2006, I started working with a theatre group for one and a half years, then as an assistant in ad films, and as an assistant director and writer in production units. I approached many directors with scripts and ideas. Some were rejected, some were liked but nothing happened,' says Akhilesh.

Akhilesh and Sachin are working in a production unit when their paths cross Zeishan's.

They have been idle for quite a while. The unit's project has been benched and the two are frustrated over the lack of work. With Zeishan in the picture, and his newbie enthusiasm over the films he sees during the day, late-nights at the flat become a common occurrence. And then one day, Zeishan watches *City of God.* That evening, while discussing gangster films, Zeishan begins to recount tales of Wasseypur that enthrall and excite his listeners. This is it, this is the story they have been waiting for.

Akhilesh has grown up watching what he calls the 'Indian hero type of cinema' and has become disillusioned by it. 'Even I had better stories to write. When we heard this story, we realized, that, yaar, this is the film we have to make but apna level itna nahi tha that we could do it,' he says.

They need the right person for job. They decide to approach director Hansal Mehta. 'Throughout this we were searching for Anurag Kashyap because we were sure that he would like this but he was never there in the office,' recalls Akhilesh. It is Zeishan who insists on pursuing Mehta, overriding Akhilesh and Sachin's protests that they didn't even have a script; it was still just an idea.

The call is made and Mehta asks Sachin to come over and join him for his evening walk where they could discuss the story. 'It wasn't a story,' says Mehta. 'It was just an idea; it was full of colourful characters. The characters were Faizal Khan, Ramadhir Singh and Saabir Alam. It starts with Faizal Khan firing a hundred bullets into Ramadhir's body; there was the concept of vengeance for his father's death. I saw the film as an epic. I wanted to call it "Dhanbad". I asked them to build a story on that. I am on, I said.' Mehta, however, has not made a film for quite some time. It will take time to find a producer and raise finance. He is, however, excited enough about the project to rope in Manoj Bajpai for Fahim Khan's role.

Towards the end of May 2009, an advertisement in a newspaper catches the writers' attention. 'Anurag Kashyap presents *The Skeleton Woman*, a play written and performed by Kalki Koechlin and Prashant Prakash on 2nd and 3rd June, 2009, at Prithvi Theatre.' Deciding that this is one place Kashyap will surely be, Akhilesh and Sachin reach the theatre and hang around till they catch Kashyap's eye.

Kashyap's *Dev D* is just out and *That Girl in Yellow Boots* is in the wings when he produces *The Skeleton Woman*. 'I remember that was the first week of the shows at Prithvi Theatre and because I was a first-time producer, I used to hang out at the theatre. So that's where I met Sachin and Akhilesh. They were hanging around and simply looking at me,' recalls Kashyap.

When Kashyap finds out that they want to discuss a story idea for a film, he asks them to wait. Akhilesh and Sachin do so patiently. The screen bell rings once and the theatre-goers begin to move inside when Kashyap remembers the two. Okay, he tells them, tell it, and tell it fast. They give him a one-liner which surprisingly none involved remembers except that *City of God* is referred to. 'We spoke for thirty to forty seconds. It was the rise and fall of Faizal Khan and the story of the teenage gangsters with him. There was no scope for a star cast in the film. We had written the contemporary story – Fahim Khan's story. And he was portrayed as an older man. "Have you written it, registered it?" Kashyap asked us. We said yes, so he asked us to get it the next day,' recounts Akhilesh.

Mehta is told that Anurag wants to meet them; he asks the writers to narrate all the stories they have with them, including the Wasseypur one. 'I was taking time to give them a confirmation, and the guys were getting impatient,' he says. The next day, back at Prithvi Theatre, Anurag reads the synopsis and asks who else has been shown the script. 'We said Hansal Mehta. Then he said, don't take it to anybody else, I will make this film. Kahin mat jaa, main banata hoon picture.' Kashyap introduces them to producers Richa Pathak and Vikas Bahl from UTV who are with him, takes the writers' numbers and says he will get in touch. Kashyap is at this time in a nine-film deal with UTV.

Kashyap recalls it a little differently. 'It was one of those moments ... I never ever get time to do things like this. Sachin and Akhilesh met me at the theatre and I agreed to read their script. I liked it but it was too much like *City of God*. I said I have seen lots of gangster films. They said, *nahi, nahi*, sir, *ye* real story *hai*. I said where is the real story? They got very offended at that. I asked them to show me the research, show me how true it is. I knew that I liked the idea, I liked the potential of it, but I was not sure whether I wanted to do it,' says Kashyap. He, however, called up Mehta.

'Anurag said, "If you are doing the film, I won't touch it." I replied, "No, you go ahead." I was yet to get a producer and Anurag at that time was on board with UTV,' recalls Mehta.

However, by now, Kashyap is busy with *Yellow Boots*, and the writers have to bide their time. 'When I got back to them after *Yellow Boots*, they came back with Zeishan Quadri and a whole lot of newspaper cuttings.' The newspaper articles are the final hook. The writers have got them along as proof that the incidents they described did happen. Kashyap, however, is intrigued more by what they have not talked about. 'See, when I was given the story, it was an interpretation of *City of God.* They used that film as a template, but with real incidents. There were just a lot of violent scenes as it was only Fahim Khan's story and I wondered why I should do this, this is like any other gangster film. Then they got the paper cuttings, and I wasn't interested in just the headlines. It wasn't the characters that spoke to me; it was the history, the context, the atmosphere, the world around them that spoke to me,' says Kashyap.

Zeishan then begins to tell the stories – of how Fahim Khan was arrested by the police on a train for carrying illegal guns, of how he had purchased the guns a second time and hid them in the train and marked the bogie with his initials. 'There was this story of this man who was killed while buying fruits and vegetables. The guy escaped in his Maruti car from a shooter who was chasing him, little knowing that there was another man hiding in the back seat, who easily shot him,' says Kashyap.

There are other seemingly absurd stories too. There is one of how a boy in Wasseypur got the nickname 'Definite'. Zeishan narrates how he and his elders and other people were sitting and talking: 'And this little boy squeezes through a small hole in the door of the house and comes out and his father promptly quips, yeh definite chor banega, bada hoke.' The locals delight in recounting the anecdote so often that any comment about the boy would include the word 'definite', so much so that it became his nickname. Kashyap is fascinated by the way a single dialogue could create a name. The stories intrigue him, they pique his interest; he wants more.

'What got it for me was when he told me the story of Sultana Daku. I had grown up on his stories and I thought, Yeh Dhanbad kaise pahunch gaya? Sultana Daku's myth is so strong. You go to Faizabad; they tell you Sultana Daku was from there. If you go to Bundelkhand, they will tell you Sultana Daku was there. Every region has its story about Sultana Daku and how he belonged to their region. In real life, he was hanged to death in Calcutta but Wasseypur has this story that he was a Qureshi. That he ran away from kaalapani and settled here. So I decided to use that – Sultan being a Qureshi in the story – to play on the myth of Sultana Daku. Those are the things that got me interested. I wanted to go back there and start exploring the story.'

By August 2009, the writers get the nod from Kashyap, they are under contract with UTV, and their first job is to go back to Wasseypur. Kashyap asks them to research incidents and the people involved – the history referred to in the newspaper cuttings. He wants them to start from the beginning. 'My point was, how could a story about Dhanbad not discuss coal? When Zeishan started telling me stories about Wasseypur's past I asked him why is this not a part of the script? Those stories were to be a part of this; it was necessary since I didn't want to make a mafia film just for the sake of it. I wanted to get into the whole background, the history of it; right from how and where it started because that gave me the scope to explore. I could have just shot the contemporary version of it (Part 2), and it would have been any mafia story in a city where people are killing each other. The whole terrain and landscape that we see of coal mines – the sense of history would not have come in.'

In September 2009, Zeishan, Akhilesh and assistant director Jai Mehta go to Wasseypur and Dhanbad, and spend the next forty days there. Creative differences with Sachin have led him to drop out of the project. The writers talk to old men in Dhanbad whose stories are of an earlier age, they spend time with local troubadours, they get in touch with journalists and then they get to speak with the men who worked with Fahim Khan. 'Most of the recorded material was after the 1980s [the heyday of crime in Wasseypur]. Prior to that it was difficult to find official sources. So a lot of information came from the old people who had lived in Dhanbad all their life. Travelling through generations, the story must have changed or been exaggerated – what we have tried to do is capture the soul of these stories,' says Akhilesh.

The locals are more comfortable talking to Zeishan. The others are seen as outsiders. 'We met a few who used to work with Fahim Khan but they would talk more openly to Zeishan. We tried to talk to Gopi Khan but we couldn't as he was transferred to Patna jail. It was difficult in Qasai Mohallah, for the teenagers were half gangsters. They would threaten, "Who are you, what do you want, why are you roaming around with a camera?"' recalls Akhilesh.

When the writers get back, they attempt to write the

script but Kashyap is not satisfied. 'I asked them to write it as it happened, make a story – don't worry about the script. I always write the final script,' he says. This novella became the basis for the script, and parts of it were used for the voice-overs in the film.

Kashyap finds that Zeishan has used original names in the novella. 'That was a problem. We couldn't use the original names – I had tried it in *Black Friday*, and in our country that doesn't work. It was a Catch-22 situation, for if they changed names it would end up being a strange, confusing story. Besides, in the story that was given to us, life was happening at its own pace, leaving a lot of gaps in between. There were periods when nothing happened with the characters, then suddenly they become active. So I told Zeishan, "Dost teri kahaani kahen, toh kaise kaha jaaye?"'

The answer was to fictionalize the whole story. 'I kept the incidents the same and decided that I would start mixing up characters. Contemporary stories are mostly verified and remembered by people, and they are reported in the newspapers. A whole lot of the stories of the earlier generation had the element of myth, which I wanted to retain. We did, however, try to reduce it, which is why we conducted independent research on the history of Dhanbad. So, there were the elements of the hand-me-down stories that the writers brought in from Wasseypur and, there was our production team's research for timelines, incidents and places,' says Kashyap.

By this time, Kashyap knows how he is going to approach the film. Three experiences are the trigger points.

The first is the landmark *Heimat*[3] series of which Kashyap had seen part I and II. The second is Rainer Werner Fassbinder's *Berlin Alexanderplatz* (2007). Kashyap saw the entire series at one go – it took him twenty-one hours. The third is an Italian film called the *Best of Youth* which Kashyap describes as a six-hour movie about the history of Italy told through the life of one person.[4] 'In this day and age, visual medium is becoming what literature was to us when we were growing up. When you see *Heimat,* it's like a visual novel. That started getting to me. It felt like I could tell a longer story. From then on I wanted to make a film that tells the whole story of a place. It was while I was digging into the Wasseypur stories that a whole lot more emerged and that's when I felt I could tell the whole story, and with *Heimat, Berlin* in the back of my mind came this idea of chronicling a time zone.'

The film then would be the story of three generations of the Khan family. 'My characters were forming in my head,' says Kashyap. However, to write it down, he needs to get away, far from Mumbai. In mid-2009, as the production team is being assembled in Mumbai, Anurag

---

[3] *Heimat,* written and directed by Edgar Riez, comprises three films, serialized over thirty episodes which encapsulate life in Germany from 1919 to 2000.

[4] *The Best of Youth* (Italian: *La meglio gioventù*, 2003), directed by Marco Tullio Giordana. Originally planned as a four-part mini-series, it was presented at the 2003 Cannes Film Festival. It was then presented on stage in Italy in two three-hour parts in which forty minutes were edited out.

Kashyap begins looking for a place where myth, history, urban legends and the reportage and research would come together in his mind to recreate Wasseypur.

2

Between Fact and Fiction

'I was having fun, I was actually laughing at the absurdities of things and I wanted to get carried away with those absurdities.'

– Anurag Kashyap

By mid-2010, Kashyap is involved in the post-production of *That Girl in Yellow Boots*, which is to be released later that year. He is also exploring international markets for the film. Then there is *Udaan*, directed by close friend Vikramaditya Motwane and produced by Anurag Kashyap Films Pvt Ltd (AKFPL), which is all set to go to Cannes 2010. In the middle of this, he is making notes for his next film titled *Production No. 7*. Kashyap plans to go to Romania to write the script but that falls through. In June, his wife Kalki Koechlin and the rest of the cast of Zoya Akhtar's *Zindagi Na Milegi Dobara* pack their bags for their shooting schedule in Spain. Kashyap decides he will meet up with his wife and then go to Madrid.

He is booked in a hotel in the centre of the city. 'When I am writing, I like to walk around, sit in the pubs in the evening, and write through the day – that's how I work,' says Kashyap. The hotel turns out to be a meeting point for transsexuals. 'They were fascinating,' he says. Here, amidst the revelry, he would finish the script in five days.

Apart from his notes, Kashyap has Zeishan's novella at hand – the story of three generations of the Khan family and the research from the writers' trip to Wasseypur. Now he needs to '...make sense of time and create a place and fictionalize the story; to synchronize myths, reality, history and people. Mixing all the elements, the story came out in an organic way and I knew which character was what and what he will do. In my mind I had made the rough family tree,' says Kashyap.

Zeishan's novella is about the rise and fall of one family in Wasseypur – beginning with the grandfather Manovar Khan, his son Shafi Khan, and his grandson Fahim Khan. In Kashyap's script these change to grandfather Shahid Khan, son Sardar Khan (while Kashyap is writing the script, this character is named Zeishan) and grandson Faizal Khan.

Kashyap decides that the film will be in two parts. Part I will be the story of Shahid Khan and Sardar Khan, covering the era from the 1940s to the 1980s; Part II, the contemporary story of Faizal Khan, will be from the '80s onward. The story will unfold in Wasseypur and Dhanbad.

The script begins in the late 1930s with Shahid Khan. Wasseypur doesn't exist at the time so Shahid Khan, like his real-life counterpart Manovar Khan, is from the village Mutkariya. The East Indian Grand Chord railway line has become a man-made boundary separating it from Qasai Mohallah, the base of the Qureshis who in real life and in the script prove to be the catalysts driving the fate of the Khan family.

As already mentioned, Shahid is based on the life of Manovar Khan, who makes a living out of looting grain from trains that carry supplies across the north on the Grand Chord railway line. This doesn't sit well with Mohammed Sharif Qureshi, the leader of Qasai Mohallah who considers the railway line to be his territory. Local lore has it that Qureshi was none other than the infamous Sultana Daku.

It was in the 1920s that stories of Sultana Daku[1] began to surface. Legend has it that this dacoit who specialized in train robberies so terrorized the local police forces that often policemen in lonely areas would run out of their stations and give him their arms when he passed by.[2] The British government set up a special Dacoity Force headed by Deputy Superintendent Freddy Young, who proved to be the dreaded dacoit's nemesis.

Around that time, a popular play portraying Sultana Daku as the villain and Freddy Young as the hero did the rounds of fairs and festivals. However, as time passed, and resentment against the colonial rulers grew, the play cast Sultana Daku as a Robin Hood figure, robbing

---

[1]He belonged to the Bhantu tribe which was deemed criminal by the British Criminal Tribes Act of 1871.

[2]From Philip Mason, *Men Who Ruled India: The Guardians*, Volume 2, p. 13; and E.A.H. Blunt, *The Caste system of Northern India*, 1931, p. 160.

British trains, with Freddy Young as a fat and cowardly officer. From being a dangerous dacoit Sultana Daku was recast as a patriot.

'Sultana Daku was never reported to be from the region of Dhanbad. He has always been talked about as being from eastern UP. But his stories were famous. Every train robbery came to be attributed to him. When he became famous, koi bhi train robbery karta, sab Sultana Daku ho jaate thay. There are conflicting stories but Wasseypur ke logon ki ek apni history thi,' says Kashyap.

Sultana Daku was hanged in 1924. Many of his comrades were said to be deported to the Andaman and Nicobar Islands. However, Wasseypur's home-spun history has Sultana sentenced to kaalapani, from where he escapes by digging a fourteen-kilometre tunnel from the jail, swimming out into the sea till he stows away on a private ship. He reaches India and settles in Dhanbad because he has relatives there. 'So I decided to use all these stories and let the myth be a myth. That's how we started with ek Sultana Daku hai. There is another man who also professes to be Sultana. We do not know who is the real or the fake one here. Are both real or are both fake, we do not know. So in the script, the myth and fact were married to the fiction of Sultana Daku as Mohammed Qureshi, who drives out Shahid Khan from Wasseypur because he would rob trains in the Qasai Mohalla territory posing as Sultana Daku,' says Kashyap.

While the exiled Manovar Khan dies of natural causes, in the script Kashyap has Shahid Khan becoming a coal mine worker, who is later promoted as a pahalwan by a local coal contractor Ramadhir Singh. As Shahid Khan becomes more and more ambitious, and a threat to Ramadhir, the latter has him killed.

The next generation comes into the picture. The script has Sardar Khan vowing vengeance on Ramadhir Singh for his father's murder. In real life, after the death of his father, though there are no official records, Shafi Khan began looting petrol pumps, government officials and then ventured into illegal coal trade. Here the original story reaches a dead-end and there is no information on Shafi Khan from the 1950s till he surfaces in Wasseypur in the 1970s, ostensibly on the request of the village elder, Qamar Makhdoomi, to combat the increasing nuisance of the arrogant Qureshis.

Kashyap's research doesn't throw up any stories/legends/news reports which he can fictionalize in the script. He uses this space to chronicle the actual history of the coal industry and related political developments in Dhanbad like the nationalization of coal mines and the birth of the coal mafia. This is used to tell the story of Ramadhir Singh's rise to power.

It was in 1839 that the British discovered the Jharia coalfields in Dhanbad[3] which at that time was a subdivision of the Manbhum district. (The district belonged to the region the British had named 'Gondwana',

---

[3]There are several theories about how Dhanbad acquired its name. As per the *Indian Gazetteer of Bihar* written by one P.C. Chowdhury, Dhanbad was derived from *dhan* (paddy) and *baid* (third class) which would make it third-class paddy land. In 1918, the additional deputy commissioner of Dhanbad, a Mr Luby, dropped the letter 'i' in 'baid' and made it Dhanbad.

parts of which they later allocated to the Bengal state.) This led to the rapid industrialization of the area with the establishment of collieries and growth of subsidiary industries. With the Grand Chord Line of the East Indian Railway reaching Dhanbad, the area grew in leaps and bounds. In 1956, Dhanbad became a district in the state of Bihar. The boundary lines have since been redrawn, with the district now in the newly formed Jharkhand state.

Under the British, private colliery owners used to employ contractors who brought in workers from the villages to work at the coal mines. The owners looked to these contractors as 'peacekeepers' to keep the mine workers in line. These peacekeepers, locally called pahalwans, grew into trade union leaders when mine workers began to get organized. After nationalization (1970-71), contractors and trade union leaders became interchangeable as is aptly demonstrated by Ramadhir Singh, the chief antagonist in the film.

Kashyap, however, skews conventional logic when he views Ramadhir as tangential to the whole story. 'That was a very conscious decision. I was trying to tell the story of this family for whom their world was Wasseypur. So the story stays with the family. The antagonists come in when it is convenient – Ramadhir comes in only when the stories about the family stop, to take it to the next level. He is used to cement various incidents. That was a very tough call. But you know there are so many stories; you cannot tell it all until and unless you are making a TV series. That's why I was doing this,' says Kashyap. The rise and fall of the main villain, Ramadhir Singh, is woven into this story, to provide context and the environment surrounding Wasseypur as it grew into a power base within Dhanbad.

The character of Ramadhir Singh is an amalgamation of two men from Dhanbad: B.P. Sinha and Suraj Deo Singh. B.P. Sinha, a farmer turned contractor turned trade union leader, used to be a member of the Socialist Party until he was expelled on corruption charges by Jayaprakash Narayan in 1950. He went on to lead the Rashtriya Colliery Mazdoor Sangh (RCMS), which was affiliated to the Indian National Trade Union Congress (INTUC). Under his reign, the coalfields became an INTUC stronghold. Money poured into the Congress party coffers from the RCMS.[4] Allegations were made by the rival union Bihar Colliery Kamgar Union (BCKU) led by A.K. Roy that the RCMS union bosses owned multiple residences, movie houses, factories and several hundred acres of agricultural land.[5]

In the late 1970s, Sinha found a rival in his former protégé, Suraj Deo Singh, a Rajput from Ballia district in Uttar Pradesh who set up his own union, the Janata Mazdoor Sangh (JMS). In 1977, he was elected as the Janata Party MLA from Jharia .[6]

---

[4]Arun Sinha, 'Dhanbad: Dogs of Corruption', *Economic and Political Weekly*, Vol XVIII No. 38, 17 September 1983.

[5]Ibid.

[6]The private colliery owners used trade union leaders and contractors to subdue workers and break strikes. The strategy continued after nationalization. On 5 February 1979, when a

(Contd…)

'We could not use the original names – not of people who have streets and monuments named after them. Once you have been put on a pedestal you are free of all sins. So, we mixed the alleged crimes with the rumours. B.P. Sinha's mafia elements were taken out from him and put in Ramadhir's life. So it became slightly black and white,' says Kashyap. The black goes into Ramadhir Singh; the white is retained in a character called S.P. Sinha who in the script is a Bharat Coking Coal Limited (BCCL) officer.[7] This character is hacked to death by Ramadhir Singh when he does not comply with the mafioso's demands.

This murder is based on the actual murder of B.P. Sinha on 29 March 1978 by unknown assailants. According to news reports, at around 7 p.m., a man

---

(Contd…)

day's token strike was called by trade unions of the coalfield, JMS got workers from Simlabahal, Horiladih, Rujapur, South Jharia and Basudeopur collieries into the mining pits. When BCCL officers sat with trade union leaders to discuss workers' demands two months after the strike, one of the trade union leaders was Suraj Deo Singh. A.K. Roy's BCKU boycotted the conference. Arun Sinha, 'Dhanbad: Dogs of Corruption', *Economic and Political Weekly*, Vol XVIII No. 38, 17 September 1983.

[7]BCCL was incorporated in January 1972 to operate coking coal mines in the Jharia and Raniganj coalfields, taken over by the Government of India on 16 October 1971 to ensure planned development of the scarce coking coal resources in the country. Source: http://www.bccl.gov.in/.

asked for Sinha at his residence in Gandhinagar, Dhanbad. Confirming his presence at home, half an hour later, armed men in two cars attacked the house and shot him dead. This led to a war between the RCMS and the JMS, with six of Suraj Deo Singh's men being murdered in the months to come. The violence attracted media attention and the matter was brought before the government. A special investigative cell for Dhanbad was set up in the home ministry and a one-man committee of J.G. Kumaramangalam was appointed to investigate the activities of BCCL and curb mafia presence.[8]

With the death of B.P. Sinha, Suraj Deo Singh became the face of the coal mafia-political nexus in Bihar. There were other Rajputs in the game too. These came to be known as the Five Deos (gods) of Dhanbad, namely, Suraj Deo, Narang Deo, Satya Deo, Sakal Deo and Panch Deo Singh.

In the late 1980s, the chief minister of Bihar, Bhagwat Jha Azad, began to back the efforts of Deputy Commissioner Madan Mohan Jha, who was trying his best to clean up the coal mafia in Dhanbad. Jha filed charge sheets against Suraj Deo Singh, Navrang Deo Singh, Ramchandra Singh, Mahabir Singh, Satya Deo Singh and others.[9]

---

[8]Arun Sinha, 'Dhanbad: Dogs of Corruption', *Economic and Political Weekly*, Vol XVIII No. 38, 17 September 1983.

[9]A hundred mafia-related cases were registered against some 160 people and charge sheets were submitted in 85 cases against 140 men; 436 cases were registered under the Essential

(Contd...)

Suraj Deo Singh was arrested and put in judicial custody but he used his health as an excuse to evade court dates. At this time, Janata Dal leader Chandra Shekhar (prime minister of the country from 10 November 1990 to 21 June 1991) publicly offered support to the charge-sheeted mafia don. Chandra Shekhar is reported to not only having attended rallies demanding the release of Suraj Deo Singh but is also believed to have written to the CM and the PM pleading Singh's case.[10] Political pressure worked. Azad had to resign and Jha was transferred.

This meteoric rise of Suraj Deo Singh is used as a basis for Ramadhir Singh's political background in the film. Chandra Shekhar[11] finds space in the script as Ramadhir's

---

(Contd...)

Commodities Act (1955) against the mafia and charge sheets filed against 112 men; 26 cases of usury were also registered under the Protection of Workmen Act and charge sheets filed in 22 of them. Indu Bharati, 'Usurpation of the State: Coal Mafia in Bihar', *Economic and Political Weekly*, Vol XXIV, No. 42, 21 October1989.

[10]Indu Bharati, 'Usurpation of the State: Coal Mafia in Bihar', *Economic and Political Weekly*, Vol XXIV, No. 42, 21 October 1989.

[11]Years ago, Kashyap had written a film on Chandra Shekhar called *Ballia Bakatu*. 'It's about this guy who is very ugly. But he thinks that if my daughter becomes Miss India, indirectly I will also become good looking.' The idea was squashed by his horrified family, who were on good terms with the former prime minister. This, Kashyap remarks, is his revenge on his family.

mentor. 'Our laws don't allow us to use original names; I suffered a lot in *Black Friday* for the same. The character of the mentor of Ramadhir Singh who looks a lot like the real person was not named in the film, and in the script too he is always referred to as CS.'

Though officially there is no proof of any connection between Suraj Deo Singh and the Wasseypur gangs, Zeishan's novella mentions a local legend where Shafi Khan is said to have slapped Suraj Deo Singh when the two met at a police station in Dhanbad. This is some time in the late 1970s when Shafi Khan had risen to power in Wasseypur through his illegal coal trade. This incident is used by Kashyap in the script. In Part I, the fictional Sardar Khan is shown to slap Ramadhir Singh's son, J.P. Singh, and have him arrested and put in jail. He escapes and hides in Qamar Makhdoomi's house where he meets Durga,[12] the Bengali woman with whom he has an affair and a child.

With Shafi Khan back in Wasseypur battling his old family enemy, the Qasai Qureshis, the area around Noori Masjid in the locality becomes the battleground. When the dust and blood from the warfare settle, the Qureshis' strength is considerably diminished. Many of their gang members are arrested, while many leave town. Wasseypur is now under the thumb of two gangs: Shafi Khan's and the Naya Bazaar gang. The script tracks the same trajectory.

---

[12]The character of Durga is based on an alleged involvement of the real-life Shafi Khan with a Bengali woman.

Sardar Khan finds an enemy in Sultan (the script retained the name of the actual man who led the Naya Bazaar gang). It is said that Suraj Deo Singh supported Sultan and his Naya Bazaar gang in his efforts against Shafi Khan. Suraj Deo Singh's patronage of Sultan finds a parallel in the film in Ramadhir being advised by his mentor to use Sultan to strike at Sardar Khan. There is another story that has been put into the script. 'Everyone knows this story of how Suraj Deo Singh was taken from his car by Shafi Khan, of how his car was pulled apart. You ask any kid and they will say that in Wasseypur everybody says that Shafi Khan ne ungli kiya tha Suraj Deo Singh ko. For them that's a high. So these elements that everyone knows and remembers have been kept as they were in the script. Everything that happened in that incident, including the lines, I have kept intact in the film. The line that goes itna goli marte hai ki driver saari khaali khokha bech bech ker rais ho jaata hai is taken verbatim,' says Kashyap.

By now the third generation had arrived on the scene from whose lives several incidents become part of the script. Shamim Khan (Shafi Khan's eldest son) is injured trying to protect his father from the Naya Bazaar gang's bullets. In the film, Danish Khan (based on Shamim Khan) gets shot in the arm while protecting Sardar Khan. When the real-life Shafi Khan turns from his criminal activities into something more legal – the fisheries business in Topchanchi – his filmic counterpart Sardar Khan does the same.

The death of Sardar Khan[13] is recreated in exact detail as happened to his real-life counterpart. Shafi Khan left his house for his fishery in Topchanchi in an Ambassador car with two of his friends and a driver. Four shooters on two motorcycles attacked the car in Barwadda at a Bharat Petrol outlet. The villagers, hearing the gunshots, converged on the scene. Three of the assailants escaped but one was caught. The shooters were said to be from Sultan's gang.

A key person who planned the attack is said to be a man named Fazlu, a local youth leader and childhood friend of Shafi Khan's second son Fahim Khan. This is also used in the script. 'The betrayal is true. Fazlu betrayed Fahim. We have even kept the dialogue of Fazlu. Every kid knows the story of how Fazlu had called his co-conspirators and said, "Doctor bina alla (stethoscope) ki Topchanchi se nikla,"' says Kashyap.

To avenge his father's death, Shafi Khan's son Shamim Khan killed one of his father's murderers, a man named Asgar, at the Rajhans Mansion in Dhanbad. It's gruesome: Shamim shot Asgar, then plunged his knife into one of his eyes. Shamim Khan then walked into the police station and surrendered to the local cops for stealing wood – a common enough practice to evade murder charges. 'This is how it goes. Suppose I steal some iron scrap. And someone files a case that iron scrap of fifty kg

---

[13]The killing of Sardar Khan in the film, though based on the real-life murder of Shafi Khan, has been compared to and said to be inspired by Sunny's killing in *The Godfather* by reviewers.

has been stolen, okay? Now I kill somebody the next day and then I go and surrender for stealing iron scrap. So then I am put in jail and then get bailed out,' explains Zeishan Quadri.

The incident is played out similarly in the script.

Again, as in real life, Danish/Shamim Khan is killed at the court house when he is released on bail. The Madrid draft of the script ends Part I with Danish's murder, shot dead by Sultan and Fazlu.

As the time zone shifts to the 1980s, which is well-chronicled with much more research material available, Part 2 of the saga takes a different approach. 'Part I is rooted, with more emotions, while in Part 2 everybody is having a ball … I was only trying to see these people as they are which I found absurd. Most of their actions are pointless. I found these characters extremely amusing. The gun is an extension of their hand. Their personality without the gun is non-existent. Their world is so small. I find them so strange, because Wasseypur is two streets. There are just two streets. What are they fighting for? Why?' asks Kashyap.

The script imbibes this sense of absurdity as it tells the tale of Faizal Khan, the second son of Sardar Khan and the hero of this story. It takes the story back into the past[14] – Sardar Khan's marriage, young Danish assisting his father's escape from prison, Sardar Khan abandoning his wife and kids for his Bengali lover Durga, the friendship of Faizal and Fazlu, Faizal throwing stones at Durga's

[14]These scenes were later pulled from Part 2 and put in Part 1.

house. These scenes provide a foundation to Faizal's character development.

With the action shifting to the new generation in the 1980s, there are references to the influence of Hindi cinema, seen in the way the characters model themselves after their favourite stars. 'M Sasikumar's *Subramaniapuram* which shows how cinema impacted Rajnikant fans was a trigger point for highlighting the effect of cinema in Wasseypur. Without *Subramaniapuram*, this script could not have visualized the impact that popular film has on the life of people,' says Kashyap. Further vindication of the depiction of this 'Bollywood obsession' as Kashyap calls it, comes from Wasseypur itself. 'There was this report of how a murder was planned on the release date of the movie *Munnabhai MBBS*. This is because they were sure that the targeted person, even if he was in hiding, would definitely come for the premiere of the film. Everyone comes for the premiere, you see,' says Kashyap.

Faizal Khan, in keeping with his times, is shown to be an Amitabh Bachchan fan – he constantly refers to himself as Vijay of *Trishul* and to his father as Sanjeev Kumar.[15] The constant identification with a Hindi film hero is emphasized in the way the dabanggiri of a person is

---

[15]Directed by Yash Chopra and written by Salim–Javed, *Trishul* (1978) is the story of an illegitimate son Vijay (Amitabh Bachchan) whose mother has been abandoned by his father (played by Sanjeev Kumar), and the son's revenge for his mother's suffering.

represented – some do it the Amitabh Bachchan style; some prefer Sanjay Dutt and some are modelled on Salman Khan.

This imitative behaviour is rather cheekily underlined in a scene in the film where Faizal Khan poses in front of a mirror with a gun in his hand. Kashyap cannot stop laughing as he says, 'This is my anti-*Taxi Driver* moment. Here Faizal pretends to fire the gun in the typical way Hindi film heroes of the era do. You can see this in western films from Hollywood, where the cowboys shoot their revolvers and then spin the cartridge chamber. Our people copied it without understanding that here they are using pistols which do not have a chamber.'

Kashyap uses Ramadhir Singh to drive home the influence of cinema in India. 'The sequence where Ramadhir Singh says that he has remained alive and successful when his enemies have died because, "mein cinema nahi dekhta" is the key. That was my driving force for Part 2. Woh scene soch ke likha hua scene hai. What I wrote are my actual feelings, the words are my actual thoughts on the subject. Those are my feelings about this country, about the world we live in. Everything comes from cinema; people here take cinema so seriously,' says Kashyap.

Faizal Khan's rise to power in the film begins with the macabre killing of Fazlu. Fazlu is beheaded and his head is delivered to his mother. This again is something that his real-life inspiration Fahim Khan had allegedly done. Street lore has it that after the beheading, Fahim walked up to a sweet shop called Shankar Mishtan Bhandar in

Ara Mor and bought sweets which he gifted his mother, telling her that he had avenged his father's and brother's deaths. The murder established the varchasv of Fahim Khan in Wasseypur and he set to build on his father's empire. His counterpart in the film follows the same fate – he becomes the overlord in the iron-scrap dealing business.

Ramadhir Singh's presence in Part 2 abates a bit; his real-life inspiration Suraj Deo Singh died of a heart attack in 1991. In the film, Ramadhir's political savvy serves as a contrast to the naivety of Faizal Khan who is set up for one betrayal after another. The first of the betrayals is by his friend, Fazlu. The second happens with Shamshad, based on the real-life Saabir Alam. The script followed the real-life friendship between Fahim Khan and Saabir Alam which had turned sour. Their eventual enmity resulted in the death of Fahim Khan's mother which unleashed a gang war that continues till date.

In real life, Saabir Alam's office was attacked by Gopi Khan. In the film, Shamshad is severely injured when Faizal Khan's stepbrother, Definite, bombs his office. This is followed by a scene where Sultan, chasing Definite, reaches Faizal Khan's home, finds Danish's widow, Shama Parveen, and shoots her in the head (again a reported incident in the real Wasseypur where Shamim's widow met with a similar fate). 'After writing the scene of Sultan killing Parveen, I went back in the story and made them brother and sister in the script. While the murders really happened, what was fictionalized was Danish's wedding to a daughter of the rival Qureshi clan. This was done to provide an emotional thrust because it then becomes a family saga – of inter-family and intra-family rivalries, of the stories of two wives, son's wife being from the enemy family and all that kind of thing. I also wanted to give Sultan more dimensions. So I wrote of Danish falling in love with Sultan's sister and his talking to Badoor Qureshi and the wedding happening. Danish marries Sultana Daku's granddaughter. I kept making these connections to get the story together, otherwise the story was too spread out,' says Kashyap.

This 'family saga' aspect is also underlined by Kashyap making Definite the son of the Bengali woman Durga. 'The idea was that he is still in the family and there is a rivalry between Definite and Faizal Khan, a certain tension. Definite and Faizal Khan are based on real people in Wasseypur who have this rivalry going. What is shown in the film actually might happen. It is predicted to happen,' says Kashyap.

Definite is based on Gopi Khan, a former associate of Fahim Khan, who is currently residing in Patna Jail. Many of Gopi Khan's stories have been used in the film such as the scene where Definite takes a snake from the snake charmer and walks about with it hung around his neck. Making Definite the stepbrother also provides him with a motive, gives him a reason to kill Faizal Khan. 'So that the audience understands his vendetta. Hindi cinema audiences are like that. They need to know why he would want to kill Faizal. They want their heroes to stay alive; they are used to him getting away with things,' says Kashyap.

At this juncture, the script is heading towards a pause. Kashyap is now just writing bare outlines of what is to come. The character of Perpendicular, Faizal Khan's younger brother, is introduced. Perpendicular is based on Chottna Khan, younger brother of Fahim Khan. The stories that Zeishan chronicles, the incidents of his crime spree which started as a teenager become part of the script, as does Chottna Khan's habit of carrying a naked blade on his tongue. His death at the hands of Sultan is used in the script.

The character Iqlakh is introduced, inspired by one Shahid Mansoor Alam who gives Fahim Khan the idea of subverting the auction that the railway holds to sell its iron scrap. He was also allegedly the person who introduces Fahim Khan to the BCCL Internet auction scam. 'Iqlakh was necessary to explore what happens now in the mafia – the auction and the manipulation. I had to tell that, as for me that was more important than anything else. I wanted to know the machinations of the mafia. I needed to show how they rig auctions and how the government tried to avoid corruption by holding it on the Internet. To bring those elements in, I had to bring in these characters,' says Kashyap.

These scenes have not been fleshed out as yet. There are just three-four lines to give an idea of what should happen.[16] Kashyap writes a couple of lines about Iqlakh being introduced to Faizal, and a half-done description

[16]The scenes were developed during the shooting of *GoW* Part I.

of the Internet auction process. He ends the script of Part 2 with the brutal attack on Faizal Khan's house. This is set up as a prelude to the climax. Right after this, the script wraps up the story with the killing of Ramadhir Singh. This again is just one line which says that Faizal Khan comes to a hospital and pumps more than 700 bullets into Ramadhir.[17] This scene is based on the actual murder of the real-life Sultan, the leader of the Naya Bazaar gang. This happens after Sultan has killed Chottna Khan. A grief-stricken Fahim Khan on getting the information that Sultan is at his home, watching television, loads up his white Ambassador car with carbines, repeaters, pistols and some thousand bullets. Sultan is caught unawares and is unable to fire a single shot in retaliation. He dies, his body riddled with bullets. 'There was this other incident of a man getting killed when he was buying fruits and vegetables. In the script I used that incident to show how Sultan in my story is killed and I used the death of the actual Sultan in the murder of Ramadhir Singh,' says Kashyap.

There are other scenes in the film which are not present in the Madrid draft of Part 2: the Faizal–Mohsina romance, the booth-capturing scenes, several scenes that connect characters to one another. These scenes would be written on the set.

Right now, Kashyap is on his way home. There is a stopover in Delhi to attend to some work but there is a

---

[17]The scene was developed just ahead of the actual shooting of the murder.

minor hiccup. 'When I landed in Delhi the airlines lost my bag which had my script. That was the worst moment of my life. I stayed at the airport for two days till they found my bag,' he recalls.

In Mumbai, a news report by Subhash K. Jha refers to Kashyap's next production being about the gangs of Wasseypur. Though the film goes into its shooting schedule as AKFPL Production No. 7, the phrase 'gangs of Wasseypur' is now entrenched in their minds. By December 2010, the shooting schedule of the film begins. 'Once we went on the set, we forgot the actual story. It is like the whole idea was, set pe jaane ke baad, jo original story hai, woh bhool jao, hum ek separate film banaa rahe hai. We stopped dealing with Fahim Khan, Shafi Khan, and Manovar Khan, and Gopi Khan and Suraj Deo Singh. We started dealing with Faizal Khan, Sardar Khan, Shahid Khan, Definite and Ramadhir Singh. They became our characters, they became our world,' concludes Kashyap.

3

The Not-so Stars

'The most intelligent man in the film is the villain and the rest of them have a collective IQ below him. The film has very unintelligent heroes.'

– Anurag Kashyap

October 2010: No. 29, Aaram Nagar, Andheri – the newly formed production unit of Anurag Kashyap's Production No. 7 is coming together as a cohesive unit. A few blocks away, aspirants are queuing up at the casting director's office. Anurag Kashyap's usual suspects in the casting department are missing in action: Gautam is working on a script and Vasan Bala is involved in his own project. Kashyap needs a new man. Mukesh Chhabra is welcomed aboard after Kashyap sees his work in *Chillar Party*.

Mukesh Chhabra has his work cut out. Though some of the principal cast are in the bag, Ramadhir Singh, Sultan, Durga and about 200-odd minor characters are still to be cast. Armed with the script, a character list and a family tree to explain the various connections, Chhabra begins his work.

With his theatre and film background, Chhabra brings a certain sensibility to the casting process. 'I had a certain process. I read the script, I shot the complete scene with the actor and then I went through every audition and gave the selected tapes to Kashyap.' The director gives him a free rein. 'The only brief I got was that attention must be paid to the language skills of the actors. They need to get the dialect right. So, I focused on actors who came from the north, mostly from Bihar,' says Chhabra.

The process of casting goes on through the shoot. Improvised scenes mean added characters. There are scenes where the crew members themselves pitch in. Akhilesh, the writer, plays Ali, one of the henchmen of the Sultan gang. In the scene where Nagma goes running through a brothel, the assistant directors play the prostitutes and customers. 'Banaras is a very conservative place. No one would come for shooting as a prostitute. Karuna Dutt, our second assistant director, was the rape survivor. Neeraj, Shlok and Shilpa are in the hunter song. Prerna can be seen dancing in the "*O womaniya*" song. Then there is a scene in which Definite has made love to a woman and there are two legs shown under the bed sheet. Those are mine!' laughs associate director Anubhuti Kashyap.

Ramadhir Singh: Tigmanshu Dhulia

It is Mukesh Chhabra who recommends Tigmanshu Dhulia. Kashyap is on board immediately. 'Ramadhir's character was based on a character from Ballia so I wanted a north Indian. I knew Tigmanshu's potential as an actor. When he directed me in *Shagird*, I knew this guy should have been an actor. But then it was about how to convince Tigmanshu to play the role,' says Kashyap.

Tigmanshu Dhulia is emphatic that he is not an actor despite the fact that he specialized in acting at the National School of Drama (NSD). 'I realized in my second year that I was a very bad actor and I should not act,' he says. 'I understand the fear that an actor goes through and I do feel that I have the ability to rectify it but khud acting karna mushkil tha.' He could enact scenes to actors and ask them to do it that way but when they would say, 'Sir, why don't you do this role?' he would demur, 'No, mujhse nahi ho payega.'

Dhulia is busy with the post-production of *Saheb Biwi Aur Gangster* when he gets a call from Chhabra. 'Anurag wants you in his film, I was told. The role was explained to me. Then I said leave the script, when I have time I will read it,' says Dhulia. He doesn't read the whole script, just the first part, and bits and pieces. He finally gets around to it when he is on location. The role, he realizes, is a bit more than he had estimated.

Kashyap feels that Ramadhir Singh, because he is a combination of many significant figures of Dhanbad, turns out to be the most intelligent character in the film. 'He is the most learned, intelligent, objective person who, if you look at it in a certain way, was actually very progressive. The only man – despite the fact that we are not telling his side of the story, our point of view was from the other side – who was evolving.'

Dhulia has not realized that it is the main villain's role. He knows Manoj Bajpai is in the film, which meant he would be the central character and so he surmises that his would be a four- to five-day shoot. 'And then I was told that my character would age from thirty-five–forty to seventy-five years and the prosthetic guys were called and I had to lie down and they were making casts. And slowly it dawned on me that I should not have got into this. But it was too late, and I could not say no,' he says.

Playing an older person worries him. 'Playing my age is fine. I am forty-four. So playing up to fifty years was not a problem. But playing a man of seventy-five – it's not just about good dialogue delivery, physically too you have to act. So when you need to do that, you need an actor who is solid, who knows his skills. Any actor can't do it. I did it though, and that I could do it was because of Anurag. If it was any other unfamiliar director I could not have done it. I knew that even if I did some gadbad, we could meet up later after the shoot and sort it out,' says Dhulia.

He does his bit to prepare. 'Beedi peeta tha and then I would drink cold water immediately so that my voice would be a bit hoarse. Anurag had given me some political references. And then the context was that it's a small town, and the costume was dhoti/kurta. So the basic, simple derivation was that he would definitely be of feudal values. He doesn't smoke cigarettes. Kabhi pahalwani bhi ki hogi. He is very ruthless, very.'

But Dhulia needs more. 'As a director, I always give an emotional thread to my protagonist, whether he is the villain or not. I ask the actor to play him like this: that you are a villain but you love your family and agar woh thread pe perform karoge you will be able to connect with the audience. If the role is substantial, kahin na kahin you need to make the character endearing, even if you are playing the villain,' explains Dhulia. 'When the shooting started I had a discussion with Anurag one night, I asked him, bhai, give me an emotional thread to the guy, for without that I will not be able to perform. So we kept talking about it and though he never quite pointed it out, he said quite a lot about other things in the film. From this I developed the idea that this guy, he kills before the other guy kills him, he does this to survive. I played him cold, not emotional and aggressive but ruthless. But I played it casually and subtly, not loud like "I will burn your Lanka, I will reduce you to ashes, you bastard"; so it came out good. Har profession ki tameez hoti hai, woh tameez bhul jaate hain when you do it stereotypically,' says Dhulia.

There are some scenes about which he disagrees with Kashyap. One is the compromise scene between Ramadhir Singh and Faizal Khan. 'It was a crucial scene, very important, two sworn enemies are meeting. If I had directed it, it would have been an important scene, because bhai aap dushman ke saath baith kar baat kar rahe ho, and you have killed his father and grandfather. I would have not done the scene like that. I would have taken him around, bahar khana waana pak raha hai … given him something to eat and asked, "bhai namak theek hai na?" I want to bring him to our side and I would not do it sitting across him. I would do casual things but talk serious stuff. Anurag wanted all that subtext to come out just through performance and that was a huge challenge for me.'

The scene he is particularly displeased with is when Sardar Khan humiliates Ramadhir Singh. 'I couldn't kill the director inside me, the writer inside me. In the scene, I am a powerful MLA. This man is not an ordinary man, he is a gangster, he carries a gun and he has people around him. And a young, just mushrooming gangster Sardar Khan, he stops my car, takes me in his jeep, takes the car to the garage and dismantles it; he fingers me and talks dirty. So I disagreed that one cannot do this with a powerful man. You could humiliate me but not in this way.'

Dhulia's endnote is emphatic. 'People said that I did well but I won't ever act again.'

Sardar Khan: Manoj Bajpai

It is late at night and Kashyap is talking with his assistant directors about how appropriate Manoj Bajpai would be for the role of Sardar Khan. They decide to call him right away. Bajpai is surprised and delighted. The two have been out of touch for a long time, a misunderstanding, says Bajpai, which is resolved during the *Wasseypur* shoot. 'I have known Anurag for fifteen years. He was a young boy; he had a lot of energy, a lot of restlessness in him, lots of chaos in his mind. He had seen my plays in Delhi, and we started talking and I came to know he was interested in writing films. I was looking for somebody to write

Satya ... Ramu[1] had put me on the job to look for a writer. So I told Anurag about the film. That's how the whole relationship started,' recounts Bajpai.

Kashyap recalls asking him, 'Sir, ek script hai, sunoge? He said, "Haan bilkul sununga yaar." I asked him, "Abhi aa sakte ho?" It was around 11.30 p.m. He said, "Abhi?" I said, "Haan sir, aajao na." He said okay and I asked what will he have to drink. He said red wine. I got a new bottle, he came, heard the story, liked it, finished the whole bottle, got a little drunk and agreed to do the role. He had just one request. In the script the name was Zeishan Khan and on Manoj's request it was changed to Sardar Khan.'

It is in the middle of the marathon narration that Bajpai decides he will do the film. 'I was drunk but I knew I was going to do the film. No matter what the script was. The narration started on a good note and it was flowing very well.'

Bajpai reads Sardar Khan as a person who doesn't have any values, any kind of thought system. 'He just does, there is no deep thinking behind it, no deep moral value. What you see is what you get. He sleeps with many women but at the same time when he sees a woman being molested, he goes and punishes the person.'

He keeps on working on his character's look. One day he feels that he should shave his hair off completely. He feels that this entire character will come through if there is no hair on his head. Kashyap, however, says, 'The head

---

[1]Ram Gopal Varma, director of *Satya*.

was shaved because I wanted to undo the image of Manoj Bajpai. His hair is curly and everyone is used to seeing him that way. So I needed to make him Sardar Khan. To make him a sexual beast, a sexual human being. There is an added animal sexuality that comes in with a shaved head. That was a visual call. Then I connected it with the revenge motive because in the north they don't normally shave heads just like that.'

The film was challenging, feels Bajpai. The challenge was to make people believe that, '...they are watching real life. I had to unlearn everything. Make it so real that people should forget they are watching a film. It was not just about being realistic for cinema; it was about being real in real life and that's the most difficult thing to do.'

There is a lot of improvisation. 'Anurag just gives me that freedom and he knows I will give him what he is looking for. Before shooting there were three-four days of reading sessions, workshops, many people talking many things, I just kept on listening to them. I came to know the girls I was going to work with. It's important considering the scenes I have with them. It's important to become friends with them,' says Bajpai.

Long conversations with Anurag help. 'Anurag loves to talk. It's very difficult to work with reserved and quiet persons. With Anurag it's not difficult. It's always important for the actor to listen to the director, for in all these conversations, there are some points hidden. So I look for these points all the time. He is the best director I have worked with. I have worked with many good ones and I always thought it was difficult to find anyone equal to Shekhar Kapur. Anurag understands my quietness and my loudness; he understands my search and restlessness.'

Manoj Bajpai considers Sardar Khan his best performance to date.

NASIR: PIYUSH MISHRA

Nasir is to be the voice of conscience. 'A person who watches everything, the silent type, he is the one who is telling the whole story,' says Kashyap. He is the guy who has nurtured three generations of Khans and his role is limited to that. 'I did not need to know where he came from. I didn't need to know what else he did except that he was there, always. It is like Sanjay's role in Mahabharata,' states Kashyap.

Piyush Mishra is given an option between Ramadhir Singh and Nasir. 'He was confused for a long time, but while writing the script I realized I needed him as Nasir and he wanted to do Ramadhir Singh.'

Mishra finally selects Nasir because, 'I felt that there would be shades to the character, that it would match my temperament. All I was told was that the character has one of his hands cut off and that he would be in the film throughout. When I got the script, I was not quite there; there were just glimpses of Nasir. I was told that the role was like that of Sanjay in Mahabharata. But who was Sanjay? He was a person too. Was he good or bad, lecherous or ethical? He is there at the beginning and at the end. Everybody dies but he is still there. What would I do with such a character? But I trusted Anurag that something would develop during the shoot.'

Though Mishra gets the script quite early he cannot understand the character. 'When I got the script, I threw it away. I just didn't know what to make of what he had written. I could not understand what the character was all about. It was all in Anurag's mind, which in a way was good, for he knew what needed to be done. At the same time, it was infuriating that actors didn't know what was happening. If you get the proper script, you work on the background; you create an imaginary background on the basis of which you act. Here what we got were scenes and we were told what to do.'

Then the character keeps changing, which irks Mishra. First, Nasir's hand is cut off. But that is off the table because of budget issues – it is too expensive to create that effect throughout the film. 'And he kept improvising. If I thought of a track to play the character, it would be changed overnight. So I gave up, surrendered, put myself in his hands, let him do what he wanted to do,' says Mishra.

Kashyap agrees that there are not many scenes of Nasir with dialogues. 'I wanted to just use his silence a lot in the film. Piyush bhai's biggest issue was that there were no dialogues. I said your voice is omnipresent in the film but he thought if he had got nothing to say, if his character was not talking much, he was doing nothing. He just didn't believe in it and he was very upset … especially the part about the whips,' rues Kashyap.

Four or five months after the shooting schedule is done with, Mishra is called to do some more scenes. 'I had to whip myself. And it was horrible. It was not a real whip but the way it was asked to be done, it was painful, very painful. But I would do that for him; actually I would do that for any director. I was told that whenever Nasir would feel guilty he would whip himself. When I was doing the whipping scenes, I was not told what particular actions had made the character feel guilty. I had no idea what those scenes were,' explains Mishra.

The self-flagellation was something that Anurag got from his former driver who used to constantly report to duty injured. He would explain, 'Hum se kabhi koi galti ho jaati, toh I whipped myself.' His back was criss-crossed with marks. 'The irony was, he had two women in his life and he would drink every night, but this false morality that he lived with stayed in my head. Nasir's self-flagellation is because he is feeling guilt. The first time he whips himself is when Shahid Khan's wife dies. He thinks, because he couldn't fight the pahalwan his friend got delayed.[2] A key whipping scene happens after the incident with Nagma which Faizal sees and runs away from. There is one more scene in Part 2 but that was purely for humour,' says Kashyap.

Piyush Mishra does not believe in the way Kashyap works with his actors, even if he agrees that the end result is brilliant. 'I don't believe in this kind of acting. This is

---

[2]Refer scene in *GOW* Part I where Nasir is asked to fetch Shahid from the mines, as his wife is having trouble in delivering the child. Nasir is not allowed inside the mines by the Pehalwan, the muscleman, and therefore there is a six-hour delay. Shahid blames him for this which makes Nasir feel guilty.

not his usual way. He wasn't like this in *Gulaal*,' says an indignant Mishra.

Mishra gives credit where it is due, however. 'He is good with actors in that he is crystal clear about what he wants of them but he never makes them feel claustrophobic. His instructions are minimal. He just tells them what not to do and he extracts brilliant performances. There were no acting exercises of any sort, even in the workshop. You see the performance and you feel that the characters are well-defined. That's how it is with him. The result will be good; you will like what you see on the screen. But if you ask whether I enjoyed the experience, whether I had fun doing it, it would be an emphatic "no",' rues Mishra.

There is, however, the conviction that an Anurag Kashyap is very necessary for Indian cinema – 'Two of his kind bhaari padega but yeh ek jo hai is vital,' quips Mishra.

RICHA CHADDA: NAGMA KHATOON

Casting Nagma Khatoon is a problem. 'No one wanted to do Nagma's character as they didn't want to play a mother,' says Kashyap. His first choice is Shilpa Shukla who refuses – she has just done a gangster film called *Bhindi Bazaar*. Then he calls Sharda Goswami who doesn't get back to him. At one point, they think of dividing the character into two, with Shabana Azmi playing the older version.

Then he remembers Richa Chadda from his *Dev D* audition. 'I really liked her audition in *Dev D* and offered her Durga's role. She had never been cast in a role like this and though it was challenging I thought she might do it. So I decided that she will be Nagma, but I knew there would be a lot of problems internally. UTV would never agree so I didn't tell her. See, when the film was being developed, everybody assumed it will have bigger names and faces because I had told them I am going to make it my first commercial film. So I first pitched the idea inside UTV. I spoke to Vikas and everybody, and they were happy. Then I told her, "I want you but there is going to be a long fight to get you to do this role,"' says Kashyap.

Richa Chadda is a newcomer to the industry. She remembers being clueless when she came to Mumbai. 'They asked for pictures for an audition and I gave them passport-size photos. I was that naïve,' she says with a laugh. She, however, gets two auditions within days of each other. One is for *Dev D* and the other for Dibakar Banerjee's *Oye Lucky Lucky Oye*. She lands the latter although both her auditions were appreciated.

In August 2010, she gets a call from Anurag. At first the role offered to her is of Durga and 'then he said, "I would like you to do Nagma's role. It is very challenging." He said, "I will be very frank with you, I approached a couple of actresses but they have not got back because it's an unglamorous part." I wasn't bothered by that, and I said I would do it,' says Chadda.

The brief given to her is that she is Sardar Khan's wife. The character ages from eighteen to forty-five. 'At that time I was doing a play by Khalid Mohammed where the character had a similar graph from twenty to fifty. So I had already thought of how I was going to do it. The weight gain, the skin, physically how it's going to be etc. So I said I could do it. But I didn't know it would be so hard. What gave me a lot of confidence was how easily Anurag trusted me to do the role,' says Chadda.

Nagma, she feels, is a woman who is very much attached to her religion, her land and has not seen the world outside her house. 'She is a strong woman, knows her place in patriarchy and is aware of her dependence on her husband. What made the character interesting for me was the possibility of her relationship with Nasir. That is the only weak moment for her and you can't judge her morally,' feels Chadda.

One of the critical scenes is Nagma's breakdown at the brothel where she finds her husband. 'I tried the emotional-recall exercise – use a sad memory to cry – it didn't work. We took two takes. It was a very difficult shot, taken by a steady cam which followed me through these small, small rooms, coming out and chasing my husband with a knife. And then Anurag came – this is the sign of a genius, a master director – he just said that till the time you keep thinking about crying, you are not going to be able to cry. After that I imagined I was just like Nagma. I felt so betrayed that this guy has made me pregnant and now he is screwing around and I howled. We did it in one take,' says Chadda.

Nagma's character requires a lot of prosthetic work for Chadda. 'I had this huge prosthetic stomach for my pregnancy scenes. In Obra, while walking to the set, women passing by would ask me very kindly, "Kitna mahina ho gaya, kahan hai tumhara pati?" ... and if I walked fast, they would admonish, "Dheere chalo, dheere chalo, kahe bhag rahi ho."' As Nagma ages, padding is added to her hips and thighs.

The shot where she has to hit the kids proves difficult. 'I really don't approve of violence. It was a difficult shot. And then I had to hit the kids properly, not fake it. He didn't tell me, however, that a kid would hit me back. I was so surprised! Anurag said, don't worry, I asked him to do that. Imagine getting hit by a thirteen-year-old boy! They have a lot of strength. Anurag is pretty smart at this. He hugged and consoled me and the kid never went out of his sight. He was constantly telling him sorry and taking good care of him,' recalls Chadda.

Working with Anurag is very comforting, feels Chadda. 'He tells you the structure, the space and then lets you interpret it your way.'

Faizal Khan: Nawazuddin Siddiqui

Hailing from a small town, Morana, near Muzaffarnagar district, Nawazuddin Siddiqui first comes into contact with theatre in Baroda, Gujarat, where he goes for an entrance exam for microbiology. Theatre leads him to Delhi, where he works for a group called Sakshi (which boasts of players such as Saurabh Shukla and Manoj Bajpai). He works backstage for five to six months, cleaning the stage, getting tea and then gets a few speaking roles here and there. And then the roles get bigger. The next step is to join the National School of Drama. 'I loved NSD. But I still lacked confidence. In the third year, I was in a play directed by a Russian director, Valentin. When I worked with him I realized that what I was thinking I was able to execute, I am able to do what I am thinking. That was an important moment,' he recalls.

After his graduation in 1996, he tries his hand at theatre in Delhi but lack of funds is always an issue. He heads to Mumbai in search of work. He is offered bit roles in films so he turns to television. 'I got a few dialogue roles in television – mostly in the true crime series. Then came a time when that also dried up … six-foot handsome guys were being cast and patta wahan cut ho gaya toh majboori main phir film karne laga. I started getting one scene in films. I thought it would develop further, ek scene se do scene milenge but that didn't happen. I was still getting one scene per film. It was a long drawn out silsila … for nearly four years. Then I did *Black Friday*,' he recalls.[3]

Around this time, he gets a substantial role in a film called *Bypass*[4] directed by Amit Kumar where he co-stars with Irrfan Khan. With *Bypass* and *Black Friday* in hand, he is beginning to be taken seriously though he is still playing side characters in films like *New York, Peepli Live* and so on.

---

[3]Nawaz played the role of Asgar Mukadam, Tiger Memon's manager.

[4]*The Bypass* was awarded with the Audience Award and the Best Cinematography at Kodak/BAFTA Short Film Showcase in 2003, Best Short Award at IFFLA and Turner Classic Movies Shorts Award at London Film Festival.

The call for *Gangs of Wasseypur* comes when he is away on a trip to his native village. He is surprised when his wife tells him on the phone that Anurag called and said to tell Nawaz that jaise woh chahta tha waisa hi role mila hai. 'I called back and he said, "Come whenever you can and read the script." When I read the script I realized what he said was true but I had never revealed this wish to Anurag and I don't know how he understood. In most of the work I have done earlier, I was the small-time thug who kept getting beaten up. But I was not like that in real life. So I hated that, there was this frustration. I wanted status-wala role, where I would do the hitting. I had never expressed this wish, this desire to anybody. But he made it happen for me,' says Siddiqui.

Kashyap first sees Nawazuddin's performance in *Sarfarosh*[5] and he is impressed. It is, however, while shooting *Black Friday* that he really understands Siddiqui's charm. 'He is a good actor, but I never paid attention to him till Aparna, my assistant and also my co-writer in *Gulaal*, kept exclaiming over him after seeing the rushes. I felt that maybe I had missed something, not seen something about him. So I went back and saw the rushes again. I saw the actor for the first time there. The special thing about him is that if you meet him just like that, he is almost invisible but once you start really looking at

---

[5]Nawazuddin plays a two-bit criminal – the scene has him in jail with another man. The inspector fires a gun at his companion, the bullet grazes the ear. The criminal played by Nawazuddin breaks in fear and says that he will confess all. The scene is exactly 33 seconds long.

him, he sucks you in. This is why the camera loves him. The camera loves anyone on whom you can linger and Nawaz is like that, you can just stay and explore him.'

Kashyap calls him to play one of the 'Patna ke Presley' singers in *Dev D.* He then wants to cast him in *Gulaal* but that does not work out. 'When I was writing *Gangs of Wasseypur*, he came to my mind again and the only question was: this was such a larger-than-life character, how will he pull it off?' says Kashyap.

According to Kashyap, Faizal Khan is a complex character, we really don't know what's going on in his head. A key element in developing his character comes in a scene which is written during the shoot where a young Faizal catches his mother Nagma and uncle Nasir in a compromising position. 'See, there is this superstition which I call the Indian concept of magic realism. People would tell me that my daughter, who is eleven, looks like she is seven or eight because she has taken my separation from her mother to her heart – that is why she has stopped growing. In the villages it's called barsai hona. When mangoes turn black, they call it barsai. They reasoned that the mango has tightened up inside too much, pulling itself in and turning black. I borrowed this for Faizal Khan's character, for his growth is stunted and he grows darker because he saw his mother with a person who has been like a godfather in the family,' says Kashyap.

This gives Faizal Khan an emotional basis – a man who takes everything personally, and this shapes his character. He is a loner. There was a voiceover in the draft, which was cut out: 'Yeh Faizal kya karta tha, kisiko nahi maloom. Voh andar hi andar rehta tha.' His only emotional connects are the woman whom he loves and cinema. The only two times he cries in the film are when he is watching a film and when he is in his home with his wife, talking of how everybody has betrayed him.

Siddiqui gets the script a couple of months before the shoot. 'I went to Wasseypur a month before the shooting. I was there for a week. I met people with whom Faizal interacted and I became friends with one of them and I spent most of my time with him. He was very close to the character I was playing and was like him. So I got many pointers from him, and I picked up how to talk from there; they dope a lot, they live on the edge. They can kill anybody thoughtlessly. They don't think of the consequences.'

He develops an understanding of the character but something is not sitting quite right. 'My first scene was when Faizal is talking to Definite in jail. I was reacting to the moment, according to my reading of the scene, but that was not the track Anurag wanted. The next was the hospital scene where Faizal Khan is recuperating after breaking his leg during the attack on his house. So I had to say my dialogues and I was saying it loud and aggressive – "ki kya kar lenge, usko wahin jaake maarenge".' The character that was being created was driven by what Nawaz found comfortable – what came to him easily. 'I am very energetic and according to my energy I had visualized the character. An actor wants every role to be done in his own energy. If there was powerful dialogue, I would speak it forcefully. It could also be because of the frustration I had in me. It happens to actors when you get work after a long time, you get a little bewildered. Bokhala jaata hai. So Anurag called me at night to his room and told me that sur nahi pakad raha tha,' recalls Siddiqui.

Kashyap explains what went wrong. 'He came to play a gangster, he had the burden of carrying the film and he thought this is the first time he is doing a film where he was the hero so he came on as a hero. So first day he came to shooting, he was very aggressive. I said to Nawaz, "Tu paagal ho gaya, kya kar raha hai? Have you gone mad?" I said, "This is not the Nawaz I know." I told him that if you are powerful you don't have to show it. And any person who tries that is just trying to attract attention, he is not really powerful,' says Kashyap.

Siddiqui recalls, 'I did it the way he wanted but during the takes I was not convinced. I felt there wasn't enough force in the words. But when I saw the rushes, it was much more beautiful, the way he wanted me to do it. You have power, you feel it, but don't spell it out. That day, I got the correct sur. That was the third day of the shoot.'

For Nawazuddin, the defining scene of the character is the one where he promises his mother that he will avenge his father's and brother's deaths. 'I put glycerin to make my eyes red shot – I was playing a junkie. But there is this stinging pain when you put glycerin and that was incorporated into this thing ki maa ka badla lena hai, the pain reminded me of this all the time. Every actor has tricks like this. The Nasir-Nagma angle adds a dimension to the character. Basically he is a *charsi* … and he wants to stay like that … but the mother's insults jar his ego. So without thinking he jumps into action, feels his life has been useless, this will give meaning to his life. So based on emotions, without thinking, he jumps into action.'

Siddiqui feels that Faizal does not really want to kill. 'It's basically the working of a small-town ego, he kills for reputation. *Uske baal* hero type *ke hain,* he is innocent, he loves his girl. He is loyal to his love. Unlike his father – in real life too, if the father is langot ka kachcha, the son tries not be like that. During the first stage of his life he thinks that there should be no negativity in his mind, but in the second stage, he is a little mature but he has to maintain his reputation, the khauff, and concentrate on business. He starts avoiding murder because he wants to be a hardcore businessman. Sometimes he thinks of revenge, but he also tries to compromise. But when it does not work, he comes back to his auqad … he has to come back to his first instinct, that is to kill.'

Siddiqui discovers a quality in himself through the film '…which I never realized was there. We have everybody within our skin, a child, a woman, a man, a criminal, a bad man –you need to discover it. I discovered the fearlessness in me. In real life too, I started to talk slowly, and friends started to tease me, saying that I have changed into Faizal Khan. I took two months to get him out of me. There was a chance that subtle touches of his would be there in the next film I was shooting, but I was careful. If you give yourself to the character, he takes something out of you; he claws something out of you.'

SHAHID KHAN: JAIDEEP AHLAWAT

It is Manoj Bajpai who recommends Jaideep Ahlawat for the role of Shahid Khan, having worked with him on Bedrabata Pain's *Chittagong*. 'We auditioned Jaideep and he was spot on,' says Kashyap. Physically, Ahlawat fits into Anurag's perception of how Shahid Khan will look. 'I just had to grow my beard and hair. And I had about a month and a half to do that. And what one gets to see is Shahid Khan as a very raw person who is in touch with his land, his roots. My character belonged to the pre-independence time, so though the most of the characters' looks were influenced by cinema, mine wasn't,' he says.[6]

For Ahlawat, it is the emotional and mental make-up of the character that is difficult to place. It meant getting into the skin of a person who is not bad but not too good either, who is dabangg but a bit of a coward too. Ahlawat cannot understand how this character, who despite being warned, goes against the Qureshis and then runs away, leaving his men behind when they are attacked. 'I remember Anurag telling me that he is a character who will run to save his life first. I wondered why. He is a leader; he should save everyone. But I realized that he is just a man and he will run for his life first. Talking with Anurag helped me to build this character and the script helped too.'

Ahlawat feels that, 'It's the situation that makes a person good or bad, and Shahid Khan was a victim of the

---

[6]Faizal styled himself after Amitabh Bachchan, Definite was styled after Salman Khan, and so on.

situation. He was dabangg in Wasseypur but kept a low profile in Dhanbad and was just doing his work and earning his daily bread. Till one situation changes everything for him. Once he becomes Ramadhir Singh's pahalwan he too sees the opportunity to be powerful and strong. He gets ambitious.'

Sultan: Pankaj Tripathi

Several options are being explored for the character of Sultan when Mukesh Chhabra suggests Pankaj Tripathi. Tripathi is from a village called Gopalganj in interior Bihar. He likes to tell the story of his village where electricity reached just a year back. 'It comes for two hours. Even before electricity came, there were mobile phones because the service providers had put a tower there. The people would go to the next village, where they had a generator, to charge the batteries,' laughs Tripathi.

His parents, who are farmers, want him to become a doctor so they send him to Patna for higher studies. Tripathi gets involved with student activists, with the ABVP.[7] An agitation lands him in jail where he meets with students of the left-wing movement who introduce him to theatre, plays and literature. 'All I knew of theatre was the plays I did in the village. There were two performed annually – very basic, low-brow plays. When we came out of jail, my left-wing friends took me to a

---

[7]Akhil Bharatiya Vidyarthi Parishad is the student wing of the Bharatiya Janata Party.

play written by Lakshmi Narayan Lal. I saw the play and I was in tears ki bhai aisa bhi hota hai,' recalls Tripathi.

Twenty-five plays later, he seeks the help of a guy at a cycle stand in the area who knows most of the theatre groups in town as many of his regular customers are actors. He is introduced to one group and his theatre career takes off. He has been working for about seven years when a NSD faculty member sees his performance and asks him to work with her. After that experience, he decides to join NSD. He gets through in his second attempt and spends the next three years in studies which he hates. 'Our theatre in Patna was impulsive, less of craft, more of instinct. I could not get the theory in NSD. It was much later that I realized my mistake, that NSD had everything an actor needs to train himself. But I didn't take advantage of that. I was a rebel. I questioned what they taught us,' says Tripathi.

After NSD, he tries working in Patna. He is married by then and theatre is just not enough to support a family. He decides to come to Mumbai. He runs into Bhavna Talwar during one of his audition attempts and gets a role in her film, *Dharm*. *Omkara*[8] comes next and then a Tata Tea advertisement which gets him noticed. Then he plays the chief antagonist in a television series, *Powder*, which had a successful run. Tripathi is working in a daily soap – *Gulal* – when he hears about *Gangs of Wasseypur*. By the time he gets to Mukesh Chhabra, the

---

[8]Tripathy plays Kichlu, an aide of one of the rivals of the main character Omkara.

casting is almost done. Chhabra promises to call if anything opens up.

He is travelling to Jaisalmer for his daily TV serial when he gets the call. He has to come to Mumbai and no, he cannot send an audition tape. Though sick, he walks in armed with antibiotics and steps into a gruelling audition which takes all day.

Tripathi is in awe of Kashyap. 'I was scared. I didn't think at all about the character, I just did it. I am a director's actor. If they give me three lines, I will not do a fourth. I will not improvise – I will do it the way he told me to do it.' However, it is tough for him. 'I could not understand the character at all. I was a zero. The first thing I thought was that since I am from Bihar, I have seen such people, in fact even been with some of them. So it was familiar. But the brutality, the dabanggiri that I didn't know, that aspect I needed to adopt, how to internalize that ... that was difficult. I was told, don't interpret the character. Just do it the way of the script. See, there is a human in every character. So I search that humanity in him. My character is a butcher. Now it doesn't mean that he is brutal. I thought of him just as me. Normal.'

There are two scenes that he connects with. One is where Sultan's power is challenged by Sardar Khan and the second where he kills his sister because she marries Danish Khan, the son of his enemy. Tripathi was upset about the second scene, and could not figure out the logic behind killing his sister. Then one day prior to the shoot, Anurag wrote a new scene where Sultan tells his sister before her marriage, 'Don't marry otherwise I will kill you.' 'I was happy, ki chalo yaar logic toh mila ... so I was comfortable with that,' says Tripathi.

But there is a problem. Kashyap insists on a controlled performance. Tripathi has to whisper that one line into his sister's ear – don't do this. In that one line, he has to project the anger at what was taking place as well as his love for his sister. 'Normally one builds up the emotion to this scene, you look at the sister, then say something and then build up the emotion in the fourth or fifth line. Here it's just one line, one take and I have to get it right. Now if I become very technical, it would feel fake. So it's a small scene but it was creating havoc,' says Tripathi.

Kashyap realizes that Tripathi wants to pour out all the emotion he can in the scene of his sister's wedding, because that's how an actor is trained here. As Kashyap puts it, 'Indian cinema has long been about dialogues, dialogues, plot and dialogues. It's all about mera emotional thrust kya hai? It's like the old story of Hitchcock. Actors ask him about motivation. He says it's in the script. When I started shooting Tripathi, I started shooting him like that. In most of the scenes I have kept him silent. I took away his dialogue. In the script where he thrashes Ehsan Qureshi (Bipin Sharma) with the chappal there was supposed to be a lot of dialogue. I cut all that out. I said just keep it silent and let the rage come out like that. It was difficult for Tripathi in the beginning because his acting, the whole idea of how to approach the character was influenced by the theatre he has done, and the daily soaps. Most actors think if they have nothing to say, they are not doing anything.'

Though a bewildered Tripathi accepts his director's instructions, it's not till he sees the film that he realizes the effect of his character's presence. 'I never imagined it would be like this,' concludes an excited Tripathi.

Reema Sen: Durga

Reema Sen comes in at the last moment. The team has auditioned a lot of girls and zeroed in on three: Pallavi Sharda, Bindu Chowdhury and Paoli Dam. Kashyap's brief is very clear. 'I needed a Bengali woman who could fit in the milieu very well and looks like a woman from that time. Bindu was too much of a girl. She could have very well played the younger Durga, but the older version was a problem. Besides she was toned. Women those times didn't attend the gym. I was keener for Paoli Dam at that time. Reema Sen was not in my thought process.'

Kashyap also wants an actor who will bring out the sensuality of the character. 'Many of those we auditioned didn't have a problem exposing but they could not bring the kind of sexuality of the nineteen sixties and seventies, which I wanted. My thing was, this is a woman who will not take her clothes off, will not wear a short skirt, and she will be in a sari and not a wet sari and yet be sensual. It has to be sensual, not sexual, and her eyes should reflect this. This was very important for me,' says Kashyap.

Sen comes into the picture after Kashyap sees *Aakrosh*. 'Because I had never worked with her, even though I knew her for a long time, I asked her for a screen test. She gave the screen test and I was sure, for me it was locked,' says Kashyap.

Zeishan Quadri: Definite

Zeishan Quadri's casting as Definite is the condition the writers place before Kashyap when he agrees to do the film. Kashyap, however, tells him that he would have to audition for it. Zeishan is very bad at the auditions. 'Terrible auditions' is how Kashyap describes it. At one point, they think of casting Rajkumar Yadav, but Zeishan keeps working on his character. When Reema comes on board, the team realizes that there is a kind of facial resemblance. They look like mother and son. 'But till the last moment I kept Zeishan hanging and only in the very end I told him he would play Definite. And that's how Zeishan came to do it and he is brilliant in the film,' says Kashyap.

Huma Qureshi: Mohsina/Anurita: Shama Parveen

Kashyap is looking for imperfection. 'My brief was just that I want a girl who is almost Madhuri Dixit or almost Hema Malini. One look at her and you feel if she was a little thinner, she would have been Madhuri Dixit. If her teeth were a little smaller, she could be someone else. Slight imperfections create the small-town beauty whom the whole town thinks of as Miss India. That slight imperfection makes them beautiful. So that's how I wanted to cast these two characters,' says Kashyap.

Huma Qureshi had acted in one of the advertisements that Kashyap directed. 'Huma was big and very stunning, and somehow the camera misses her size, it's the face that the camera captures. I felt Nawaz and Huma would make for a very odd and interesting pair and that's why I wanted to cast her,' says Kashyap. Anurita is also cast in the same way for Shama Parveen. 'When I saw Anurita I knew that she is right, but I needed to know how brilliant an actor she is. So we screen tested and she was fine. She was immediately locked in.'

Huma Qureshi recalls that she was shooting an ad with Anurag when he asked her to work with him. 'It was much later that he told me about his film and a character he wanted me to play. I didn't know much about the character and I was instructed by Anurag not to read the script. So I didn't even know my character's name.'

Qureshi feels that Mohsina is a small-town girl, much influenced by cinema. 'Even the Mohsina–Faizal romance is cinema-influenced. Their relationship is very real, very passionate but has a certain amount of stupidity and innocence. Physically, Faizal is not like Amitabh Bachchan but in his mind he feels and behaves like him. Mohsina loves Amitabh Bachchan and for her, Faizal's physical appearance or his profession did not matter,' she says.

Other Characters

Kashyap spots Rajkumar Yadav in Dibakar Banerjee's *Love Sex aur Dhoka*. 'While I was writing *GoW*'s script, I thought his role (that of Shamshad Alam) will become bigger and bigger but it did not develop. So I told him that it had not developed so much and if he wanted to step out of the role he can, but he still wanted to do it,' says Kashyap. Two actors are cast based on their physical abilities. 'I have these strange reasons for casting people,' says Kashyap. Mukesh Chhabra is cast as Nawab (Shamshad Alam's friend and business partner) because Anurag wants him to dance to the '*Electric Piya*' song, though in the rest of the scenes he is just sitting there doing nothing. Sandip Achrekar is chosen as Tangent only because he runs well and is lean. 'I wanted that in the chase sequence.'

Aditya who plays Perpendicular gets the role after stalking Kashyap for months. 'I had worked with him on a short film and he would come by daily and ask me, "Sir what am I doing next?" I used to get very irritated and push him out, saying, "Go find work for yourself, I am not going to give you work for a lifetime." But still he stalked me and then I got this idea. I told him, "I will give you a role on two conditions. One, you have to look like you look now, like a child, when I start to shoot the movie." He said, "Done." Second, I said, "This character plays with a blade in his mouth, you need to do that and you have a lot of time to learn the technique. I want you to play with a blade in your mouth – that is your audition." So he took on the challenge and he practised that every day for six months with a blunt blade. Then one day he came to me and said, "Sir I have to show you something." Out of the blue he just took out the blade and started playing with it and I was like "Wow." That is how he got the role,' recalls Kashyap.

The role of Faizal's elder brother Danish was initially going to Irrfan Khan. Irrfan was the first guy to read the story in the *City of God* version that Zeishan gave. He said he wanted a role in the film. But when Anurag started writing the script, Danish didn't develop as much as planned. The other roles had already been cast. So the idea of casting Irrfan was dropped and Vineet Singh was cast as Danish.

Satya is cast as J.P. Singh after Kashyap watches a low-budget film made in Nagpur by a film-maker called Chatrapal. Satya played the main lead in that film. 'The film was very weakly shot, but incredible screenplay and incredible performance by this actor. I did not know then but I found out that he was married to my secretary and I told my secretary, you have been here for two years, you have never introduced me to your husband. She said if it is in his destiny, he will get the role, why do I have to introduce him to you for a role?' says Kashyap.

Yashpal Sharma comes on board after a chance meeting with Kashyap on a flight. 'He was sitting next to me and wanted to read the script. He loved it. He wanted to be a part of this. I told him, "There is no role for you; he said something has to be there." Then I thought and asked him, "Will you do the role of item girl?" and he said, "Why not?"' laughs Kashyap.

Yadavji, the gun-runner who kills Shahid Khan and later on is killed by Faizal Khan, is supposed to be played by Anurag Basu. 'We cast Anurag Basu, made him grow a beard. He grew his beard for two-three months but the shooting got postponed a little bit and he lost his patience and shaved it off. My team insisted I should do it but then people would have got a chance to talk about my vanity. With no option left, I was going to do the role myself but thankfully we found Harish Khanna. I decided a long time back during the making of *Gulaal* that I am not going to let my team manipulate me and put me in a shot. I have no aspirations of being a star,' says Kashyap.

Gaurav Sharma, who plays Iqlakh, impresses Anurag with his audition. There is unfortunately no role for him. The decision to cast him happens at the last minute. At this point of time, only half the script has been done, so the character has only a few lines. When the script is developed, which happens during the shooting of Part 1, Kashyap turns Iqlakh into a prominent character. 'At that time, the rape sequence was being shot and two days later we were going to shoot the Iqlakh portion. The four guys who played the rapists were to be to be picked from local casting. But then I got an idea, why not use Gaurav Sharma for this role and connect it to Iqlakh in the second film? The connection would be that he is the son of the rapist who is forced to marry the woman he raped. So Iqlakh wants to avenge his father, and this is the motive for him to betray Faizal Khan. There is one other double role in the film, with the same actor playing Sultana Daku and his son Badoor Qureshi,' says Kashyap. He must be the only director in whose films minor character actors get to play a double role.

A key role in the film, Guddu, Faizal Khan's confidant, is to go to Sanjay Dadhich. The man, however, has just played the lead in a film called *Shahrukh Bola Tu Khoobsurat Hai* and is upset with the casting team of *Gangs of Wasseypur*, as he is not called to audition for the lead role. But what Kashyap doesn't know is that his own assistant Murari is eager to play the role. 'Murari knew that I would reject him outright. So he went and prepared his own tape with Chhabra. When I came to know, I fired Chhabra: why did you test him for Guddu? If I wanted him as Guddu, I would have told you. He was like "Sir, please watch the test" … and I saw the test and it was amazing. He just grew from there, he just flew. The role became so large that he bloomed as an actor and ended up doing *Peddlers*, and many other films. Suddenly a new actor was born,' exclaims Kashyap.

The Kashyap School of Acting

In November 2010, with most of the principal characters being cast, a workshop is organized where the actors get together to meet, discuss and talk about the film. It is an important exercise to establish a bond between the actors, to feel secure and comfortable around each other. This would happen if the actors opened up, bared their soul, so to speak. 'I do this with all my actors. I call it getting emotionally naked with actors. I spend a lot of time with them. It starts slowly, with the actors apprehensive to begin with – how will I be able to share the worst things in my life? I began with how I cheated on my wife, how I ruined my life by stepping out of my marriage, kaise main chhup chhupke daru peeta tha. Then slowly people started crying, they started saying things,' says Kashyap. This would continue up to a certain point. 'You know how much you can bond with the actors. It happens with very few actors. I find that women are less conscious but men keep thinking what others will think of them. The women are not worried, they start opening up. Nawaz completely broke down and we developed a close bond. On shoots our rooms would be next to each other and there would be long conversations. Huma was not in the workshop because her part had not been written yet. So for the first two weeks on the shoot she was very quiet and would not interact at all,' says Kashyap.

This sharing was critical in developing trust. 'My actors trust me. On locations, the doors to all rooms would be open; anybody could walk in and out. So the actors stay together and get comfortable with each other and there is no sexual tension on my sets which usually happens between men and women. I would break that until and unless I require it, then I do it the other way around and create it for the actors. I don't let them meet, and keep them apart. I did that in *Paanch* and *Dev D*. Usme gadbad kya huva tha ki I fell in love,' laughs Kashyap.

However, the difficult part is yet to begin. On the sets, during the shoot, often the actors do not know how their characters have been shaped. 'I can't always explain. Many a time, the actors who are used to the conventional method of storytelling find it difficult to understand this kind of cinema. They don't have a reference point of what cinema can be. The only cinema they know is the conventional, mainstream cinema,' feels Kashyap.

One of the things that Kashyap does to break this deadlock is to pick up DVDs of world cinema from his mammoth collection and make his actors see these films at the shoot. 'So they understand the zone they are working in,' says Kashyap. But it does not work all the time. 'None except Rajeev Ravi understands my working process – none of my ADs, none of my actors. They are always questioning, what is he doing, why is he doing this? I go by instinct, which Rajeev understands.'

Kashyap does not believe in developing character sketches, which bewilders actors who are constantly seeking their character's emotional motivation. 'I believe that what makes a character is the presence of contradictions that bring in complexities. Complexity is not just verbal. It is about actions, it is about what I am doing now and what I will be doing two hours later and what I am doing in the night and what I am doing five days later, which cannot be put together logically. It does not happen every moment in an individual's life. If you give a character sketch to an actor, he becomes very one-dimensional. For example, if there is a back story that the character is psychotic, that becomes the defining characteristic, the actor will play the psychotic all the time, his eyes will all go wild and all that. I don't want it to happen like that.'

Kashyap's challenge is to make the actors unlearn everything. 'I didn't want them to prepare too much. Nawazuddin and Richa came very prepared with their ideas of how to play their roles. I had to pull the rug from beneath them. After her first shot, I saw Richa hunched over the script. I peeked over her shoulder and it was the script and she had made notes, ki yahan pe main emotional ho jaoongi, here I will cry. It was like compartmentalizing her emotions. I took her notes and tore them and threw them in the dustbin. Richa was shocked initially but then she slowly became confident. Manoj came with complete faith and trust in me because we had worked together earlier. He would come in every day and ask aaj kya karna hai?'

At times, individual characteristics of the actors are picked up and changed to help them create the character better. 'I did this in *No Smoking.* John Abraham was very hard-working but whatever he was thinking was not seen in his eyes so we gave him spectacles. We created a character out of his vanity; I made him vain in the film. Two aspects of Abhay Deol in *Dev D* took away from the character – his jaw and his hands with its long fingers – very feminine. I gave him two things to do, a chewing gum for his jaw and made him roll a cigarette to give his hands something to do, a habit I ended picking up because I had to keep a supply for the shoot,' says Kashyap.

For *Gangs of Wasseypur,* he makes Piyush Mishra change the way he walks. 'I asked him to take longer strides and constantly corrected him if he forgot – what happens is that he is concentrating on his stride, and he stops thinking too much about his acting and the result is a very natural performance,' says Kashyap.

For Huma, the challenge is that she has a complex about the way she looks. 'I had to make her understand that she is beautiful as she is. I cast people who are just short of perfection physically. That's what is beautiful about them. That's what I find beautiful. Women in my films are always real, not "heroines",' says Kashyap.

Kashyap has a tough time with Zeishan initially. 'He

was very filmi. I was shooting the scene where Definite meets Nawaz, and I asked Nawaz to slap him hard. Zeishan was not expecting that. And the line that came out after that came very naturally. It was his best performance. "Aapne maar ke achha nahi kiya." So I figured out that he was thinking too much. So before every shot, I would hit him hard and he would be stunned and then I would say "Action!" without looking into his eyes and he would be wondering why I hit him and the lines would come out naturally. I had to break his self-respect to make him an actor. It's a risk because many take it personally but I knew he would not mind. He broke down, felt shattered. That small-town attitude was stripped out. You give a performance because your psychological walls break down. Because you realize that it's not you, it's the character.'

4

How Anurag Shot His Movie

'It is very difficult for a creative person to talk about his process.'

– Anurag Kashyap

It's October 2011, and team *GoW* is just about in place. There are the usual suspects: Rajeev Ravi, who has worked with Kashyap since *Gulaal*, is the director of photography (DOP); Wasiq Khan, who has worked with Kashyap since *Last Train to Mahakali*,[1] is to be the art director; another old comrade, Kunal Sharma, is in charge of sound design. Kashyap's usual practice is to appoint the heads of departments, leaving them to choose their own assistants.

Crisis strikes when the production team's associate director Kshipra Jain quits, citing personal reasons. Anurag places a frantic call to his sister Anubhuti Kashyap, asking her to step in. She drags her heels. She is uncomfortable – she is just three films old, it is too much of a responsibility

---

[1]Short film for Star Plus channel's television series *Star Bestsellers* (1999)

and she doubts that the unit will take kindly to a sibling being appointed as their head. Anurag insists. The shoot is scheduled for December, and this is a mammoth project. He needs someone who can understand him. She hesitates. 'Anurag works in such a disorganized fashion. He is a genius but a painful director to work with for the ADs,' she says. She would know; she worked with him on *Dev D*.

Kashyap's obvious distress makes her change her mind. Anubhuti spends her first day reading the script. 'It was half-baked. He had written Part 1 and that too not in proper screenplay fashion. Part 2 was only half written. And it looked massive,' she says. Anubhuti fears that two months is going to be too short a time but Kashyap is optimistic, 'Ho jayega', he says, 'kar lenge, kar lenge.' Anubhuti is not as sure as she looks over her team of assistant directors which, apart from Prerna Tiwari, consists of eight newbies. Kashyap's penchant to take on board those with skills and passion keeps his production office brimming with young talent, which usually means a new crew of assistant directors for every film.

Her second day in the office has the line producer warning her that she can take only five ADs with her when they go on shoot. Anubhuti makes up her mind: she needs an experienced chief assistant director and she knows just the person for the job – Sohail Shah, who has worked with her before in *Peter Gaya Kaam Se.*[2] Sohail

[2]Film produced by UTV Motion Pictures and directed by John Owen.

joins the team mid-October. Anubhuti knows him to be a thorough professional and very hard working. 'He was a little introverted. So initially there was a little friction with the team but I trusted him to do the job well,' says Anubhuti. Assistant Director Neeraj Ghaywan recalls how at the end of one day, Sohail told them that he was thinking of leaving an hour early, for his sister was getting married that day. 'The whole day he had been getting calls from his family and we realized why. His commitment to us and the film overwhelmed us.'

The team is further strengthened by Shlok Sharma who has worked with Anurag as an assistant director since *No Smoking*. He has graduated from an AD to making short films and is prepping for his own feature debut. When he hears of this project, he is ready to go back to being an AD just to be a part of the film. Kashyap reacts in his usual blunt fashion, 'Pagal hai kya? I am making you second unit director for this project.'

At this point of time, the schedule is not ready. The newbies are not yet familiar with the process wherein the script is broken down into scenes, against each scene the requirements from each department are jotted down: costumes, art work, properties, camera and so on. The work begins in earnest after Sohail joins. The schedule is created and power point presentations are prepared for each department for each scene. All this involves a lot of research and referencing and the entire team of ADs is roped in. The schedule is ready by the end of October.

While the production team begins to draw up the shooting schedule and its requirements, Shlok is asked to go for the first recce since he is the most experienced in hunting locations. Though Kashyap prefers to shoot at the locations where the story is based, going to Wasseypur and Dhanbad is out of the question. Jai Mehta, the assistant director who had accompanied the writers of the film on their research trip to Wasseypur, makes it clear on his return that it is next to impossible to shoot there – the spaces are too contemporary.

Kashyap needs locations that will not only be used for the period sequences of Part 1 but also for the contemporary time zone of Part 2. 'Wasseypur's history is divided into three time zones: in the beginning it's a village outside Dhanbad, next the village extends into Dhanbad, and in the third zone it becomes the centre of Dhanbad. I asked my team to search for real locations based on this. Wasseypur became an excuse; it was used as a metaphor to explore the whole of the northern region,' says Kashyap.

Kashyap has already identified his childhood home in Obra (Uttar Pradesh) to portray the early years of Dhanbad. 'While I was writing the story all the places that were coming to my mind were the ones where I spent my childhood. I went back to my roots, where I grew up and the scenario there is not very dissimilar to what's happening in Dhanbad. Instead of finding and discovering Dhanbad, we went to something parallel. Meri recce toh bachpan se chali aa rahi thi. I knew the location like the back of my hand.'

Obra is a small town which hosts a thermal plant that at one point boasted of being the biggest in Asia. The entire belt is dotted with open-cast coal mines. 'You have hills on three sides and water on one side. Every fifteen to twenty kilometres, there is a government colony. At some places there are water bodies too. The colonies have retained the look of the time they were built in. The combination of hills, water and the old colonies made a very scenic landscape,' Anubhuti remembers.

The power plants are significant to Anurag who says he likes shooting on real locations. 'I like things very real and rustic and raw and rough.' He hates making things unnecessarily beautiful. For *GoW*, he wants the landscape to be exaggerated emotionally and physically which is why they shot a lot of places like Obra's thermal power plants. Though the coal mines have nothing to do with power plants, they give a sense of the kind of place Kashyap wants to capture. They were brought in to create that exaggerated larger-than-life landscape and a sense of time – they gave a sense of a town that is emerging.

For the rest of the locations, it is decided that the starting point will be Banaras and it is here by the end of October 2011 that Shlok ends up conducting the first rough recce. Anubhuti, who is busy organizing the actors' workshop and other pre-production jobs back in Mumbai, joins him after fifteen days. Shlok keeps the time zones of the film in mind as he hunts locations: the first from the 1940s to the early 1950s, the second in the 1970s and the third, the contemporary time zone. 'For the seventies and eighties I looked for houses made of bricks, as that was the norm at that time in villages. No cement was used. I was backed by efficient ADs whose research gave us pointers for each decade,' says Shlok Sharma. The ADs had contacted several people from Wasseypur and Dhanbad to figure out the feel and look of the places in that era. Zeishan and his friends are a big help here. For example, several shoots are located at petrol pumps placed in different decades. The research helps Shlok to identify how a petrol pump looked in the 1960s and 1970s.

He looks for locations close enough to Banaras to facilitate travel but suitable for the period look they require. He zeroes in on Ahraura, a village which is about a one-and-a-half-hour drive from Banaras. It is more of a kasba, with a small railway station. The architecture of the houses within a small colony in the kasba where Muslim households are clustered looks perfect for the Qureshi Kasai Mohallah scenes.

Another place identified is Chunar, a predominantly Hindu town, and different from Ahraura in look and feel, which is important. This is because in Wasseypur there is a difference in the spaces occupied by the two communities – the Qureshis and the Pathans – which needs to be reflected in the film. It is decided to keep Chunar for the Pathan side (the Khan family). Besides there are 200 sub-locations, houses, alleys, marketplaces that are needed and Chunar can fulfil these needs. Locations for Ramadhir's bungalow and some scenes placed in the Patna jail are identified in Banaras proper.

As Kashyap points out, 'We divided the time zones in different towns and villages, so if you see in the film the landscapes are changing with the times.' Obra in Uttar

Pradesh, which has an early 1970s industrial town feel, becomes Dhanbad. Wasseypur is largely Ahraura. For the contemporary period everything is in Banaras city and Chunar. 'We have not just shown the development suddenly. We have shown it happening in phases.' In the scene where Ramadhir is talking with his mentor you can see a bridge being built in the background. The scene is shot with the complete bridge which is then broken down using computer graphics (CG). 'The whole idea of a time zone was that development is going on. So this was the way the time zones were created,' says Kashyap.

While Kashyap knows exactly what he wants in Obra, the team is frantically trying to get approvals of the other locations from both him and Rajeev. It is becoming difficult to synchronize their time with that of the art director Wasiq Khan. 'It was tough. For every sub-location we had to speak separately to the production designer, the DOP and Anurag, and all three had different opinions because they themselves had not shared their vision within themselves. Normally, Rajeev is very clear on how Anurag sees the space. For *Dev D* and *Gulaal*, he and Anurag would spent a lot of time on each location, even discuss things like, "Yeh room ko pinkish kar lete hain poora, aur usi tarah ka world rahega, ajeeb sa dollhouse world jaise jisme Chanda lives." For Wasseypur, there was no feedback so it was very stressful and confusing before we finally reached a decision,' recalls Anubhuti.

Anurag's plan is to go to the location on the day of the shoot with a fresh, open mind, take in the look and feel of the place and then decide how to go about it. For him, the script is a map and each location on it a space to be explored. His cinematic vocabulary does not restrict the word 'location' to the physical nature of the space where the process of 'lights, camera, action!' rolls out. It is an integral element in his approach to film-making – the location is where the ideas walk in, characters evolve, where the physical environment is a source of context for the characters and the incidents in the film. 'Once I am on location I start to explore it and then ideas come about. This way the film becomes more rooted in the place I am shooting in,' says Kashyap.

After much persuasion, Anubhuti gets him to agree to a three-day recce. Anurag gives the go-ahead for Ahraura and Chunar but does not give any specifics regarding what he wants done there. At the end of three days, Shlok and Anubhuti are still confused. The team works out a plan. They think they might get him to agree and approve specific places during the first week of shooting, with both him and Rajeev on the scene. The three with the most experience would be in charge of this – Sohail and Shlok would go on recce for locations while Anubhuti would manage the set. 'It didn't always work,' says Anubhuti wryly. 'It is always tough to keep up with Anurag and Rajeev with the speed at which they shoot.'

The instinctive understanding between Anurag and his DOP keeps the unit on its toes. Before one shot is completed, assistants are setting up the next shot. 'So yeh cut hota hai and next shot is ready. You need that kind of alertness on the set. And both of them are very impatient. If the next thing is not ready, if there is any wastage of time, they start shouting and then it's difficult to get back in the mood,' says Anubhuti.

With Anurag bent on exploring characters and scenes in conjunction with the location, the team learns to deal with impromptu decisions. This starts right at the beginning of the shoot. Anurag decides that instead of using Banaras for the interior shots of the Sardar Khan – Nagma marriage and of their first house, he will shoot these in Obra and Anpara (the adjoining village). 'Three days before the shoot, Anurag said, "Yahan mazaa nahi aa raha, let's go to Obra." The script showed interior scenes – that could happen anywhere, so why Obra?' questions Anubhuti.

For Kashyap, the script has led him to spaces rooted in his personal history. 'Main woh pahadi pe jaake baithta tha where young Faizal sits. Uss ghar main jaa ke shoot kiya, jahan pe hum log rehte the. The bridge you see where Sardar Khan and Asgar are walking is the bridge where I used to go. While growing up, I would often think that this would make a great location for a film shooting. I have used all those childhood locations in the film. My childhood is etched on the screen.'

Sequences are built around the Kashyap siblings' romping ground. The hill nearby used to be where they caught porcupines. How do you catch a porcupine? Carefully. You put a bamboo basket on it and then you keep shunting it till you get it home and keep it as a pet, feed it, play with it, till mother finds out and thrashes you. The hill is used in the scene where a young Faizal Khan sits after running away from home. The scene is also inspired by another childhood memory – Abhinav, Kashyap's younger brother, had run away for three days before he made his way back home.

The shift to Obra for an extended interior shoot makes for a logistical nightmare. The base camp has been set up in Banaras. The cast and the crew will now have to travel five hours to reach Obra. There are no trains; they have to travel in hired cars and buses on a busy truck route. The production team reaches Obra two days prior to the shoot, with the production designer and the art team. Last-minute permissions are applied for and quickly obtained because of Kashyap's connections. 'But my team could not find the desired locations, like where Sardar Khan's house will be and all that. So I just gave them the directions that there is a colony there where you will find the house and that was the house where we lived. And they went there and sought it and we got it,' says Kashyap.

The first three and a half days of the shoot take place in a house two doors away from Kashyap's childhood home. There is a huge amount of excitement combined with nostalgia. Anubhuti and Anurag argue over the gate at which he lost the tip of his little finger while swinging on it. Friends of the family pour in, aunties and uncles who indulge in memories that neither Anubhuti nor Anurag seem to remember.

Kashyap's exploratory activities using his script as a map means scenes being added overnight, rewritten beyond recognition. 'Bound scripts are very boring,' shrugs Kashyap, a fact that is painfully obvious to Anubhuti.

Anurag has assured everyone that Part 2 is nearly finished – there are about eighty pages done and it is just the matter of writing the climax, 'chhota sa climax' as Anurag calls it. But as the shoot progresses, so does Anurag's writing and it dawns on the team that the small climax has developed into something that could make an entire film in itself. Anurag accepts, 'I did toy with the idea of making a third film during the shoot.'

The Obra shoot is also an eye-opener for the team as to what Anubhuti calls Kashyap's 'organic way' of shooting. Despite all the preparations that Anubhuti and her team have made, the shooting often progresses as if it has a mind of its own. It keeps changing as per location, as per the circumstances that the camera finds itself in on that particular time and day and venue.

They shoot a scene here which characterizes the entire schedule. One of the scenes to be shot is a crisp two-liner in the script: Sardar comes out of the house, Nagma does the ritual to ward off evil eyes, and he, Nasir and Asgar drive away. Anubhuti and the others assume that the action will be located in the drawing room, with actors Manoj and Richa. But by the time Anurag reaches the location, the scene has changed.

'The house layout was such that it had a bathroom, a verandah, and a room from which you could exit the house. There was a kitchen and then another bedroom inside. Anurag planned a single-take sequence which he placed through the entire house. Sardar Khan is in the bathroom, so he comes from there and passes the kitchen where Nagma is doing her preparation for nazar utarna.

So then you follow Nagma, she is working in the kitchen and then she goes into the room, Sardar ki nazar utarti hai, and then she comes to the living room and then she goes into the other room where Nasir and Asgar are and she does nazar utarna on them too. Then they go out, get into the jeep and ride away. All this is choreographed in a way that you see the entire house in one scene,' explains Anubhuti. The single-take shot was later edited to several scenes.

The team is nonplussed – they are just not prepared for it. They have set up just the drawing room, the rest of the rooms are still being painted. The art team reaches the set early morning, comes up with a plan of how to get the rest of the rooms required in the shoot, ready and executes it in half an hour. This is a valuable lesson to the team, making them open their minds to the fact that anything can happen in the shoot. Anurag can shoot anything in a given location and not just where the team thinks, going strictly by the schedule.

Three scenes shot in Obra when combined last thirty minutes. With such continuous long scenes, Anubhuti worries about what will happen on the edit table, how long the film is going to be. Rajeev Ravi later starts calling up their editor Shweta Venkat, warning her about the enormous amount of footage that is coming her way. Kunal being an old-timer in Anurag's crew, knows of Anurag's fondness for improvisation. 'Once he writes the script, he is not bound to it, which is what is brilliant about him. He can improvise any time on the shoot, change anything he wants, which also makes him a very frustrating guy to work with. But that is also the magic with him. Anurag will come on the sets, stay there for a while, look around and come up with something brilliant that neither Rajeev nor I would have thought about.'

'This, however,' rues Kunal, 'is particularly hard on the ADs who have to constantly be on their toes. Since they don't know what he is going to ask for, they are prepared for everything and anything and make sure they are ready to give him whatever he asks for.'

That the three of them complement each other is amply clear, as Kunal narrates how they would reach a location and wonder what to shoot there only to have Rajeev setting up an amazing frame, keeping the unwanted things away. 'He has got the eye, Anurag has got the idea and I have got the ear,' is how Kunal puts it.

Questions about Anurag's camera technique elicit a crisp answer: 'I follow the character, that's my only camera technique.' Kashyap and Rajeev Ravi have stopped using cranes and trolleys. 'Those just enhance a certain emotion that you are trying to create. I have stopped doing that in my last four films. It takes a lot of time and also unnecessarily enhances the melodrama. I have completely discarded all the paraphernalia. *Dev D* main bhi gin chun ke do jagah thay, uske alawa kahin nahi tha.' For this film Rajeev suggested shooting the earlier parts in classic-film style, and as the story becomes contemporary, so does the shooting style. 'So we started shooting cinemascope, then it became Super 35 and then we started using Alexa and all 5Ds and 7Ds as we went contemporary,' explains Kashyap.

With Kashyap, the sound design usually lies in the script. He describes the moods, the lighting and the location. This time Kunal finds that it is the situation that is set up rather than the scene. 'I had to mike every actor for I didn't know who is going to say what. Anybody could improvise.' This leads to him abusing and yelling 'Quiet' on the sets very often and the ADs retaliating by calling him 'Gabbar'!

'Much more happens when you are doing a shoot with Anurag,' says Anubhuti. 'The story grew with the place. It started the first day itself. Like the scene of young Faizal getting up in the middle of the night and seeing Nagma with Nasir. That scene was written after the first day's shoot. Anurag connected this scene to Faizal running away from home and sitting on a hill, with a voiceover saying that the image stuck with him and he somehow aged quickly due to which he always looked older than everybody else.'

Many scenes are based on Anurag's memories. 'I have picked up elements in Obra. See, for me to relate to a character's childhood, I had to bring in elements from my childhood. When I was young, I used to wonder why my parents would lock the door. I would try to get a glance, a peep inside. I was very curious. From there came the idea of Faizal peeping into his mother's room. Mom used to hit me right in this aangan, bam bam with chappals and jhadu. She remembers this and she feels bad about it. I used that in the scenes where Nagma hits her children. You draw a lot from your own life to interpret somebody else's,' says Kashyap.

Every night, Anurag writes new scenes or expands or rewrites scenes while assistant director Neeraj sits waiting patiently for him to finish. Neeraj is one of Kashyap's protégés. After quitting his corporate career (he has a MBA degree) to follow his passion for cinema, Neeraj was working as a spot boy for UTV. He also worked part-time as an editor for the now defunct Passion for Cinema portal. A call from Madrid where Anurag is writing the *GoW* script makes him rethink his position. 'If you don't take the risk, how are you ever going to realize whether you have a film-maker in you or not?' Anurag tells him. Neeraj puts in his resignation. In July 2010, Neeraj was the first, along with Karuna, the AD in charge of costumes, to join the *GoW* team. Though he is the script supervisor and in charge of continuity, he is also responsible for the massive amount of research that goes into the film. And one part of his job is deciphering Anurag's scribbles and typing them into his laptop, and taking printouts and copies for the cast and crew for the next day's shoot.

'The first night Anurag was narrating and I was watching the clock. We had to wake up next day at five a.m. for a six a.m. shoot and I thought these guys would be sleeping early, like ten p.m. The clock showed two and then three and he was still writing. And then he gave me the book. With the story spanning generations I had to calculate each thing, the individual, the age he or she was in and match it with the time period and location. Then I had to put the scenes in the right places in the screenplay which was very crucial. By the time I went to my room, four to five people were already there.'

The space is crammed; someone or the other is always in the room. The government guesthouse in Obra has just twenty rooms, so four people have to share a room. There are times when Neeraj sleeps on the couch with his feet in the air. 'Now I had to type it out, take a printout and give it to the actors and not only that, I had to punch it into the screenplay for continuity. I could not work in the room because I could not turn on the light. So despite it being cold I had to sit outside and I was shivering and typing till four thirty in the morning.' Neeraj begins to hate the small printer that seems to have become an accessory during the entire shoot – he has to lug it around daily. 'The vile printer will be thrown from the heights of Chunar fort,' he promises.

The sight of Anurag scribbling away in his notebook becomes a familiar sight on the sets. The scenes are rapidly written because Anurag has been ruminating over them during the breaks in the shoot. 'Anurag normally walks with his head held straight but if he is thinking, his head tilts on one side. So we had this joke: we would say, "Sir ko bulao," then we looked at him and would say, "Abhi chhod do, sarr teda hai," Anubhuti says, laughing at the memory. Often Anurag gets so lost in his thoughts that he does not realize what is going on around him. 'Once, just after the petrol pump shot, we were walking back and we saw Anurag sir deep in thought, walking right in the middle of a busy road,' recalls Neeraj.

A day in Chunar has the team frantically searching for Anurag who is in one of his thinking phases. 'And of course his phone was never with him and even if it was, he would keep it on silent. So we were coordinating with each other on walkies, "Arre Anurag sir ka shot ready hai" and one by one the ADs began responding that they hadn't seen him,' says Neeraj. 'And it is a small town but you can get lost in the gallis,' interrupts Anubhuti. The team finds him at a food stall, having gulab jamun. The walkies squawk in relief – 'Anurag sir mil gaye, gulab jamun kha rahe hai.' Then Anurag realizes he has lost his bag, so the walkies go back in action, 'Arre Anurag sir mil gaye par unka bag nahi mila.'

Neeraj is often handed a scene scribbled on paper that he has to add to the screenplay. This at times happens just minutes before the scene is to be shot. For example, the scene in *GoW 2* in which Iqlakh is to be introduced. The script calls for Faizal in his office with Guddu and Nasir. He would be talking to the police and inquiring why Definite has been shifted from Dhanbad to Patna jail and then Nasir and Iqlakh would walk in. The set is prepared, the actors know their lines and Neeraj goes to Kashyap to tell him that they are ready for him. 'Ek minute', says Kashyap, 'aaj ye scene aise karte hain.' The actors are handed a new set of dialogues. 'For one scene, not only did he talk about Faizal enquiring about Definite, he added quirky dialogues to reveal the collective IQ of the people there – and Iqlakh is introduced as a character more educated and sensible in contrast to this whole chaotic bunch of morons. He wrote that scene in a way that set up the events that would come later in the film,' says Neeraj.

'It was quite an improvised set up,' agrees Nawazuddin.

'There is a scene when my character is in jail and I have to walk along a corridor talking to my wife on the phone. We have just begun the shoot, the lights are on and then he comes and describes this scene, and he describes it so fast that sometimes one does not understand. The dialogue keeps changing even as he talks to you. You are in character, and next thing you know, he has added five to six dialogues, and you don't know quite how to and where to place the line. Sometimes dialogues were added during retakes!'

Several incidents are inspired by conversations in the acting workshop conducted prior to the shoot. Anurag picked up elements from the lives of the actors and put them in the film. One person in the workshop narrated how he saw his mother in a compromising position with his grandfather and how he left home after that, cutting all ties with his family. That became the basis of the Nasir – Nagma angle in the film and was tied to Faizal peeping into the room, which came from Anurag's childhood.

Sometimes the additions/improvisations happen purely due to the actor cast in the role. But the nature of changes is such that it enriches the script by adding a dimension to the characters and establishing connections between the past and present of the film's story. The character of Ehsaan Qureshi was barely a dot in the script of Part 2, a minor henchman. 'Ehsaan's character was written as a silent character but when Bipin came and said he wanted to do a role, uske liye dialogues likhe thay and that was the turning point in the film. If Bipin Sharma was not playing this role, these scenes would not have been there,' says Anurag. Two new scenes in Part 1 are added during the shoot for Bipin. When Shahid Khan is sent to Kolkata, Ramadhir sends Ehsaan to kill Nasir and Shahid Khan's son Sardar but he doesn't find them there as they had escaped. Ehsaan goes back to Ramadhir Singh's house and lies that they have been killed and the bodies disposed of. The other scene is laced with dark humour as Ramadhir discovers that Nasir and Sardar are alive and calls Ehsaan to ask him about it.

Another scene which grows on the spot is when Sultan beats up Ehsaan at Ramadhir's home. Pankaj Tripathi, who plays Sultan, recalls, 'That scene was given to us on the day of the shoot. Now I think every genius has a child within him and it was that child that thought up this scene. I was told that when you walk out of Ramadhir Singh's house after being berated by him, you will pick up a chappal and Bipin will start running. Sunn ke hi hasi aa rahi thi and everybody loved the idea.'

Elements of the Faizal – Mohsina romance come from Nawazuddin's memories. 'That was Nawazuddin's first date in a small park in the town where he lived, when the girl said, how can you touch my hand and he broke down,' says Kashyap. The scene where he wants to take her to see a film happens with Anurag calling the actors, writing the scene there and then and shooting. The scene where Nawazuddin is being teased about his age is shot because of his self-consciousness about an earlier scene. 'When Danish dies, Faizal is comforting his mother, he and Nagma are sitting next to each other and they looked the same age, there was a moment when it seemed that they were about to kiss,' says Kashyap. They decide not to use the scene but the image haunts Anurag to the extent that it leads him to create this scene where it is emphasized that Faizal Khan is younger than he looks.

A mistake in continuity happens during the sequence showing Faizal Khan's release from jail, which is shot in Chunar. 'There was very little time and only one senior make-up artist was designing the looks for everyone. Richa Chadda (Nagma) had to look old, a mother of a forty-something man. We did the wrinkles on her and it turned out well but when her turn came for prosthetic make-up we were running out of time. So the make-up man tried to do the make-up with shading,' recalls Anubhuti.

The action is being seen on clamshell monitors which are usually used for outdoor shoots. The reason: bigger monitors would attract crowds and disrupt. 'So when we shot those first few scenes with Nagma in old age we checked in the small monitor and did not realize that she wasn't looking very old. Her makeup is not good in the whole film and because we couldn't change it we stuck to it because by that time we had already shot so many scenes with her in old age,' says Anubhuti. Post-production CG helped to shade her hair to look as if she had applied mehndi and to accentuate the dark circles under her eyes in an effort to make her look old.

Sometimes scenes were also used to provide motives to certain characters' actions, 'to make it obvious to the audience', as Anurag says wearily. For example, the scene in Part 1 when Ramadhir insults and beats up his son J.P.

Singh after the humiliation they suffer at the hands of Sardar Khan at the police station, is added because the angle of J.P. Singh's involvement in the death of his father and Faizal Khan are added later. So his hatred towards his father needs to be explained. In fact, most of Ramadhir's sequences are written during the shoot.

Anurag's insistence on context and environment also leads to a lot of details being added to the scenes. As Anubhuti points out, most scenes have a lot of actors in them, and they can't just be sitting there. They have to be doing something, which calls for dialogues. For example, there is a scene where Sardar and Danish talk about changing professions. In the background, one can see Nagma going about her household cleaning or Nasir teaching a boy who is reading a poem.

This, however, also means that the local production team has to go scrambling for a prop about which they are informed a night before the shoot. It becomes so bad that the team puts its foot down – no requests will be entertained after seven p.m., they say, which eventually gets pushed to nine.

The scene where the father and son are discussing their new business venture has the mother Nagma using a vacuum cleaner. Anubhuti has to pick up her mother's vacuum cleaner for the sequence. 'Anurag told us, we will create period without spending money, if it does not meet our budget, we will establish period through little tricks. So if it is a train robbery set in the forties, we will show a seal on the gunny bag which was the norm during the British rule. The lock will be from British times. We don't have to worry about creating an entire village for that period,' says Anubhuti.

Sometimes props entail added dialogues – in one scene a fridge is used to denote the time zone but the one they get is ancient and the door doesn't close properly. So dialogues are added during the shoot where Nagma wonders why the door is not shutting properly and shouts at others about not knowing how to use a fridge.

The added background scenes often provide a context that adds layers to a scene. A scene in the beginning of *GoW Part 1*, which has Sultan calling J.P. Singh to tell him that Faizal Khan is dead, gets new background dialogues during the shoot. J.P. Singh is having dinner with his father and a group of fellow politicians. He gets up to attend the call. The conversation at the dinner table continues. In the background is an out-of-focus television set where a barely discernible voice is asking a politician what the national anthem is. Reacting to this, a guest at the table laughs derisively. 'The idiot', he says, 'that is not the national anthem!' Ramadhir Singh looks at his guest and asks him, 'So do *you* know what our national anthem is?' 'Of course', he says, humming '*Saare jahaan se accha*...'

'This goes back to the time I wanted to make a film called *Bihar*. Part of that script was based on Apple Singh, the character Sanjay Mishra made popular during the Cricket World Cup. He was later used in another television programme during the elections (NDTV's *Khol Pol*). In one of these episodes, he spoke to a few candidates and asked them about the national anthem. One of them said '*Saare jahan se accha Hindustan hamara*' another was humming '*Tum chalo tum chalo*...' I used that in the script where Apple Singh became a central character who is looking for Bihar. That film was never made. This was instead added to the scene where J.P. Singh betrays Sultan – he is on the phone and his father Ramadhir Singh is having dinner with other politicians and in the background they are referring to the Apple Singh episode,' says Kashyap.

The impromptu additions to the film also have the local casting team working overtime – they never know what Anurag will come up with! When the production team is hard-pressed to find a suitable location for a nursing home for the Nagma delivery scenes, Anurag suggests doing it in the house, with midwives, like how it would really happen in those times. So the local production team go scouting for actual midwives from the nearby villages who are then cast in the delivery scenes of Shahid's wife and of Nagma. Richa laughingly recalls the valuable input she had from her midwife. She asked the midwife what she could do to make the performance more real. She told me, just think that you are really constipated – woh expression dijiye or zor zor se chillaiye,' says Richa, laughing.

Context and environment are keywords for several scenes in the film. The decision to shoot in an actual slaughterhouse – a scene that will serve as an introduction to the character of Sultan – is in this spirit of creating the right environment. 'There was this twelve-year-old boy there who was slaughtering buffaloes with such efficiency and he was so enthusiastic about being in a shot. He said,

"Sir, I will cut the buffalo on my own!" That little boy was the scariest person there, a twelve-year-old who has no sense of fear and who can cut down a buffalo became, for me, a person to fear. That violence in him formed the back story of Sultan which was narrated in the voiceover that Sultan "baarah saal ke umar mein poora bhaisa akela hi kaat deta hai. Abhi din mein saath bhaisa kaat-ta hai." There was this man who was the main guy, very proudly telling me that he cuts sixty buffaloes a day and he showed me how he did it. Everybody listened to him. So that whole sense of hierarchy in a slaughterhouse came from those two – a boy who was the only boy working there, for children are usually not allowed, and this man whom everybody feared. For me Sultan became that butcher who everybody fears,' says Kashyap.

Shooting the scene in the slaughterhouse is an experience that has the cast and crew shuddering. For one, the actors who need to be in the scene are pure vegetarians except for Pankaj who plays Sultan. Tripathi is in the thick of it, literally. 'I thought there would be some four-five buffaloes being cut. And where I stepped in, there was blood everywhere. The buffaloes were being cut during that time and it was all manual. They would tie the rope, draw the buffalo up. And we had to act in that. We were up to our knees in blood. We didn't know what we were stepping on. To shoot that one scene inside we were there for two hours – there was our DOP and two other actors besides myself.' Anurag could only manage to shoot bits and pieces of the intended scene here. 'While we were shooting, the butchers cut sixty buffaloes and one camel. I couldn't walk in (to the slaughterhouse). I went in with my eyes closed then checked the shot. *Sirf actor ke face pe concentrate kiya,* then I walked out and stationed myself on the roof next door,' says Anurag.

Outside the slaughterhouse, a huge hostile mob grows to nearly 3000. The team has landed in Allahabad with required permissions and police protection. 'But what we didn't realize was that we were in the middle of a predominantly Muslim area. It is a sensitive area. We were just three ADs to manage the crowd. As we pushed the crowd back, there were teenagers who began threatening to pull out their knives,' says Anubhuti.

For Kashyap, shooting at real locations also means capturing 'aspects of things previously unseen, something the audience hasn't seen before, something I have not seen before but that exists. Like the fire that still burns in Jharia mines. I wanted to know how it happened and I shot the whole thing with the voiceover.' Though the Jharia shots are not used as they don't work well with the story, there are other sequences that come out of this approach. 'I wanted to see the sand mining, maine kaha jo bhi yahan pe criminal activity ho raha hai, sab shoot karo. We shot it like a news video. Then we tried to bring as much as we could in the film. This is how I usually make films. I go into a world and then shut out everything else and try and explore that world within.'

This is how booth capturing turns into a massive scene in Part 2. Anurag wants to show exactly how a booth is captured during elections in India. It is not as if the booth capturing is integral to the film but these little details are important to him. As he says, 'We keep hearing about such incidents that are common during elections in smaller cities. Because we don't see these, we usually use our imagination. So I wanted to show how it happens. For me the whole process of how they rig elections was important,' says Kashyap.

Neeraj is given the job of finding out how it is done. Till the eve of the shoot, the team is clueless about what needs to be done. Neeraj digs around for information and gets a lot of it online, including a blog by an IAS officer who writes of his experiences in Bihar. Information also comes from Zeishan who has seen it happening. A sixty-page document is handed over to Anurag who writes the scene which has the action happening in four booths. 'Art Director Wasiq was quite pissed about how late he got the info,' laughs Neeraj. Besides this, the camera crew positions need to be worked out and permissions taken but the team manages to pull it off.

Similarly, the hand-made gun sequence in Part 1 is shot after interviewing an actual blacksmith. The team has benefited from research for Anurag's film on Bihar which is the inspiration for the sequence. Anurag interviews the blacksmith in detail on the process of making the gun. The same details are used in dialogues between Manoj Bajpai and the blacksmith. Then they get another blacksmith to make the gun. The scene in the film requires the characters to take handles from actual trucks which would be used to make guns. Anurag recalls, 'We shot the whole process of it, took every separate shot.

We had to find trucks, take their handles out – and then we cut it together. So the whole approach to the film always has been that you know the entire process, shoot it and take editing calls later on. Shoot everything, shoot every atmosphere.'

This is also why Anurag decides he wants to show how sand is stolen. The job is handed over to the second unit. The second unit team has already shot small-time crime earlier near the open-cast mines, where they had gone to take wide shots of the coal mine. 'There was this mountain of coal in the outer cast mine, from where they were sneaking off coal and selling it on the road in small heaps. They were just poor people who were engaged in small thefts. I realized that here one can either find very, very rich people or very poor. There is no class in between,' says Shlok. Armed with a film and a digital camera, the crew reaches the location their local guy has directed them to. 'What happens is that the approved contractor is told to get manual labourers and pick up sand with their help in a day. What he does is he uses machines, which is illegal. Manually about three-four small tempos can be filled but with the machines they can fill up eighty trucks,' recalls Shlok. The team gets the shots needed and Shlok is packing up his cameras when he finds his team surrounded by a hostile crowd. 'We were so much in their area of control that if they killed us, no soul would know,' he says. Surrounded by men with guns, it takes some quick thinking and fast talking to get the crew out with the film intact.

Trouble becomes the middle name for the second unit

team. Often sent to shoot at locations without required permissions, they would end up in the local jail. Shlok would call up Anubhuti and say, 'Yaar, main jail mein band hoon.' 'First time we got really worried, second time we were laughing and our line producer would get upset because he had to go and talk to the police and beg them to leave the crew,' says Anubhuti. She can hardly stifle her laughter as she recalls the incidents. It helps that the line producer is a very influential person from the area but even he has his limitations. 'And he was really upset with the second unit. He didn't want to see their faces.'

'Even the police began to get tired of us,' says Shlok. 'Once we were at the police station for three hours. They kept asking, "Will someone ever come for you or not?" I said, "I don't know." Finally, they got tired and asked us to leave. Imagine! Being set free only because the police was irritated that no one was coming to pick us up.'

When Shlok is offered the second unit director's job he is elated, even if he thinks that at the most he will be asked to shoot the routine, 'scenery, sunrise, a goat, a cow'. However, from open-cast mines, to facing gun-toting goons to spending time in jail, the experiences that the second unit go through are anything but ordinary and the scenes they shoot add immeasurably to the film. Shlok recalls a four-day trip across north India. The first unit was in Dhanbad at that time. His team had to go from Banaras to Patna (jail) to Bhagalpur (station) to Ranchi (airport) to Kolkata (road scenes). 'First we went to Patna to shoot the jail sequence where Durga comes to meet Definite. In spite of permission, we had to bribe a local goon who was serving his sentence in that jail to allow us to shoot there. After shooting our sequences, I had to take one wide shot covering the jail from outside. While checking my shot I could see a man standing near a window of the jail. So I asked them to move the person. The jail personnel told me not to ask him to move as he wouldn't. You are getting to shoot because of him. So I realized he was the goon the police had to take permission from and whom we had to bribe for shooting there. The police did try and get that guy moved from one window to another. He was still coming in my frame but nonetheless I shot it,' says Shlok.

The team faces a dangerous situation while travelling through hostile territory in their journey to Ranchi and Bhagalpur. 'In one area we passed fifteen to twenty shaadis in one hour. These shaadis have exactly ten baaratis, one groom and some music. They were basically there to loot people who travel at night. They would stop the car to let their procession pass and then loot the people in it. We had been warned not to stop,' narrates Shlok.

The team has learnt that real locations mean unique problems. In Ahraura, the villages are away from the main road. Narrow, unmotorable paths lead to them. For night scenes, the team needs generators – there is no electricity. The generators are parked on the highway and long power cords run from there to the shooting location. The roads are made of stone blocks, which need to be covered in mud to maintain the period look. 'It was a production nightmare,' recalls Anubhuti.

Then Kashyap decides that it needs to rain when Shahid Khan, on orders from Ramadhir, destroys the workers' house. The team has to get rain machines connected inside the village. Six to seven huts are created on an empty ground. Rains, burning and breaking of huts, people running amuck, the camera following – all this is to be done in evening light which has a small window of ten to fifteen minutes. The tanker runs out of water. To top it, it gets stuck in the waterlogged mud. It just doesn't start. With a single narrow pathway, unless the empty tanker is out of the way, the back-up tanker cannot be brought in. 'We were getting ready to pack up, thinking this is not going to happen when all of sudden we see Anurag walking towards the tanker and pushing it – uphill. It had been a tough day, we were tired and wet and just wanted to wrap up for the day. And there was Anurag pushing the tanker and saying, "Come on, ho jayega," and one by one every last member of the crew joined in and we got the tanker out of the way,' narrates Neeraj.

Ahraura is also used to film the 1970s portion. The entire initial sequences of Durga – Sardar are to be shot here when Manoj falls sick. 'We shot for one day but he was burning with fever. That was 5 December. Early next morning the sequence was of him bathing in cold water and he was running high temperature. Many of the sequences required him to be bare-chested – sleeping, bathing, or roaming around. And the cold was making it worse. So we decided to take a break for a day,' says Anubhuti.

Manoj is not any better the next day. He insists on shooting, however, and the team can't afford to say no. The scenes are of Manoj at the tube well. The ADs run around making sure there is hot water for the actor. There is no electricity in the village so a bhatti is used to heat water.

For the cast and crew, despite improvisations and surprises, dealing with goons and violence and the ever-increasing cast of characters, the experience is an enjoyable one. From the spot boy to the overworked ADs to the department heads, from junior artistes to the principal cast, it has been an enervating experience. In the midst of this bustling schedule, at the foothills of Chunar fort, a tragic accident takes the life of Sohail Shah.

It is 25 December 2010, and the plan is to shoot the Sardar and Asgar jail sequences in the historic Chunar fort which housed a jail earlier. The area being deep in Naxalite territory, the team has permission to shoot for just one night and two days. On the way to Chunar is a bridge where there is half a day's shoot. It's a small bridge that connects Banaras and Chunar and allows one-way traffic at a time. The scene to be shot here is Sardar Khan blocking Ramadhir's car and kidnapping him. It's a traffic and security nightmare. The crew has to coordinate with walkies and at the same time conceal themselves from the camera in a place where there are no structures to hide behind. One camera is stationed on the fort to follow the action.

One of the shots is of the jeep leaving at sunrise which would also establish the bridge as a part of Wasseypur.

'The whole unit moved to the fort very early morning, with a few staying back to complete this early-morning shot before joining the rest at the fort. I was to go to the fort and Sohail was to do the bridge shot with Anurag. I was waiting in the jeep for the shot to finish so that I could cross,' recalls Anubhuti.

The bridge is a pontoon bridge – a very wobbly one that moves both ways. Sohail is the one driving the jeep; Sardar isn't required to drive it for this particular shot. The unit has a driver but it takes so much time to explain the intricacies of timing and speed required for the shot that Sohail gets impatient and insists on taking over. The jeep is halfway across when it crashes through the rail of the bridge. It lands half into the water and half on the banks. 'Someone came in Sohail's way and to save him, he went little more on one side but the bridge wobbled and he lost control. The water wasn't so deep that he would drown but as the jeep crashed Sohail fell from it and hit his head on the railing which was made of metal,' says Anubhuti.

Two of the crew members immediately dive in and pull Sohail out. Anubhuti's vehicle is the easiest to access and the closest to the road. 'We sped towards Banaras which was nearby and had the best hospital. He was lying in our laps – Shilpa was rubbing one hand and I the other. He was so cold; we removed his wet clothes on the way to the hospital and wrapped him in whatever warm clothes we had. Since it was early morning it took us forty-five minutes to reach there. When we reached the hospital we found out that he had passed away in the car. Sohail died in our arms.'

The whole team arrives at the hospital, shocked and shattered. 'Rajeev and Anurag were the worst hit. Anurag sir cried and cried. It was a difficult situation, with Sohail's family being understandably upset. They couldn't accept the fact that he was driving. Everybody kept asking us about it but we couldn't say anything. He was in control of the situation; he took the decision to drive himself. The mood was tense. All of us were grieving and trying to come to terms with the situation. To convince the rest of his family, to talk with them, Anurag had to fly to Mumbai on the third day. He also wanted to speak with Viacom Studio 18 to do something for his grieving family. Viacom 18 spoke to Sohail's family and said they would take care of Sohail's parents for their entire lives,' recalls Neeraj.

Anurag finds it difficult to talk about Sohail. 'It took us forever to recover from it. Every time I see the picture, I go back to the scene. Every time I see that jeep shot, it just reminds me. That jeep shot is the most difficult shot for me to see and I cannot deal with it. He was incredible. We tried to be like, the show must go on, but we just couldn't do it with everybody still thinking of him, missing him all the time. But Manoj had to leave. If Manoj didn't have to leave, I don't think we could have started shooting.'

Rajeev takes Sohail's death rather badly, for it was he who had asked for this one extra shot. The last shot. 'He took quite some time to come to terms with it, that he was not responsible for it. Anurag had gone into a totally different zone. One day in the middle of the shoot he suddenly started crying, and when I say crying, I mean howling uncontrollably. Each one of us felt responsible for it in some way, people kept thinking that they could have avoided this,' says Anubhuti.

5

There Will Be Blood...

> *'My take on violence is that the more real or actual you show it, the more it puts you off, it has a larger impact and it's less gratuitous.'*
>
> – Anurag Kashyap

Violence is the way of life of the gangs of Wasseypur. The gangs literally live and die by the sword or rather the gun. Whether driven by ambition, greed or vengeance, in this tug of war between life and death played in this minuscule arena, everyone loses. It is the futility and absurdity of this that Anurag Kashyap seeks to capture in the *Gangs of Wasseypur* films.

What Kashyap wants from action director Shyam Kaushal is to make the violence feel real and to shoot the sequences as single continuous shots. Having been associated with Anurag since the *Black Friday* days, Kaushal is an old hand at interpreting Anurag's ideas. 'These are not larger-than-life characters who need exaggerated action sequences. The approach had to be very honest; the action needed to be believable and real without technical gimmickry. Usually, cuts are used in action sequences to underline elements of a shot. In *GoW* that was not the case. Anurag did not want to underline the gore or the blood, just the impact of the violence,' feels Kaushal.

The killing of Ghanshyam pahalwan by Sardar Khan is shot this way, a continuous shot; it begins in an alley and then continues towards the main road, right in the middle of Ahraura market. 'Single-shot scenes make you feel breathless, they build up tension. The impact of violence should be that it repels you,' explains Kashyap. The scene begins with the pahalwan walking in the lane; he has a chicken in either hand. Sardar Khan will attack him here. 'Anurag wanted to show how agile Sardar Khan was. It made the scene more believable because the difference in [the built of] the two was such that he would not be able to throw the pahalwan down. Anurag told me that Sardar Khan would have to move in, stab him, move back, and stab him again. I had to make it convincing. I needed to show the stabbing and the blood staining the pahalwan's sweater. Now this was a live shot, there were no special effects to be used. So we hid plastic bags filled with fake blood under the sweater. Manoj knew the spots he was supposed to stab but the knife was a fake one, where the blade retracts on pressure so it could not pierce the bags. We could not put tubes because there was movement, so the stuntman who played the pahalwan had a ring into which a pin was welded. The idea being that when Manoj would stab him, the stuntman would bring his hand up as a reaction to cover the wound and prick the bag. So when the hand came away to cover another stab wound that Manoj inflicts, the audience sees the blood on the first one. And since the fight was shot in one long continuous take, both of them are tired and that shows on their faces, adding to the impact. If there were cuts, both of them would have looked fresh,' Kaushal explains.

The scene then breaks when the pahalwan manages to get away – Sardar Khan and Asgar follow in the jeep, hit him and then drag his body to the jeep. 'The local people were very curious; our team told them what was going to happen and how. They however kept staring into the camera. It took almost half a day, five to six re-takes and we didn't have expendable costumes so we requested them again to look at the action that was happening and not into the camera,' says Anubhuti. The team had to finally push the people out of the frame. The scene originally ended on a darkly humorous note with Sardar Khan and Asgar trying to put the body into the jeep, clumsily pulling at it in opposite directions. 'I cut that scene because I wanted a voiceover here and laughter would have broken it,' says Kashyap.

The single shot rule is not applied to the sequence where Shahid kills the pahalwan of the mines. 'This was the beginning of the film. This established the base of the Khan family, where they come from – where the anger comes from. It's the first time Shahid shows his aggression. So the close-ups taken enhance that feel. It justifies the terror that he inspires in workers later,' says Kaushal. The script has Shahid Khan attacking the pahalwan with a knife; on the set it is decided to use a rock instead. The stone he uses is actually a dummy made out of thermocol. 'You could sense that it was touching the face, it was not like it usually happens, Jaideep's performance made the brutality very real.'

'It was a very difficult scene,' says Jaideep Ahlawat who had done push-ups to work himself up for the scene. 'It is here where his inner animal instinct comes out. Anurag said this scene is important as Shahid Khan has led a life in Wasseypur where people knew him to be powerful though in Dhanbad he is lying low; no one knows what he is or can be. The character's new journey starts here. People will recognize his strength and will fear him after this.'

The death of Sardar Khan is written and shot the way the real-life Shafi Khan was killed, except in one aspect. In real life, Shafi Khan was accompanied by a driver and friends, whereas here Sardar Khan is alone in the car. The death scene is shot at an abandoned petrol pump which ironically, the team later learns, used to belong to a mafia don. 'It had to be executed well since the scene required men on motorcycles firing into the car, and the windshield and windows shatter,' says Kaushal. As an injured Sardar Khan gets out of the car and staggers onto a cart, the gun slips out of his lifeless hand. Kashyap explains, 'We took that shot later on, of the gun falling and the cart going away because that became a good note on which to end the film. When we were writing the script, it ended with Danish's death. But when we started shooting the film, we realized that something was not quite right. We needed to end it on a much larger note so

I decided yahan pe main khatam karunga, Sardar Khan ke maut pe.'

As the scene was being shot, the wheel of the cart ran over the gun that fell from Sardar Khan's lifeless hands. 'It was a fortuitous accident – the idea to make it seem that the gun fires as the wheel runs over it came later and this was done with computer graphics. My editor Shweta Venkat made it mind-blowing by putting a voiceover, a dialogue that Sardar Khan had said in the beginning of the film – "goli nahi maarenge,"' says Kashyap.

Another instance of art imitating life is the scene based on the murder of the original Fazlu, a tale that is a legend in Wasseypur. Kashyap doesn't have a clear idea of how he is going to shoot it but the location helps him to construct the scene. The actual mechanics of the action is researched by Neeraj. 'I found a website where I went through videos of beheadings. I finally found one video which showed clearly how it was done so I downloaded that and gave it to Shyam Kaushal. He saw it and then said, "Never show me this again." I even gave it to the sound guys. And to the actors, as there were many nuances to pick up, like the hand movements when you slash at the neck. And when you come to the middle of the neck, you have to hit hard for the bone to break,' explains Neeraj.

The scene has Fazlu and Faizal Khan sitting on a platform, with the camera focusing on their backs. They share a joint and then Faizal holds Fazlu in a neck lock and slashes his throat. 'It's my favourite shot,' says Nawazuddin. 'It was not quite how I envisaged it. I thought I will take a chopper and put it to his neck. I think this was done suddenly in Faizal's mind. The problem was that the camera was behind us and I had to act like I was slicing his neck open. It had to seem that it was being done with full force but my hand was going awry ... it had to be done precisely. The amount of force I would use would have to be proper. We had done the rehearsals but it had to be done in one take. I had to get the timing right.'

The stunt team, out of sight of the camera, is huddled near the legs of the actors. One of them has a Bisleri bottle full of fake blood which he will press with each slash of the knife to show the blood spurting out. When Fazlu falls to the ground, avoiding the blood and the prosthetic head designed by the National Institute of Design, Nawazuddin has to follow, bending down and lifting up the prosthetic head. The action is being prompted by Kashyap who says, 'Abhi swing kar, abhi sar dheere dheere utha.' The scene is wrapped in a single take.

The Perpendicular killing sequence starts with him watching *Munnabhai MBBS* with Tangent in Ray Talkies. This scene is shot in Chandan Talkies in Mumbai because they cannot take the *Munnabhai* prints to Wasseypur. The scene then shifts to the duo walking out and being followed by Sultan. Perpendicular heads towards the railway track while Tangent runs to get Faizal Khan.

'Sankalp (Tangent) was cast just for this one shot where he had to do a lot of running. He is being chased by Sultan's henchman (aka Akhilesh the writer). The chase has him get into a bus which was supposed to keep running. The bus went a bit ahead and stopped, they just could not understand what we wanted and so he had to get down and run again. This is just one of the problems when you shoot in real locations,' rues Kashyap.

The next scene where Sultan corners Perpendicular on the railway track and kills him is shot in Banaras. 'We wanted to shoot the killing on a railway track that is connected to a road and we didn't have an ideal location for a long time. While travelling to Chunar we came across railway tracks which suited our requirements,' says Anubhuti.

The scene requires Sultan to bash Perpendicular's head with a stone. For this a fibre body is used. 'It was a difficult shot to do. I kept hitting the dummy but the head was not breaking at all,' recalls Tripathi. Kashyap is disappointed. 'The idea was not to show brutality but give the idea, the feeling of it to the audience. We wanted to take the action to the next level where we see the impact point which we could not because of the faulty dummy,' says Kashyap. Some of what Anurag intended does come through with the help of computer graphics.

It is a tough shoot because its success depends on the movement of the trains and the timing of the choreographed chase. The shoot gets postponed thrice due to lack of official permissions, so tempers are running high. The scene requires Tangent to lead Faizal and the men to the body, lift it up and leave. The fake fibre body is replaced by actor Aditya who lies on the track with the make-up of blood and gore. The whole set is ready for the shot. But during the take, Singh, who plays Tangent, instead of looking for Aditya, comes running in, spots the fibre body which was kept somewhere behind the camera and takes Nawaz and the others behind the camera, out of the frame! 'Anurag lost it and shouted so much at that guy: "Dimaag nahi hai, dihkta nahi hai samne lash padi hai aur tum wahan ja rahe ho,"' recalls Anubhuti.

The railway track where the shot is to take place is full of human excreta. 'Whoever was walking there had their legs covered in it,' recalls Shlok. 'Anurag came there and saw the place wasn't cleaned as yet and he shouted. No one budged so he just got a bag and paper in his hand and began to scrape it up. Looking at him everyone rushed out and we had everyone cleaning the tracks.'

If a faulty prop disappoints Kashyap in this scene, in another case it gives rise to an impromptu action sequence. The scene originally has Definite walk into Shamshad's house, fire in the air, run out of bullets and then hightail it out of the house with Shamshad hot in pursuit. Definite then gets on his scooter and escapes. It is one of the early acting days of Zeishan and he receives a daily dose of firing from Anurag, who is not very happy with the way he is going about his role.

The set is ready. It's a long scene to be shot in one continuous take. 'Zeishan,' warns Anurag, 'don't fuck up.' A very nervous Zeishan manages to get through the scene, till he tries to fire the gun. The gun jams and Zeishan doesn't know what to do. Anurag has not called out 'cut', so an unnerved Zeishan starts rambling lines.

Rajkumar Yadav (Shamshad) realizes that the gun has got stuck so he carries on the scene; he picks up an iron rod. Zeishan takes the cue and runs out of the house and gets on to the scooter as planned. However, he goes the wrong way and, instead of moving out of Yadav's range, lands up right in front of him. 'When I ran and got the scooter, I saw that Yadav was already in front of me, so I just turned the scooter and drove away and he came running after me,' recalls Zeishan. Terrified, he looks at Anurag only to see him falling out of his chair, laughing. 'It happened in such a funny, bizarre way and the actors didn't stop. I decided this should continue into a chase sequence,' says Kashyap. The problem is to fit this into the shooting schedule. Kashyap takes the decision of handing the sequence over to Shlok and his second unit.

Kashyap gives a bare outline. Definite is on a bike, being chased by Shamshad on his scooter and they should get stuck in a traffic jam. Shlok, having roamed around Banaras during his location recce, knows exactly where and how to shoot. 'We were given a basic concept note of the chase. I decided to shoot the film actor/character wise. The first day I shot with only Zeishan, then the next with Rajkumar Yadav.' However, Kashyap's idea of a traffic jam is a stumbling block. The road they select to shoot in has no signals and the traffic is smooth and continuous. The traffic jam will have to be created. So the team has a spot boy take a car, have it take a U-turn and stall. Another member of the crew will follow in a second car which will stop in front of the first car and the two drivers will stage a mock fight to hold the traffic long enough for the shoot to take place. No one finds it odd that in a street in Banaras one of the drivers is abusing in Malayalam.

There are two cameras: one stationed with Shlok on a rooftop and the other in one of the cars. The cameras are hidden so that no one can notice them. Even the actors do not know where they are. They are fed cues by Vicky Kaushal, the sole assistant director to the unit, who is stationed at a bakery, its owner increasingly suspicious of the stranger who keeps hanging around every day in his doorway. Coordinating with Shlok is another nightmare; walkies are not allowed as they would attract attention. Communication happens through mobile phones but tricky networks make it difficult to send instant cues.

While shooting, Shlok feels that having kids with kites at the traffic signal would be a great idea -- the kids could be shown trying to disentangle their kites which have got stuck in the telephone wires, and then they would run and dash into the actors. The result: it looks real, not staged. It's Vicky's job to hang the kites. 'So there I am, standing on a stool and trying to hang kites on to the wires and people around me are wondering, what's happening, bandein usually patang utarte hain aur yeh tange jaa raha hai.'

After each day's shooting, Anurag watches the rushes and gives his inputs as to what to do next – do it this way, next make them turn up at the same petrol pump. Shamshad is chasing on foot, his friend Nawab is on the scooter, he stops at a petrol pump for a refill and spots Definite who has turned up at same pump.

The petrol pump scenes are shot without permission. 'We did manage to do it with a lot of action happening, like Nawab is filling petrol, Definite comes there to fill, he tries to stop Definite's bike as he is pulling away from the pump,' says Shlok. One of the vehicles at the petrol pump has a number plate that gives away the game – that the scene is being shot in Uttar Pradesh. 'And we were begging him, "Please gaadi idhar ghumaiye,"; and we could not even tell him that we were shooting,' says Vicky.

The last chunk of the chase is thought up by Shlok (Anurag thinks Shlok is obsessed with trains – most of his second unit scenes have train sequences). Definite abandons his bike and runs towards the railway tracks. Shamshad is still in pursuit. The first takes have a problem. The camera pans on Zeishan and he goes off the frame and the next second Shamshad comes running into the frame. 'He was so obviously near that Definite could have been caught. This was ruining the chase so I cut the Shamshad scene and as trains were running in the background I wrote the whole scene that Zeishan manages to get into a train but the compartment is full of military cadets and then he goes to jail. That posed a new problem – he had to be out of jail for the next sequence. So then I had to write a scene where we had to get him out of jail. So that's the organic way of making a film,' quips Kashyap.

Filming the scene is difficult. The scene required precise timing. The train is moving slowly and Zeishan is moving along with it, then he crosses the camera and then he has to run fast and get in the train. He fails to get the timing right. Anurag shouts at him. In the fourth take he is running next to the train, trying to board it when suddenly he disappears. The unit is panic stricken. Zeishan has fallen into a small gutter, hanging upside down, his legs in the air. 'He was very close to the train and his legs could have easily hit the train had not been for Vineet Singh (Danish) who held his legs. After that Anurag said, "No more doing that, I will manage with what I have got,"' recalls Anubhuti.

The Asgar and Nagma death scene is shot in Chunar. Originally, the scene was supposed to be shot as taking place during the month of Ramzan. This idea is discarded and instead it is decided that the extensive footage the crew had taken of Moharram processions in Allahabad and Banaras would be used. 'I wanted to create that whole atmosphere of the culture. The sequences were also tied in with the projection of violence. We shot both Shia and Sunni maatams, but the Shia maatam stands out because there is violence in it, because of the drama in it,' says Kashyap. Some of these shots are also used as a prelude to build up a certain environment necessary for violent sequences, for example, when Sardar Khan bombs the shops in the Qasai Mohallah and attacks the members of the Sultan gang.

With this footage in hand, the timing of the Nagma killing sequence is changed to Moharram. The team set up stalls and banners, the junior artistes wear black clothes, they are not instructed on their course of action, they are present in the bazaar, ready to move when the call comes.

Three of the characters are to die: Nagma, her sister and Asgar. Asgar is shot on the street by two men on motorcycles; one of them goes after Nagma and her sister in the shop. Nagma asks her sister to run. The man shoots her, turns and runs around to the back of the building and shoots the sister dead. This has to be done in one shot. 'We did three takes but none of them have come out very well,' says Anubhuti.

The problem is with the crowd. 'We had only three saris to shoot that bullet through so we could have only three chances. The crowd was supposed to run when the killing happens and there in the shot we had one woman walking leisurely. There is gunfire but she is not bothered. We removed her digitally,' says Anurag.

The shopkeepers in the market are told that the shoot would last two hours. They become restless when the team crosses the deadline. They start to scream, so the post-murder scenes, where Faizal Khan and his family members come to take the bodies and close the shops in protest, cannot be shot. 'This was not something we could replicate because then we would need to redo the whole sequence. And it is a critical point in the film – Faizal Khan's mother is dead and it is this emotion that leads to the climax of the film. We needed to have that transition of Faizal Khan – the news of his mother's death sinking into him – his anger is not seen,' laments Anubhuti.

Chunar is also the place where the scenes of Sultan's murder are to be shot. The team locates a vegetable market in the middle of Chunar. The killing is designed as follows: Sultan comes in his car, sees Definite and starts backing the car, bumps into something, at which point, the window glasses shatter, he takes the car ahead but gets shot. The problem is that Anurag isn't happy with Zeishan's performance.

For Zeishan, the whole day is disastrous. 'I had reached the set in the morning but was called in at four, and I knew the light would go by five. By the time the set was ready, there were just ten minutes to go. I was just about to go on when someone comes and tells me to be careful of shattering glasses lest I get hurt. Now I am worried about that and I had to act. The scene was that I would fire one shot, then run to the car, try and open the first door, it would not open, then I would try the back door and struggle with it, then put my hand down the open window and open the door and fire. So I run and do that and the first door opens. I freeze for one second; someone had forgotten to lock it. But nobody notices that it's come open and in the struggle I close it again and then I run to the back door and try to open it and then open it through the window and fire. Rajeev sir is sitting inside the car. Then Anurag sir comes and hits me on the head and says, "What is your problem? You were supposed to struggle with the back door for some time and then open." Now I could not tell him what happened.'

The whole sequence is shot again in Ramanagar near Banaras. The action has changed by then. There are men following Sultan and they report to Guddu who has to then call and tell Definite what to do next. Definite follows Sultan and as he gets into a car, kills him. 'Anurag was giving cues of four different actors to Murari (Guddu) through four different phones and he did this while directing the shot,' says Anubhuti. This time the scene runs through smoothly.

The attack on Faizal's house is planned in the old, crumbling house in Chunar – the house where Sardar Khan settles with his family in Part 1 and Faizal Khan rises to power in Part 2. It will be a one-take sequence: the Sultan gang attacks the house, Faizal goes up to the terrace and jumps to the terrace of the neighbouring house and from there to the terrace of yet another house and then comes down the stairs of that house and goes back to his home. However, to maintain the single shot, the camera will have to jump with the actor as he crosses the rooftops. The idea of using a crane is raised and quickly abandoned. The logistics pose a problem – there isn't enough time to get one to the location, not to mention the narrow pathways that will be a challenge.

The team hole up in Kashyap's room with research material – police files are referenced and films with one-take sequences are viewed. 'We started looking at *Children of Men* and *Secret in their Eyes* where there were ninety single-take scenes. How did they do it? *Children of Men* was done in a very simple way; *Secret in their Eyes* seems complicated till you realize that it wasn't actually really a single take. It was a mix of special effects and technique,' says Kashyap. Neeraj finds a technique where both the camera person and the actor are rigged with wires, so that the camera person can do the action along with the actor to get a seamless flow. This triggers Kashyap into planning out the sequence.

The action team, led by Shyam Kaushal, reaches the location two days prior to the shoot. Anurag briefs the team on what he is looking for. Anubhuti and the art team work out how to manage the interiors. The house is a three-storeyed structure with a courtyard in the middle surrounded by rooms on four sides. The sequence is going to involve a lot of bullets and bombs and that means possibilities of damage. The owners, needless to say, are not happy about this. Someone suggests building fake walls. But there is not enough space for that. They would shrink the already small house and shooting in that space will be difficult. The fake wall idea is dropped. They will keep the house as is. The owners give permission, rather reluctantly.

The ADs draw up a map. 'We were working like a FBI team,' quips Neeraj. One of the ADs makes a diagram which doesn't quite work, then Vicky draws a top-angle map of the whole area. Anubhuti briefs the ADs about where they will be and their positions and each AD's responsibility to pass on the cue which has to be perfect because if one thing goes wrong, everything will. The map points out the sequences, the movement of the characters, and the cameras that will shoot the scene. Six cameras are used. 'The house was lit up in a way where the camera would go into black and come out and we just maintained the momentum and the distance of the blacks while we changed geographically,' says Kashyap.

Then a problem rears its head. At midnight, the team realizes that terraces are not close enough for the actor to jump. A ramp would be needed and that would take away from the planned shot. The matter is resolved by breaking the single shot into three: the first will follow Faizal getting his family to safety and then going up the stairs to the terrace; the second will have him jumping across the terraces (the darkness is used to camouflage the fact that the roof does not belong to the neighbouring house), the third shot will have him coming down the house which is next door, down the unlit stairs, following him back to his home.

Rajeev follows Nawazuddin with the camera on his shoulder, up the very steep stairs. There are no ADs present in the house except for Vicky who is doing the clap and continuity. Shyam Kaushal, meanwhile, has set up the paraphernalia for the rooftop shot. He has done the jump once himself to ensure that it is safe. A platform is created with boxes covered with a green cloth to break Nawazuddin's fall. The platform will be erased by CG later.

The rigging team is briefed. They have to de-rig the camera after the jump, remove the harness without jerking the camera. All this has to be done on the move, as the shot is being taken. 'The jump shot was difficult to execute. We were just not getting the shots. Then we realized that if we wire both of them it's a problem. The camera however needed to be rigged. So then we unwired Nawaz and the moment we did that Nawaz becomes a superman, an action hero. He easily jumped from one roof to the other and then jumped down. He is just so firm and flexible on his feet and he did it without wiring in one take. We had taken eight takes and we didn't get the shot; Nawaz did it in that one take and we got what we wanted,' says Kashyap.

The interior shots take three days to shoot. While shooting Anurag realizes that while the camera is following the character inside the house he needs to show the action happening outside where Sultan and his gang members are firing into the house. He is loath to cut away to the action outside as that will tamper with the mood he is trying to convey. 'That's when the idea came that the outside sequences would be placed in the beginning and the interior sequences would be in Part 2. So they became two different single takes,' says Kashyap.

The outside sequences are shot towards the end of the schedule in Chunar. For this scene, the villagers are warned that they would hear gunfire at night. They are told not to worry; it is all fake – nothing will happen except for some noise disturbance. The villagers cooperate. The exterior attack needs the open shops, for as the Sultan gang comes here, they forcibly begin bringing down the shutters, and that needs to be coordinated. 'The opening was simply executed – following the characters, the television explodes – it was not written like that in the script but the location supported us that way,' says Kashyap.

The gang then splits in two. One set goes to the front of the house, the other group takes a lane to go to the back of the house and there the firing begins from all sides. The whole exercise calls for precise coordination so that everything falls in place like clockwork. Any lapse will require redoing the house for the bullet holes which could take hours.

Kaushal's team begins to prepare the house. The house is rigged by evening, the shoot is to commence by seven p.m. but the fighters needed for the scene reach only by midnight and by the time the sequence is explained to them it is three in the morning. Kaushal's focus is that the shot should not look designed. 'The blast impact was rehearsed with two doors. How the wood splinters when it is blasted, would it strike somebody, what material should it be made of, what if it strikes somebody? What should be the intensity of the blast? We used to rehearse in the art team's workshop, explosive lagake dekhte for safety was critical,' he says.

The action is then choreographed: who would shoot first, where they would be positioned. Tripathi recalls, 'We were called for rehearsal at four. We had a dry run and by then it was four forty-five. It was to be done in one take. We started and some mistake happened. Anurag said cut and it was cut, cut across the line. The television set needed to be changed and by that time it was near sunrise ... and the take happened perfectly. It went on for nine minutes.'

The script originally had the attack on Faizal's house as a pre-climax from which events would then build up to the Ramadhir killing as the climax. However, Kashyap's interest in adding booth-capturing scenes leads to unexpected twists in the story. While writing the booth-capturing scene, Anurag asks Zeishan to recite the scene with the dialogues. 'He was doing that and in the end he says, *jo bhi ho Faizal Khan ko nahi jeetna chahiye*. This was not even an idea at that time. And he did this because in his mind the true story was going on. That made it very interesting and then the game began. So this dialogue that Zeishan said added elements to the story and I wrote more scenes. The sequences of J.P. Singh conspiring with Definite took shape here. That scene was done after we shot Definite killing Iqlakh.'

This develops Definite's track in the film which leads to him being involved in the Ramadhir killing which grows into a more gory scene. 'It was planned that he would be shot with 700 bullets but at what scale this was to be done was not planned. Viacom had to sanction extra money to shoot the climax and we went over-budget because of that,' says Kashyap.

In the script, the scene is described as Faizal Khan coming to the hospital and shooting Ramadhir Singh. 'We didn't know that Anurag wanted to make it a grand climax shoot. Fortunately, we got this big bungalow which was unoccupied and we could shoot the whole scene there,' says Anubhuti.

The detailed scene now has Faizal and Definite walk into the hospital searching for Ramadhir who has come to visit Shamshad. Faizal leaves the bodies of Ramadhir's henchmen in his wake as he tries to trace Ramadhir; he finds Shamshad, kills him and then finds Ramadhir in a bathroom. Ramadhir, resigned, sits on a commode and Faizal keeps firing at him with all the guns at his disposal. 'Faizal is in a trance,' says Nawazuddin. 'He keeps shooting. He just wants to shoot. He takes a break, then starts again. He just does not want to come back to reality. This is the thorn that has kept me from my life. "Jitni zyada goliyan aur chala sakta tha, I will do it, main barabar ek ek goli mehsoos kar raha tha ki ek ek goli maroonga isko, ki bas mujhe goli marni hai."'

At the receiving end is an extremely discomfited Tigmanshu who has to endure this continuous explosion of special effects on and around him. 'The tiles were exploding and since these were regular tiles, sharp pieces flew at my face and near my eyes. And it was just going on. And I just wanted it to stop,' recalls Dhulia. The close-ups of Dhulia are shot on location but the final shot happens in Kamalistan where the bullets are fired into a fake body so as to get the graphic effect of a blood-soaked, bullet-ridden body.

The climax is the death of Faizal Khan at the hands of Definite. The cycle of violence that Faizal Khan seeks to end with the death of Ramadhir Singh continues. New overlords are born: Definite and J.P. Singh.

In the real Wasseypur, Fahim Khan is currently in jail, charged for attempted murder, extortion, kidnapping, and the murder of one Sagir, allegedly hired to kill him by his own grand-uncle. Saabir Alam was in jail, now released on bail, charged for the murder of Fahim Khan's mother, Najma Khatoon. As per a newspaper[1] report of September 2012, the Jharkhand police intercepted Fahim Khan's mobile calls to a contract killer, Sujit Sinha, currently residing in Ranchi jail, to take out Saabir Alam. A violent clash between Khan's brother-in-law and the Langda Chand gang follows. Fahim Khan's gang member Parvez Khan aka Pappu is critically injured in the clash and lands in hospital. The media is currently speculating on the chances of renewed warfare in the area.

---

[1] *Dainik Bhaskar*, 9 September 2012.

6

Wrap-up

'Maine story ek dum shuru se shuru ki thi'

– Anurag Kashyap

The office in Aaram Nagar is busy with post-production work. Anubhuti is trying to coordinate dubbing dates with the actors, Neeraj is desperately calling up AIR for certain audio tapes that are needed for a particular time period, the VHX guys are holed up in another office, and there are numerous others milling about.

The team is still hungover from the shooting. 'We have got to calling Anurag Ramadhir Singh,' quips Shweta Venkat, the editor. The office is being referred to as the editing office, as the film is being worked upon. Shweta is prepared for a lot of footage landing up at her table. 'Rajeev Ravi kept calling me while shooting – "Listen we have shot a lot. We have footage of approximately twenty-five to thirty hours of both the films." Getting the first cut, which was done according to story and characters, was the easiest part,' says Shweta. That was done for both films by July 2011. 'Feedback kept coming from the team and issues would crop up. Whenever we thought that we had broken through, some other idea would come up. So, somewhere Anurag and I had lost perspective. Finally the breakthrough happened in October,' says Shweta.

Kashyap is to be out of town for a few days and he asks his friend Vikramaditya Motwane to look at the first cuts. 'Because every scene was very elaborate, every scene was wholesome and I was too much in love with those scenes, I didn't want to cut them. I told Vikram, when I am not here, get into my editing room and do whatever you want to do,' says Kashyap.

Vikramaditya Motwane sees the first cut of Part 1, which is three and a half hours long, and declares it boring. He explains, 'I found the beginning too straightforward, too slow. I was told to cut scenes but while I was doing it I started rearranging scenes, moving them, compressing them. I was having fun. There were these scenes of Ramadhir Singh explaining how you wet the coal to gain weight. There I compressed four scenes into one – a longish kind of montage – and there was Sardar Khan's scene which was abruptly shifted from him as a child to a grown man. I changed it, showing him growing up gradually.'

Back from his trip, Kashyap is at first horrified at Motwane's work. 'I was shocked – he had ruined my film! Then I realized the possibilities it gave me. Vikram was so ruthless, he turned the elaborate scenes into moments and intercut those moments and completely changed the order of things. I started putting things back, but based on the pattern that Vikram had created. He changed the way the film was. One chunk that remained the same was the intercut between the coal story and Ramadhir and S.P. Sinha. Making a film is about evolution. It is a four-level process – first research, then writing, then shooting and then again redoing the film. Forget about it being a factual or geographical or political space. It's also a personal space with actors, when I start working with them. I start exploring their interrelationships, things that they would do. I start exploring the house, every single property starts getting used, making it one with them and then whatever evolves out of there comes on the editing table and then I make the scene out of it. I shoot in detail because I want to explore the place, also in the process understand the place. I spend a lot of time on editing because then suddenly I am making a new film.'

Shweta feels that Anurag's style of working is erratic. 'You have to be prepared for anything while you are editing with him. You always have to be in alert mode to keep up with his thought process. There are days where there is no work but at times his ten minutes of productivity can change the entire flow.'

Anurag feels that, 'I have a very strange way of working while editing. The editor does her work. I keep coming back, doing my own thing based on what she has done. This is a very to and fro process.'

'It was just about eliminating what was not required,' says Shweta. 'The scene where Guddu is speaking to three different people on the phone – pacing that was very difficult. In Part 1, my most difficult problem was establishing a difference between Dhanbad and Wasseypur because we didn't have shots. With Anurag there are not many options. Most of the scenes are one-takes so you really can't cut a scene. A lot of the 1940s scenes were tough to cut due to limited shots.'

Kunal feels that Kashyap's greed for taking more shots has reduced. He is very content with one take. 'For his single takes I would suggest taking one close-up somewhere just in case we needed to cut it down to something small after the edit. The Fazlu head-cutting scene was censored. But if we had one close-up of Faizal, only the face at that point, probably we could have cut it and edited it in a different way. But since he doesn't have options we can't do anything.'

Kashyap also runs into censor interference in the scene where Danish kills one of the men responsible for his father's murder. He shoots the man and then stabs him in the eyes. When the scene was shot, there was no knife, the actor uses his hand in a stabbing gesture and the knife was to be put in by CG with the apt sound effect. The scene comes up at the censors who want to cut that particular part. However, Kashyap had shot this as a single-take and there was no way he could cut the entire scene. So on the censor's insistence, the sound effect is sacrificed due to which the scene does not deliver the way Kashyap wants it.

There are instances where a single shot is edited – Shahid's killing is one such. Another is the scene where after Sardar Khan's death the family is sitting together and having dinner. 'Initially,this scene was to be a long continuous take ... we had actually kept the track for very long ... they are eating, eating, eating and we keep the camera on that ... and then Nagma says, "Tum logon ko khana kaise hazm hota hai..." But I kept the scene short though it would have been a powerful shot if we kept the longer take, I knew our audience would not understand it. I took the decision to cut it down,' rues Kashyap.

Kashyap concedes to bowing to audience expectations in some of the scenes in his film. The scene in Part 2 which has Faizal sneaking up to the terrace of his house and then jumping off the rooftop didn't have background music which is put later. 'Yes, I chickened out, I thought the audience would prefer it like this,' admits Kashyap.

Kunal is not happy with the use of music in Part 1. 'It usually happens with Anurag's films that his edit is very fast paced and if I have to add sound I need space. In Part 1 he wanted lot of music and I would go, no you don't need music and he would go music! music! So we used to have a lot of fights on this. His reason for having more music was because he felt it was falling flat. For him, if something wasn't working, he wanted it to go faster. I felt if there was too much music you don't stay with characters. I thought Part 1 was done the way it was because of a lot of insecurities. But the audience loved it.'

Shweta feels that the sound helped in establishing the bigness of the film. The scenes shot in the Dhanbad coal mines called for water rising in the mines and the workers asking the pahalwan to let them out. The problem was they could not actually flood the mines. 'It was done through lighting. We got lots of shots of water and the flood was created through sound which gave the effect of the coal falling into the water, men stumbling through it. I told the actors that you walk as if you are walking through water. When Shahid Khan had to walk out, he walked as if he was dragging his feet through water,' says Kashyap.

To recreate the sound, Kunal takes a lot of references from the location. 'There is a scene where Shahid Khan is digging and the coal has to fall in water as there is water running down. I made a mistake and took the reference of the coal falling on the ground. To correct that we added the water sound, added the low rumbling sound,' says Kunal.

Kunal is delighted that unlike his earlier experiences with Anurag, this time he actually has a decent budget to work on. 'Even in the post-production of *Wasseypur* I had the freedom to do what I wanted. My team of Zahir Bandukwala (*No Smoking)* and Mishaal Chinai (*Shaitaan*) was my backbone. Because of my team I could go much further then I had thought. There was lots of work to be done on *Wasseypur*. This was the first time we were trying to do a 7.1.[1] We did Part 1 in 7.1. For Part 2, I decided to

---

[1]5.1 Surround Sound: Speakers are placed in left, centre, right, the left surround, the right surround and sub woofers. 6.1 Surround Sound: left, centre, right, the left surround, the right surround plus a separate back surround. 7.1: Separate left surround, left back surround, back surround, separate right back surround and right surround.

go a totally different way. You have a lot of separations in 7.1. I wanted to use it only when required, I didn't want to overdo it.' Kunal decides to use 7.1 for two reels – from the attack on Faizal's house to his mother's death and then the last reel from the election sequence to the climax of Ramadhir's killing. The rest was done in 5.1.

Surround sound helps in enhancing video on screen without distracting the audience with audio effects coming from one side of the theatre or the other. 'Sudden panning of sound from one side of the theatre to the other distracts the audience; takes them away from the story happening on the screen. And in case of songs, when it starts, the audience should not look around for the speakers. I wanted the audience to remain with the story so I began to change the whole sound design. We broke all norms here.' Kunal is obviously delighted with what they achieved.

The success of this approach was evident at the film's premier at Cannes 2012. 'The first time the climax song came, I wasn't looking at the screen; I was looking at the audience: are their heads turning towards the speakers? They were glued to the screen!' says Kunal.

The music that has the audience glued to the screen has been composed by Sneha Khanwalkar who first met Anurag Kashyap through actor, lyricist and composer Piyush Mishra, with whom she worked on a song for a Tigmanshu Dhulia film. 'Anurag was working on *Gulaal* then with Piyush bhai. He sent me to Ramu where I got work. Then I wasn't working for a long time and then I got Dibakar Banerjee's *Love Sex aur Dhokha*.'

Though she wants to work with Kashyap, the schedules of the two don't match up till one day Kashyap catches hold of Sneha at Dibakar's *Love Sex aur Dhoka* party.

'Sneha is a very elusive person. Earlier I wanted her to do a film with me but she just disappeared. When she came back, the job had gone to someone else. She asked me, "What am I to do now, I wanted to work on that film." I told her, "I can't trust you, yaar, the way you are roaming I will give you a ghumakkadu work,"' says Kashyap.

Ghumakkadu, from ghumakkar, one who roams around. The name fits the job since it not only has her travel through Bihar and Jharkhand but also to Trinidad. When Kashyap tells her he wants rooted music for the film, Sneha is not too keen on folk music. She recalls a song she heard at an inter-collegiate competition. The first time she heard this music was in Trinidad where Bihari migrants had evolved an indigenous style – Bihari music combined with Caribbean beats, appropriately dubbed Chutney Music. 'I asked him, "Is it okay if it's not only folk music?" and Anurag Kashyap said yes.'

Sneha decides to first go on location – Patna, Gaya, Wasseypur, and Dhanbad – to search for references for her compositions. She is introduced to Varun Grover, the lyricist for the film. Grover, an engineering graduate from the Banaras Hindu University, left his software job when he moved to Mumbai to make a career in writing satire. He currently works for an Internet-based show, *Jai Hind*. Writing lyrics was not his first choice when he sought work in the film industry. He wanted to write scripts for realistic, contemporary cinema, for people like Anurag Kashyap, Dibakar Banerjee, Vishal Bharadwaj and Chandan Arora. 'The problem was that they usually wrote their own scripts and there was a long queue of people waiting to work for them. So I thought why not write lyrics, not too many wanting to do that,' says Grover.

His connection with Anurag began when he wrote a song for *No Smoking* and posted it in the comment section of a blog that Anurag had written on the film. Anurag got his number from somewhere and called him to say that he liked the lyrics. Unfortunately, the lyrics and music for the film had already been locked, so his song could not get in. 'Then *Yellow Boots* happened and I wrote two songs: one found a place ... just four or five lines in the film but the other, a Bihari-Bhojpuri song was not used.' This song was '*Bhoose ke dher main*' which got him a job in *Gangs of Wasseypur*.

Grover and Khanwalkar go over the research material given to them by Anurag and dissect the script. In April, Sneha leaves for Bihar and stays there through May to research Bihari folk music. She goes to Patna with sound engineer Gautam and an assistant Gangu. Their first stop: AIR. They listen to shows from the last few decades – Sharda Sinha's folk music and radio theatre of Loha Singh. The bureaucracy hinders as much as it helps. 'You cannot take the CDs. You have to sit there and then their player would not work. But I met with people who were appointed by AIR as musicians. I met a harmonium player and through him met theatre directors of AIR and tried to locate local musicians,' recalls Sneha.

Sneha had been told of a school principal, Yashwant Parasher, who would buy supplies at a particular stationery shop. He apparently owned a massive collection of music. They trace Mr Parasher through the shop. He asks Sneha and her team to come to Muzaffarpur and helps them with local connections, even taking them to a Musahar community village. In the village a bunch of kids follow her about. 'I knew that we would need a lot of songs in the background. So I had this idea. We recorded a lot of kids, some were saying their names, somebody was singing. It was a huge commotion. Some kids were laughing, we asked them to recite poems – the "*Chatano se krida karti*". This was used like a theme background.'

A jam session with the local community leads Sneha to another song. She had asked them to sing, to give a performance. 'One guy would act like he has got possessed by spirits and the rest would sing. I noticed this one guy, full of energy, and a great voice – he was short, wearing a torn shirt and a short dhoti. I used his voice for the song – the feel was very funereal,' says Sneha. This recording was mixed with eclectic music resulting in the composition '*Bhaiyaaa*', which was used in the sequence where Faizal Khan kills Yadavji in a hotel room.

Next stop: Gaya. 'We met a local politician who had opened a cultural centre. He organized some village folk singers. We didn't have too much gear, just the recorders but they were not plural recorders, we could not mike everybody and get each sound but that helped because we got the composite sound, because that's how you hear it, you don't hear it mixed,' says Sneha.

Sneha has decided to look for untrained voices for this project. 'For *Wasseypur* I thought I could explore all kind of awkward, raw, untrained khul ke gaane wale, apne aap gungunanewale singers who won't show their own singing skills but elaborate the singing style, especially lyrics. Anurag being open to it helped a lot and he too wanted it to be raw. Though I did mix the recorded songs with different beats – adding new elements, I think the soul, the essence of the music remains gawky, awkward and raw.'

The team also visits Dhanbad and Wasseypur though they don't mine any songs from there. Returning to Mumbai, Varun and Sneha meet and discuss the songs. The trip has opened their minds to the music, the poetry and the land. Varun explains, 'We would read the script and then discuss with Anurag about where he would like the songs. He was liberal about it, he said just do your thing, don't even show me the scratch, just give me the final output if you feel confident that it will work. That's a rare thing in any creative field – total freedom.'

July end, Sneha leaves for Trinidad. 'There I had to take some pre-decided songs. Get them sorted on money and contracts. I went to the Indian diaspora, met the Indian ambassador. The music I was interested in was Chutney and Parang. Chutney singers are Bihari but they have never been in India. Their body language, their accent is Caribbean but India is still their mother country. They love Indian traditional culture, music and art even if they could not speak Hindi – just a bit of accented Bhojpuri passed down from the grandparents. My favourite image is of the grandmothers at the weddings I attended there – with their frocks and cleavages, a drink in hand, they would dance to the beats but the body would be still from the waist above. "*Electric piya*" was inspired from these beats: it's Bihari music but very fast with that island pelvic vibe.'

Sneha is intrigued by studios on the island which are small scale but making their own Chutney beats. She visits one of them – Rishi Mahata's and she wants him to make separates of a song that she recorded from a CD. 'I had put this on a loop – this song with the words I thought were "hello bol". I had first thought of coming to Bombay and replicating it but I knew I would not get the original sounds. I went to this studio so that I could make separates (recording) of all the three sounds so I can use them as I want.'

Chutney music basically has three elements. One is the dholak which is used in fast beats; second, two iron rods hitting each other which sounds like a high-pitch bell; and third, an octapad. To Sneha's surprise the CD turned out to be composed by Mahata himself. 'But he was very cool about it,' recalls Sneha. The words were not 'hello bol' as Sneha thought but 'mellow bars'. The mix she gets is used for the background song '*Tain Tain To To Te*'.

In Trinidad, she meets with singers and composers – Robbie Styles, Rasika D. Rani, and Vedesh Sookoo. Sneha came across Sookoo while surfing the net. What struck her was the inoffensive way he sang double entendre songs. When she finally meets him, he looked nothing like the video on Youtube.com. He had given up singing, looked less wild with his neatly cut hair; he had left music and was managing his family business and like many singers of Chutney music, did only seasonal work, in the months of the Carnival. He agrees to work with her, says he would write the lyrics and then he would compose the music for it. 'I told him to keep the mafia angle in context,' says Sneha. Sookoo's lyrics are in English and he sings with an accent that's part Caribbean, part Indian. Anurag does not mind that it's in English so the English sections are recorded in Trinidad and the Hindi Bhojpuri lyrics are recorded in Patna, sung by Rajesh Shomu and Munna – both part of a theatre group. 'Rajesh had a natural twang in his voice that brings the madness in the song. It was sung in a very laidback manner. They sang a song with double entendre lyrics but the voices did not convey the smuttiness,' says Sneha. Munna was a theatre artist who was being recorded for another song. It was the way he answered phone calls that got him the song. 'He had a very cocky voice – every time I used to call him, the way he said "hailoo" was different. It is because of his "hailooo" that the intro in the song happened.'

Rasika D. Rani, a popular singer, is persuaded to record '*Electric piya*', the song that accompanies the launda naach in the film. She has issues with certain words: 'My loveless and luckless and screwed-up piya.' She does not want to use the phrase 'screwed up' because of her image and because it would be heard in her mother country! So the words are changed to 'messed-up piya'. Rani gets her dholak and guitar, and Sneha sort of bastardizes the music. The song has Shamshad (Rajkumar Yadav), Nawab (Mukesh Chabbra) and others dancing. 'I just let everybody go all out, do whatever they wanted, and did five or six takes and the shooting was over. Then editing table pe mix kar diya…' says Kashyap.

'*Kaala re*' is also recorded in Trinidad. 'It was a very minimalistic song then. I sent it to Anurag but he didn't react. I waited for his response but there was none. It was only back in Mumbai when I asked, "Haven't you heard the song?" he replied that he did but he had no idea where to place it. It was only later when I saw the screenplay I realized where he had placed it. The song was used as it was done in the first draft, there was no re-recording. It was taken from the cue track.[2] The song had to sound like Huma's internal voice so it didn't need to have that finesse,' says Sneha.

Another song recorded in Trinidad is '*Moora*'. It means 'fool' and is used mostly as an endearment rather than insult. The word came from the lyrics of '*Bhoose ke dher se*' and Varun had written it in rap. Varun explains, 'My experiences at Banaras Hindu University worked here. Bihari students trying to be cool use a mix of Bihari and English. So I took this lingo from there.' However, Varun and Sneha realize that the song does not work in rap. During her previous trip to Ranchi, at a tribal festival

---

[2] A cue track is a bare-bone guide track, prepared by the musician or music director, which is used as the basis for putting together the entire song. It is the basic structure of the song.

celebrating the city's annual day, Sneha had tracked down a protest singer – Madhubansari Hasmukh – whom she had heard previously in Mumbai. When she went to Trinidad, she took this to Robbie Styles and wanted him to record it in Parang. There are two versions to the song – one by Sneha with Robbie Styles in the background and the other by Deepak Kumar. Anurag had not liked the track with Hasmukh's voice and so Deepak was called to Mumbai to record.

Back in India, work begins on the songs. One of the songs – '*Bhoose ke dher mein*' which Varun had written for *That Girl in Yellow Boots* – is already in place. 'The film was about a girl's search for her father and the song was about the futility of the search so I thought it could be used as the end-title song, for the film starts with the Kabir song and it could end with a Sufi touch. But when it reached *Wasseypur* it acquired the shades of a political song – a metaphor for the disillusionment in the country after Emergency. In a way it's a satire – even the prisoners in jail are disappointed with the government,' explains Varun.

Sneha doesn't want the songs to be sung by chorus singers in Mumbai. The sound would not be authentic, it would corrupt the essence. She wants the dialects of Bihar to resonate in the songs and the best source she recalls from her experiences in travelling in auto-rickshaws in Mumbai are the auto-drivers. 'Earlier, when I travelled by rickshaw I use to get quite pissed off with the auto drivers. I felt that their drawl was borderline eve teasing. It was very irritating. But in Bihar I found everyone spoke like that. I met an AIR person and he explained the different dialects and how they sound.'

Sneha begins to enquire around, roping Varun into the search for authentic Bihari voices. 'We have lot of bastis here where the Bihari people stay and for entertainment they have jagrans. Varun finally got a number of an auto-driver and he organized couple of more people to come and do the chorus. And that chorus was fantastic. They sing in a high voice and sing from the throat not the stomach so there is a natural cracking. There were also elements of the Birha and the Chaitha in the singing.'

Unfortunately, for Sneha, they cannot trace the group after that. In Patna, she records a live session with young theatre persons – with the harmonium and singers all together. 'Then we got a singer in Mumbai, Manish Tipu, who could sing in a high pitch. We got some good energy,' says Varun. There are other voices – Bhupesh Singh who lives in Wasseypur. He has also sung the '*Salaame ishq*' number for the Danish wedding.

The song is shot in Kamalistan Studio, Mumbai. It was supposed to be shot in the Chunar fort jail where the other sequences of the prison escape were shot but that is cancelled. 'In Kamalistan, just before the shooting, a dwarf walks in saying, I can do anything, I can dance, I just want 1500 bucks. So I asked the production guy if we could pay him and he said yes. And this man just started dancing on his own and then I started improvising. He became part of the film. We didn't know his name, we didn't know who he was, he kept on improvising and he was incredible. We have no idea where he went from there. He just left after the song,' recalls Kashyap.

Sneha and Varun continue to work on the songs which continue to be written after the film is shot and everything is locked. As they watch the rushes, Anurag would say, 'Can we do something here?' They watch the scene, go back home and work. Then they match lyrics with the music to see if it works. 'If the tune was working better, I would chuck the lyrics and if Sneha liked the lyrics, she would find a different tune,' says Varun.

For Varun it is important to get the dialect and the lingo right. 'Much of the research was from memory,' he says, having lived all over north India and having studied at the BHU. According to him, the slang and the attitude were the two things necessary in this film because the language in the film is rooted to the soil. 'It's not the usual Bihari seen in films. We needed authenticity in the attitude – arrogance and innocence at the same time. The local flavour is what sets it apart.'

Kashyap, no stranger to the nuances of the language of the areas, himself suggests words which make their way into songs. For example: the words 'Chi Cha Leather' which is used in UP and Bihar to mean a bit of a mess, or a messy situation. 'The lyrics are about this fake herogiri these guys have. When it comes to actually facing danger, they lose their bravado, drop the attitude and run,' says Varun.

The song is sung by Durga, an artist with Fatfish

Records from Andhra Pradesh and the only non Bihar-UP artist in the album. 'Durga was very young when we recorded the song – she was twelve years old. She is quick at grasping. She belongs to a clan of tribal singers from Andhra Pradesh. She has an open voice and she could project. The voice had a grain that is very uncommon, a twang, an accent that was powerful. She really rocked the song,' says Sneha.

Sneha records most of the songs in Patna and Banaras and then the orchestration and mixing are done in Mumbai. 'I recorded my songs where my singers were, in their own style. They are not skilled singers, their tonal quality is different and that's exactly what we wanted. If you add elements to it and ask them to sing it, you lose the authenticity. At the same time, if you give them a song in their language – simple but new – they actually jam with it. You can see that in "*O womaniya*". There is a lot of energy in the song as it is a wedding song. So I made the chorus dance and recorded it with all their breathing sound and bangle breaking sound. And I got help from my singers. They told me about all the sounds that can be heard in a wedding; one woman sits with a dholak and another woman will sit opposite her and beat the spoon on the drum. Hence the spoon beat on the drum.'

'*Taar bijli se*' is recorded in Patna. Its first line, '*Taar bijli se Patle hamare piya, ore sasuji tune yeh kya kiya*', is taken from a Bihari wedding song characterized by a lot of what Varun terms 'chhed-chhad' or the teasing and leg pulling which are part of wedding rituals. In the hands of Varun it becomes political satire. While taking off on the wedding song gives it instant recall value, a song everybody sings and knows, it's a very sneaky comment on Bihar. Varun credits Anurag with motivating him to do something different, 'Kuch naya karte hain,' as Anurag put it. In this it echoes the songs used in *Gulaal*, where the film-maker took off on Sahir Ludhianvi's celebrated lament '*Yeh duniya agar mil bhi jaaye*'. 'The first draft of the song was about how different levels of bureaucracy have screwed the state. So it was DM and then collector then SP tuney yeh kiya,' says Varun.

'But I wanted something more political that talks about and charts the complete political history of Bihar,' says Kashyap. So the song becomes a comment on the situation in Bihar, how the state has been exploited. 'It sounds like a wife complaining to her mother-in-law that her husband is thin but it is actually about Biharis complaining to the Central government about what they have done to the state, with references to Nehru, Gandhi, Ambedkar. Like "O re Bapu" is Mahatma Gandhi, "Gulabi Chacha" is Nehru, then we have "Babuji" who is Babu Jagjivan Ram, India's first labour minister whose nickname was Babuji. He was from Ara and won from Chappra so it became "Arachappra ke Babuji". "Loknayak" is JP.'

Varun thought it was an election campaign song, but, incredibly enough, Anurag shot it in a wedding. Looking at the rushes they are dumbfounded by the weird logic but it works admirably in the film.

Anurag suggests Padma Bhushan Sharda Sinha for the song. 'I heard a lot of her CDs at AIR and other places.

Her voice sat well. It was recorded live. Sitaramji from AIR, who usually accompanies Sharda Sinha, was on the harmonium. There needed to be a chorus. I needed old voices. The first chorus I got was full of giggling girls and Rekha Jha from Mithila. Then I found some women singing in a nearby temple whose voices were untrained and raw,' says Sneha.

'*O Womaniya'* is recorded in Banaras – Anurag wants it done quickly because he needs to shoot the scene. To save on time, Sneha records it in one room with the singers and the musicians. The entire song is done in one take – I don't have separates. There were four takes taken and I used one of those. Actually all the singers were sitting in a room looking at each other and singing. Womaniya didn't get along with other womaniya too,' laughs Sneha.

Sneha decides to use Rekha Jha for '*O womaniya*'. This is Rekha's first solo. She is usually part of the chorus for state official events and till this song came along had no ambitions whatsoever. She is a homely lady and mother of five, who never imagined she could be singing in a set-up like this. She learnt singing from her father, and not for a career.

The word 'womaniya' draws from the tendency in the local dialect to drawl a word like that – chavanni becomes chavanniya, button becomes buttoniya. Rekha has trouble with the lyrics which are basically about girls teasing a bride about marriage and how to deal with her husband on the first night. She is a little stunned with the lyrics and that's why she cannot bring in that naughty touch.

'Sneha kept telling her "Thoda haske gao" but she could not smile because she was uncomfortable,' says Varun. Her voice is mixed with that of another singer, Khushboo Raj. 'Khushboo was bold and outgoing and had a great sense of humour, so the contrast we got in the song was amazing,' says Sneha.

Sneha's trip to Patna library's Bhojpuri Sangrahlaya results in the discovery of poetry and folk songs from Bhojpuri literature many of which have been lost today. 'There was this children's song, part of which was used in "*Jiyo ho Bihar ke lala*": "*Oka boka teen tadoka laiyya laathi chandan maat*". Manoj Tiwari, who has been singing Bhojpuri songs for fifteen years, was surprised to see this, even he had never heard of it,' says Varun.

The song '*Jiyo ho*', which Varun calls a tribute to Bihar and Biharis, comes about when Sneha jams with a mandli of singers in Bihar. She tells them to put in words, which they do, either improvising or falling back on their repertoire of folk songs. 'Anurag liked it and wanted to place it in a significant place in the film. So I orchestrated it in a track with two of my dear music producers Vinayak and Tarun,' says Sneha. After listening to this, Kashyap decides to put this upbeat number when Sardar is killed, to turn the situation on its head. 'There were mixed feelings about it but Anurag was sure. It is then we got Manoj Tiwari to sing it because he has that raw but clear-cut singing voice that he could project very well. Anurag showed Manoj Tiwari the scene where the song will come. Having seen that he gave us much more then we had expected,' says Sneha.

The song '*Ek bagal mein chand hoga*' is brought into the film when the plan to use old Mohammed Rafi songs for the 1940s segment of Part 1 falls through. The rights are with HMV which asks for Rs 35 lakhs per song. There are two other Hindi film songs that are to be used and for the three the sum comes up to Rs 1 crore and five lakhs. It is then that Anurag recalls a song which Piyush Mishra has written and composed. 'The song was written ages ago, before I even thought of becoming a film-maker, when I was at university. We recorded it seven times because I wanted to change the way it was sung and Piyush bhai was stuck in its old mode. The last verses of the song are sung when the huts were burning, so we needed to change it completely,' says Anurag.

Another of Piyush's works is '*Kehke loonga*'. The lyrics are initially gibberish and Mishra is roped in to write the lyrics. Sneha keeps making Piyush hear tunes on the phone. To begin with he is not at all comfortable with what he is hearing and cannot make any sense of it. He tells Sneha as much. It is not his style of composing. So Sneha calls Anurag and says she won't change the tune. 'The song didn't have the standard format of a melody that Hindi films are so used to having. It didn't have the traditional mukhda antra mukhada antra. We had some healthy debates about that. I think the problem was that the tune had irregular repetitions and he had to learn to write down. He had a problem remembering it, so he had to keep hearing it again and again. That irritated him. But I think that uneasiness worked and I had a blast doing it plus he wrote a very angry song. It is a love song that says I will take your case and who better than Piyush Mishra to say it with grace,' Sneha says.

The film-maker did not start out with the intention of creating an album with twenty-five to twenty-seven songs. Like the film itself, the songs developed organically. 'I was basically making moods. I think the music found its audience, its listeners. I was curious to know whether the liberty that Anurag and I had taken in terms of music would be accepted but it was and that was understood correctly. There was no thinking twice on what we were doing, no analysis and that worked. "*I am a hunter*" found its audience so did "*Bahut khub*",' wraps up Sneha.

7

IN FIRST PERSON
Anurag Kashyap

'Mere life se Wasseypur gaya na? Sirf ek foreword likhna hai na?

– Anurag Kashyap

Fade In…

There is a portrait of a young, lean man, wearing a dhoti, an old-fashioned leather bag slung over the shoulder. 'That was me', says Anurag, 'in another life.' This reminder of his theatre days in Delhi is the only personal portrait of his in his room at his production office. He is in the middle of script revisions of Ugly *and eager to get to his new project.*

I joined the Jan Natya Manch, a theatre group whose founder Safdar Hashmi would be murdered years later during a street play. I was a communist. Bagal mein jhola leke baith jana aur bolna, kya Coca-Cola pi rahe ho? I even grew a beard to fit the image. I was with the group for nine months and it was here that I discovered Ayn Rand and became a capitalist. So I went to the group and gave them a lecture on capitalism. I kept changing. I wanted to be mysterious to show off to the girls.

It was here that I was introduced to the world of English literature. Before joining them, I used to read only Hindi writers such as Keshav Pandit, Ved Prakash. I read so much Hindi literature in school that there was nothing left to read when I was out of school. One of my first books in English was Kafka's *The Trial*, after reading which I didn't get out of my house for months!

I came to Bombay with friends for an international film festival in 1993 and never left. I never even discussed this decision with the group. Suddenly I was on a different high. I wrote a play called *Mein* that got a scholarship award. Govind Nihalani happened to read it and asked me to write for him. I wanted to become an actor; writing was never on my mind. He said writing would pay me so I decided to write. He gave me four books he wanted to adapt into scripts. I started reading and for one year I didn't call Govindji, in fact I never got back to him at all. I didn't talk with anyone during that period. A different journey started from there.

I joined Makrand Deshpande's theatre group and did a little bit of writing on the side to survive. I started writing for television, daily soaps, anything that came my way. I was twenty-two and getting paid over two lakhs. *Satya* was the first thing that came my way where I left my sense of security. I left everything to work with

Ram Gopal Varma because for the first time somebody talked sense to me.

Satya was fun to write though there was no money in it. Everybody said no to *Satya*, as it didn't have money. My criteria was that I needed to survive and when I was making money, I made a lot of it. I earned two lakhs for two months. After two months I met Ramu and I left what I was doing. Everyone was looking for money but I was looking for excitement.

Ramu said, 'I can't give you that kind of money. I will give you half of that money for the whole film and for how much ever time it takes.' I stopped writing screenplays after *Satya*. I wrote only dialogues. I got disappointed very early. I thought *Satya* will change the industry but it changed only the people who were involved with it. Everyone became a star in their own right. *Satya* was my training. I didn't go to Harvard, I went to the 'Hard' world.

Paanch was made out of sheer anger to show the industry that a twenty-six-year-old could make a film and to tell the industry that all you need to make a film are passion and content. The whole industry loved it. But the film didn't release. There was a lot of frustration. Systematically, over a period of seven years, the arrogance of wanting to show off to people was broken down and that was the best thing that happened to me because from that I got objectivity.

I was the only guy who was doing so much. I had so much energy that nobody could deal with it. I could write a hundred-page script in one night. *Black Friday* was written in thirty-six hours. I had an insatiable appetite. I would read so much, write so much and watch so much in a day.

With *Black Friday* I was shooting with a fresh crew. I was very naïve. And because I was naïve and had that misplaced sense of idealism and that whole thing of staying true to shoot on actual locations – like a stubborn child I said I wanted to shoot the scenes exactly where they happened. At first, *Mid-Day* didn't know what to do, but they made it happen. Today when I look back I realize I was shooting inside the sea at 2 a.m., nothing is visible anyway. I could have shot it here in Versova. But it got made in that passion.

Gulaal was based on a story that Raja (Raj Singh Chaudhary), who assisted me on *Black Friday*, narrated. It is a story of college politics. I felt that the story needed a milieu, a setting, a context. The milieu became the history of Rajasthan where the story was rooted; Raja was from Jaipur. I went to Jaipur and started researching for the story. I read books, reports, found the context and emerged with the script. At one point of time I was thinking of turning *Gulaal* into a book when the film was not happening.

Wasseypur is also a mix of reportage and stories that people have narrated – people, stories and urban legends. That's how stories are told, that's how stories are written. The problem is that we are not used to storytelling any more. Our cinema is black and white.

Black is Bollywood and white is the pure, real cinema of the seventies. When I made *Black Friday*, a famous critic said that 'this is not cinema nor is it a documentary, how can you call it a film'. It was unfathomable for them. It was like, yeh kya hai, kuch bhi nahi hai.

With *Wasseypur*, people have complained that I have not paid enough attention to the pathetic conditions of coal workers. But who said that it was about that. I said in every interview that the story is about coal and coal mines till the Khan family is involved in the business, and when the family moves away from that, the story moves with them. The expectation from the film is two-fold. They want the entertainment of mainstream cinema and it should also take up social issues. Message ke bina cinema hota hai yeh unke dimag main ghusta hi nahi hai.

The visual novel approach to film-making which I have attempted in *Gangs of Wasseypur* is just the beginning. What *Wasseypur* did to me will be seen in what I am doing in the future. I have got rights to three short stories by Gaurav Solanki which I want to turn into one film. I want to shoot it like three short stories rather than make it a screenplay. Keep the integrity of a short story. Shoot the short story. Shoot the novel. The idea is to take every incident in the short story in the order in which it is written and elaborate on that. And the way the short story is structured becomes the structure of the screenplay.

Being an outsider is a big thing. That's where objectivity comes into our movies because we, the new generation of film-makers in Hindi cinema, mostly come from outside of 'Bollywood'. We have seen it from outside and we have laughed at it in the beginning and now we deal with it. I have lot of friends who are from film families and their definition of cinema forms at a very early age. Their whole idea of cinema is borrowed from old cinema. They make films but they just can't bring themselves to deal with the real world around them. So they look down upon their own surroundings. So they will never shoot in India. They will never shoot on streets, they will shoot in studios.

You will probably see this element of rootedness, of using locations that lend to the essence of the film, in all my films from *Paanch* to *Yellow Boots*. For *GoW*, I am indebted to the Madurai Triumvirate who inspired me to go to my roots. I have been watching their cinema and that's why I needed to acknowledge the three: Bala, Ameer Sultan and M. Sasikumar. These directors were from Madurai, they made their films in Madurai, and they made films from where they came from. It was Bala's film *Sethu* that triggered this obsession which continued with *Kaadhal Kondein*, *Paruthiveeran* and *Subramaniapuram* among others.

We are making cinema we believe in. We are making cinema that says where we are coming from. We are not trying to make art-house films, we are simply experimenting with the form and we intend to make films that make money at the box office. My definition of commercial cinema is a film that makes money. If my film recovers its cost, it allows me to make my next film. So if one film is very successful, you can experiment with the next film. The success of one film allows me to do other films. *Dev D* and *Gulaal* allowed me to produce *Udaan* and direct and produce *That Girl in Yellow Boots*. If *Gangs of Wasseypur* works, I will do something more extreme. Nobody in the country would touch these films. And I am doing it for myself. I am being selfish. I just want to see whether I can do that. Can I really go out and make a film like *That Girl in Yellow Boots*. Let me just shoot it like that. Let me not do anything, let me just put the camera near the actors. Follow them very closely. In *Wasseypur*, I went to another extreme – made a film of five hours in two parts.

Dibakar Banerjee and Vishal Bhardwaj are likewise selfish film-makers. We are actually making films to see how far actually we can go. To better ourselves. Hamare yahan kahawat hai, chutiya bano, chutiya samjho mat. Hindi cinema is usually made by people who think people are stupid. They actually sit down and decide that the average IQ of our audience is below 50 so they won't understand everything. That's how the film starts. They only sell posters, images and trailers. They don't make films. It was reported in some newspaper that Vikramaditya Motwane is making a film with Sonakshi Sinha and Ranveer Singh and that I am producing it. In twenty-four hours every studio in town called me. 'How much money do you need? We will give you all. Make the film with us.' There is so much desperation at the other end that nobody really focuses on the content.

Ironically, there is enough talent here. However, the film-maker makes a film only for the audience's approval. There is no self-expression. I express myself in my films – this is how I feel. But here it is not about expression, it is about catering. Like you order things from a menu – I want songs, music, romance, good-looking people, good-looking clothes...

Here nobody shares. I have this group of people who share our films right from the working stage, at the script stage with each other. There is Dibakar (Banerjee), Zoya (Akhtar), Imtiaz (Ali) and I. I read their scripts and they read mine. I know what Vishal is doing next, as I will have his script and Vishal will have mine. We are outsiders in the industry. The mainstream industry does not practise this.

But times are changing. I got funds for a five-and-a-half-hour, non-star cast film, which is my most expensive film and in a language that is not mainstream Hindi. This is because the audience is changing. The unfortunate part is that most of the audience for new cinema is a non-paying audience which downloads films from Torrent. But this audience will tomorrow become a paying audience or hopefully the world will figure out a way to generate money from Torrent. Because that will become a huge platform for film viewing and when that happens, the quality will go up and everything will change.

I always work with new producers who are willing to take the risk. Established producers want to play it safe. *Dev D* was produced by UTV Spotboy. *Black Friday* would have never been made in this country if it was not for *Mid-Day* because no other producer would have allowed me to do a film like that. *Mid-Day* believes in reporting and they were first-time producers and there was not a single person from the industry handling the production. I don't think I can make *Black Friday* again or anyone in this industry will make it till the industry changes. Because this is a country where I want to say so much but I can't.

When I took on *Wasseypur* I was in a nine-film deal with UTV. Though they were on board initially, problems began to arise. There was lot of reluctance from them when I decided that the principal cast will be Manoj Bajpai, Richa, Nawazuddin and no big stars. When the film was being developed, everybody thought it will have bigger names and faces because I had told them I am going to make it my first commercial film. They heard the word 'commercial' and they thought I would have big stars – they didn't think in terms of the content.

Then budget became a big issue. Then I was asked to forfeit my fees in lieu of rights in the overseas market which I agreed to. In spite of this, they wanted to cut down the budget and we were at the minimum.

Eventually, we went slightly over and the film ended up at Rs 18.40 crore, but UTV was not ready to go above Rs 14 crore. They wanted bigger names and I wouldn't agree to that. The bigger names would have just spoilt the balance of my film. We parted ways. That was a big turning point. I remember the day, 28 November 2010, in the morning I had the dialogue narration for Reema Kagti's *Talaash*. I had come to Mumbai for two days for this dialogue narration and this UTV meeting and the meeting was such a heartbreak. I came back and broke down. Vikas Bahl was there; he was a part of the journey, part of developing the film, Rucha and Vikas. They really wanted to do the film and it was my call to walk out. After that I did get a call from Ronnie Screwvala saying, let's get back together and we will work out something. I said no, if you don't have faith in it, don't make it, and don't do it for me. I need producers who believe in me, I need producers who back me all the way. I have seen what happens to films when producers don't believe in you. If you don't have faith in the project, doubts keep surfacing. And if someone happens to say this project is doomed that will be the last straw for the producers.

I wanted somebody who would come in with his own conviction and I was already in talks with Viacom to do *Shaitan* and *Michael*. Then Sunil Bohra[1] spoke to Vikram Malhotra who heard the story and got very excited, just like a child. And because Vikram is not

---

[1]Producer

from the film industry … he comes from the airlines background … he kind of got the picture. That was the basis on which Viacom came onboard. And I think this was the first time that a company's COO[2] came for the first narration. The very next day, his creative head, Anku Pandey, and the rest of the team came and heard the story. We all left together for the shoot which began as planned. It all happened overnight and then they were part of it, every step of it. UTV gracefully backed out. They told me that I could return the money they had already invested when I could. Not only did they not charge us any interest, they did not create any complications. Then we did *Luv Shuv Tey Chicken Khurana* with UTV. It was very unlike the way this industry functions. Both the parties were happy and there was no bad blood.

The budget constraints didn't affect the film. We didn't compromise at all. Though special effects and make-up were made to work out within what we had. The slight finesse was compromised on, but not in terms of what we wanted to shoot. What was compromised on was where we stayed while shooting, the way we travelled. We stayed in very small, cheap economical hotels, but that's what we always do. We delivered an eighty-crore film in eighteen crores and that was tough. But then a film without a star cast, a film that challenges the market conventions has to be made this way. It is a

---

[2]Vikram Malhotra quit Viacom 18 Movies Motion Pictures in March 2013.

budget we chose. It is a budget we made. You have to honour that.

Cinema has certain limitations. You are writing a book. This needs to be documented in some form. The honesty, the reality should come out. Self-censorship comes only from your past experiences. I am aware of what happened with *Paanch*, *Black Friday*. It's about how far can I push the boundaries. In *Wasseypur*, I shot the Fazlu beheading knowing fully well that it would not pass the censor board. In *Black Friday*, I had to remove the Bal Thackeray angle. I talked about Sharad Pawar's role which was born out of our research. I put that on a blog, which I had to take out.

It is worse here than in a country like Iran because there you are at least allowed to make the film and you can sneak it outside and show the rest of the world. It's only if you show it in Iran that you are arrested. Here, you take a politician's name in the film and it gets banned. In *Dil Se*, the censors objected to the climax. It's a country with a very low level of tolerance and it has no place for democracy and citizen's rights. People don't ask for rights and they don't give you the rights. How can a film like *Black Friday* happen? *Bas ek baar ban gaya*...

When one makes a film like *Dev D*, one has to deal with conservative Indian morality. One has to practise some kind of self-censorship without killing the soul of the film. I want to really go all out but I engage in self-censorship all the time. I have to rein in my camera.

Self-censorship comes in while shooting. Take the *Dev D* sequence where the boy goes down on the girl – in the script it is written out fully, but on shoot when Abhay goes down, the camera shows the sky. That's self-censorship.

While writing, my first criteria is that I write for myself. If I don't like a film how will the audience like it? I write it myself, then bring a whole team and do a narration and see their reactions. One film that nobody wanted me to make was *That Girl In Yellow Boot* but I still made that film. I had to get it out of my system. Otherwise I could not move ahead. And because it took so long I could not make any other film during that time.

The film got made only because I was in a relationship with Kalki. Otherwise, no girl would trust me enough to do a role like that, to do a film like that in this country. And also because Kalki's upbringing and sensibility is much more liberal and she keeps her work separate from her personal life. For *Dev* D, I had auditioned 2000 girls – some girls threw the script on my face, they thought I was doing a porn film. When they read the script they got all moral on me, they thought if the director has written a role like that he must be some kind of pervert. In half the meetings, I had to make my sister, who was the AD for the film, sit with me. The few who actually wanted to do the film had no clue how to interpret the character. For example, if there is a scene where the character is having phone sex, the character should not look like she is having sex. This work is just a profession they were into. These actors would not get that point at all. They would come and perform as if they are having sex.

Seriously, you have to see those auditions to know what kind of industry we are dealing with every day. For *Wasseypur*, we have Durga who starts shivering when Sardar Khan touches her, she can't serve him food because she is attracted to him. She is nervous in his presence and he takes advantage of her but eventually marries her. So I spoke to a woman who was going to audition for the part. She said it's a sexy scene. I said the sex has to be in your eyes. I need to see that you are attracted to him. She auditioned and sent me the tape. She was from Kolkata. She wore a deep-cut blouse, was fully wet in that scene and told me, 'I can go further if you want.' I said, 'No, I want you to go back.'

I grew up in a small town, fantasizing about and looking at girls from a distance. Repressed for the longest time, I wouldn't even hold hands with girls. I thought one cannot do that before marriage. The first time I saw girls with cigarettes I got very upset. I told them you can't do this. First time I went on a date, I took the girl to see *Mississippi Burning*, instead of a romantic movie, and all she wanted to do was to hold my hand. And when she tried to do that I told her, 'Don't worry, don't be scared.'

So much so, I was a safe zone for girls in college. They were not conscious of me, they would tell me about their problems. I would listen to them, mostly scandalized, but I listened to them. Women have been my best friends since then. I married the first girl I kissed. And what happened in my life after that … I was twenty-seven and nothing was going right in my personal or professional life. I had an affair with a woman who was older than me, an actress. Mere saare dhakkan khul gaye. I was the boy toy who would check into the next room at your hotel and stay in there for days because all he wants to do is to see you. I played that role for six months and I changed as a person after that. Till then I had only one perspective about women, I knew about lot of things but I would often judge them. What happened in this case was that I felt angry, feeling used at the end of it, I felt like this for next five-six months. But then it changed my perspective on women. I suddenly started seeing their point of view. That completely opened me and that's where you see most of my women characters coming from. The understanding that they are not one-dimensional … I used to be in awe of women, I used to fear them. After this experience I completely got them, recognized them as human beings. This whole thing of women being worthy of being worshipped was discarded because as long as we worship them, we tie them up with the concept of purity.

Postscript

Gangs of Wasseypur Part I hits the theatres mid 2012. And suddenly Anurag is trending – everywhere. Reviews pour in. *Part 2* releases two months later.

Hansal Mehta is amazed at the difference between what the story was and the film as it has shaped up. 'Anurag completely left behind the original idea, it's an entirely new film. There are so many new characters in it. And Anurag specializes in that. He works on the characters' peripheries and makes them an essential part of the movie. And the way he connects the three generations is amazing. He has added a lot of himself to the film. Sexual innuendoes and all were not there. I would have never made something like this, I would have never thought of something like this.'

Anurag is amused at the way the film has been interpreted by some reviewers.

'There have been really weird interpretations. The opening of Part I when the television is fired upon, someone said that it symbolized the destruction of Bollywood. It was nothing like that. We just wanted to show the episode of *Kyonki* which was playing that day when Fahim Khan's house was attacked. We went to Star Plus and picked up that episode. People do that a lot, there was this guy who said that there was a scene in

Dev D which was connected to the promiscuous nature of the character, where Dev is walking and the camera pans out and there is a hotel named 'rand' (the word refers to a commercial sex worker or a promiscuous woman). The truth was that the frame of the shot excluded one letter ... the letter G ... the name of the hotel was Grand Hotel. It was not done intentionally.'

Mehta sees a noticeable difference in Anurag's film-making in his last few films. '*Paanch* was very raw, it was a very affected film, he has broken free of all that, of overt influence, the danger for any film-maker when you see too many films, when what you see gets crowded in your subconscious. There are images and moments which are there and he has broken that in *Dev D*, *Yellow Boots* and now *GoW*. With this film he has become an auteur. When you are part of the cult, they want you to make quirky cutting-edge films; they begin to dictate what you are making. And this is what a fan following does, it starts limiting you and your work. But with *Wasseypur* and now *Ugly*, he has started to break through that also.'

Tigmanshu Dhulia notes the camera technique in the film. 'He has not used track, gyp, crane shot. The camera is static. As a director sometimes you feel the scene is not working. So I need to build it up with background music. Shaayad performance theek nahi ho, so I have underlined by tracking. But what happens if you have not done tracking at all during shooting. Even if you see *Godfather*, there is one shot in which there is a slight track, but the camera is static. It's on the strength of the director that the picture will run. He told me that

Anurag Kashyap in a pensive mode

Anurag with Chief AD Anubhuti Kashyap

Anurag Kashyap and Rajeev Ravi (DOP) discussing a shot

Kashyap with Bajpai at the doorstep of Durga's house

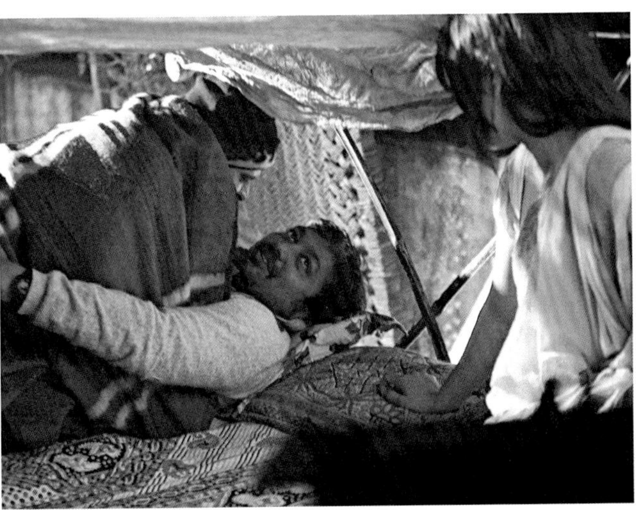

Kashyap directing a lovemaking scene on the terrace, with Reema Sen looking on

Kashyap writing out scenes on the set

Kashyap directing Tigmanshu Dhulia in the scene where Sardar Khan forces Ramadhir Singh out of his car and humiliates him

Kashyap checking a shot

Manoj Bajpai, running high fever, shoots the scene of Sardar Khan bathing at water pump at Qamar Makhdoomi's house

Manoj Bajpai (Sardar Khan) and Tigmanshu Dhulia (Ramadhir Singh): the ungli kiya scene

Manoj Bajpai (Sardar Khan) in the Pehalwan killing scene

Nawazuddin Siddiqui (Faizal Khan) in jail

Nawazuddin as Faizal Khan in jail after Shamshad Alam betrays him

Nawazuddin as Faizal Khan when he sees Mohsina at his brother's wedding

(from L to R) Kashyap, Shlok Sharma and
Neeraj Ghaywan (2nd AD)

Second Unit Director Shlok Sharma

Art director Wasiq Khan (left) at the set where butcher shops in Sultan's territory are bombed

Jameel and Bajpai in the Pahalwan killing scene

Pankaj Tripathi (Sultan) conspiring with Satya Anand (J.P. Singh)

Tigmanshu Dhulia as Ramadhir Singh

Huma Qureshi (Mohsina) at Danish wedding

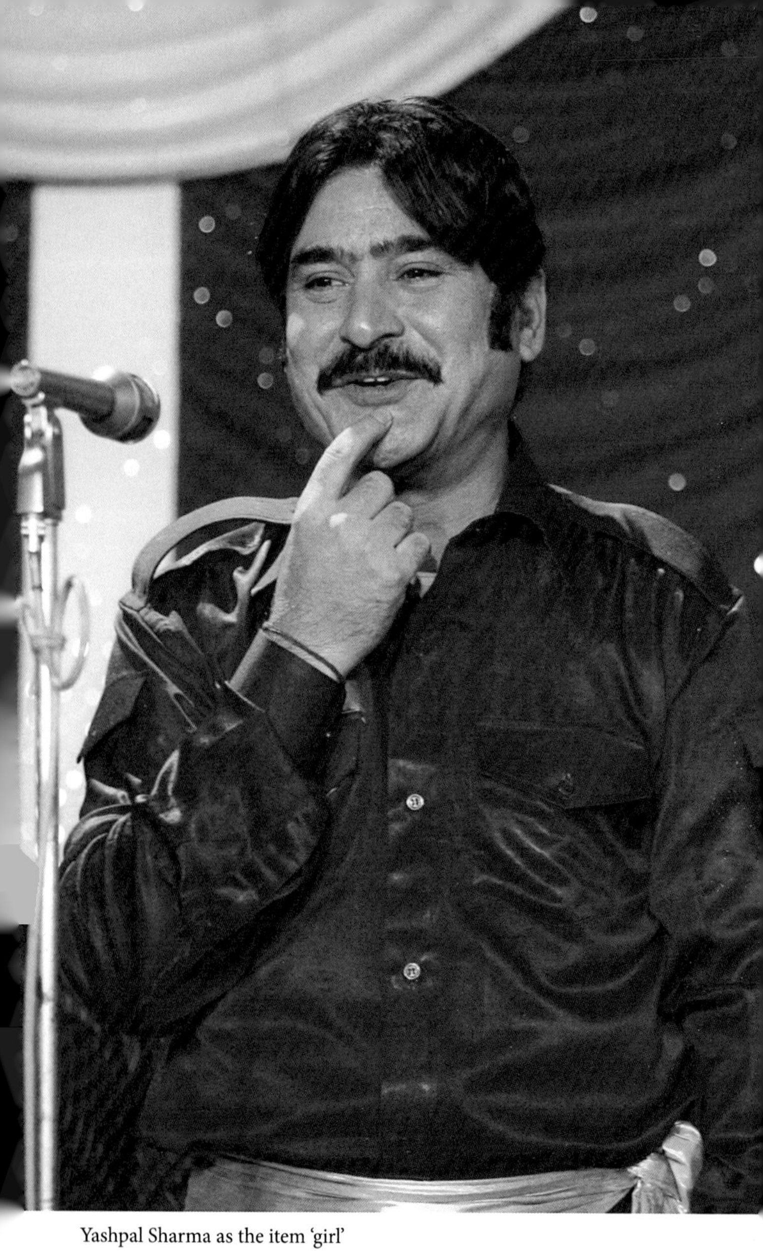

Yashpal Sharma as the item 'girl'

he would not do such things because he believes in his script and the actors' performance. Dum hai usme, himmatwalla hai.'

Anurag is tired of explaining his film. 'Doing promotion feels like prostitution sometimes. Because I don't know if film journalists really understand the process of film-making or understand anything about films. There are very few interviews in which where somebody is asked questions which you know you feel like answering. I have been doing this for two months. I have answered every question about the film and my brain is fried. I need to go and sleep, I need to rest. This film has taken three years of our lives. It has sucked me dry. I want to get it out of my system.'

FADE OUT...

GANGS OF WASSEYPUR

PART I

WRITTEN BY:

Zeishan Quadri, Akhilesh Jaiswal, Sachin Ladia and Anurag Kashyap

1 EXT/INT. PAAN SHOP-ROAD - NIGHT 2004

On Screen we see the opening credits of *Kyonki Saas Bhi Kabhi Bahu Thi* ... Camera zooms out. A paan shop ... customers engrossed in watching the episode ... The TV gets blown away by bullets. People run around in chaos. Sultan, the leader of the group, and his men come out of a Maruti van with guns. They scare people by shooting in the air. Shutters are pulled down.

SULTAN

(To a passerby who runs)
Close everything.

Sultan points at a shop.

SULTAN

Fuck off!

JABBAR

Hey shut it!

They move on into a narrow lane. Sultan fires at a man and knocks him down. As they move towards Faizal's house, some more men join them from the other side. The soap opera KSBKBT is heard in the background. They reach Faizal's house and knock the guards down.

JABBAR

I see Faizal Khan, Boss.

SULTAN

Then get in and kill the motherfucker!

Sultan hurls a bomb at the house main door.

SULTAN

Get out, Faizal. Come outside, asshole.

Sultan kicks the main door. It's locked from inside.

SULTAN

Fuckers locked it.

Sultan goes near and makes a vent into the broken door.

SULTAN

Give me a bomb.

Sultan throws a bomb inside the house. They all move away and duck. Debris.

SULTAN

Everyone down

(Pointing at his men)

Fill every hole with bullets. I want you to destroy the fucker's palace.

EXT. FAIZAL'S HOUSE- BACK SIDE - NIGHT

Qasim and his men come from the back side to attack. They march ahead with guns. Qasim gestures his men to stop and then makes a phone call.

CUT TO:

EXT. FAIZAL'S HOUSE - NIGHT

Sultan and his men continue to shoot.

SULTAN

Where are you, fucker?? Come out, motherfucker...!

SULTAN (on the phone)

What's up?

CUT TO:

EXT. FAIZAL'S HOUSE - BACK SIDE - NIGHT

I/C With Qasim (with his men) at the back of the house

QASIM

We've covered the rear. Awaiting orders!

CUT TO:

EXT. FAIZAL'S HOUSE - NIGHT

SULTAN (on phone)

Fuck orders! Just shoot everyone. Kill anything that moves.

EXT. FAIZAL'S HOUSE - AT THE BACK - NIGHT

Qasim and his men shoot at the back door and enter the house.

QASIM

Get in.

INT. FAIZAL'S HOUSE - NIGHT

QASIM

Get the bombs, quick! Blow this shit up. Shoot through that hole now. Get in the window. Women, kids … just shoot whoever you see.

They continue shooting. One of them climbs up the building and starts shooting.

CUT TO:

EXT. FAIZAL'S HOUSE - AT THE DOOR - NIGHT 2004

All stop shooting … Silence … Sultan dials a number on his phone. Jabbar walks to the door … Listens … Silence…

INT. FAIZAL'S HOUSE - A SMALL ROOM- NIGHT

The house members are hiding in a closed room and just then the phone rings. It plays out the tune *Nayak nahin* … they all keep their mouth shut and let the phone ring.

EXT. FAIZAL'S HOUSE - AT THE DOOR - NIGHT 2004

Sultan is listening to the ringtone while Jabbar is listening with his ear close to the broken door.

JABBAR

It's ringing; no one is answering.

The phone stops ringing.

JABBAR

No one is picking up.

SULTAN

Bastards are dead. Let's go. Faizal Khan is dead! Let's go. The 'villain' is dead. The newspaper will tell us if anyone survived.

Sultan and his men leave the place. On his way, Sultan calls Qasim.

SULTAN (on the phone)

Yeah, tell the boys to leave. The war's over.

CUT TO:

EXT. OLD BRIDGE - NIGHT 2004

Sultan and his men drive back in their van.

SULTAN

That was a good frontal shot.

JABBAR

That fucker came out of nowhere!

SULTAN

It's time to inform the minister.

A car passes by with a group of men.

JABBAR

Boss, that's Definite's car!

SULTAN

Let him go and clean the mess.

INT. SOME BIG HOTEL - NIGHT

JP's phone rings ... He is with Ramadhir in a dinner table meeting.

JP (on the phone)

Hello

I/C

EXT. OLD BRIDGE - NIGHT

SULTAN (to JP on the phone)
Faizal Khan's dead, sir.

I/C

INT. SOME BIG HOTEL - NIGHT
A group of politicians dining at an exquisite hotel. J.P. Singh is present with his father Ramadhir Singh.

POLITICIAN 1
So the minister was asked to sing the national anthem …
He crooned 'Vande Mataram'…! What ignorants!

RAMADHIR SINGH
You know it?

Meanwhile J.P. Singh gets a call and he steps outside. We stay on him.

POLITICIAN 1 (O.S)
Saare jaahan se acha … 'The best in the world…!' [incorrect anthem]

EXT. OLD BRIDGE - NIGHT

I/C

SULTAN (on the phone)
The mansion is now rubble. We bombed it to outer space.

JABBAR
Boss, look.

SULTAN (to driver)
Stop the car!

JABBAR
Why's there police patrol?

SULTAN (on the phone)
What's with the cops, minister?

I/C J.P. Singh cuts his call without saying a word.

JABBAR

What now, boss?

SULTAN

The bastard hung up. Sit tight … They're here for us! Sister fuckers!!!

A check-point with a lot of cops. One of the cops walks towards Sultan's van with a gun pointed at them.

SULTAN

He's coming here!

Sultan takes his gun and shoots at the cop. Random cross fire from both sides ensues. The car glass shatters with gun shots. Freeze frame.

CREDITS

NASIR (V.O)

There are two kinds of men. Bastards, and dumb fucks. They control the world. It's hard to tell when a dumb fuck turns into a bastard and vice versa. Such is the twisted tale of Wasseypur. It's a town full of rotten bastards pretending to be dumb fucks. In the final reckoning who knows what they really were, but while they were alive they thought they were heroes. The in-fighting between Muslims today is many centuries old. Initially this fight was one-sided. Everyone was terrified of the Qureshis who were butchers by profession. So the Qureshis openly ruled the town.

NASIR (V.O) (CONT'D)

This was pre-independence, when our village was a part of Dhanbad, which was a part of Bengal. Post-independence Dhanbad became a part of Bihar, and in time Wasseypur became the centre of Dhanbad. So the saga that continues today began way back then…

NASIR (V.O) (CONT'D)

… When the British seized all the grain fields and started mining for coal…
… When all the trains and modern factories were running on coal … When a dacoit named Sultana used to loot the British trains.

MONTAGE: COAL FIELDS, OLD RAILWAYS AND SULTANA DAKU.

EXT. GROUND - DAY

Sharif Qureshi talks to a young Nasir with a group of people. Ehsan Qureshi is sitting by Sharif's side.

SHARIF QURESHI

He'd attack the British trains and loot their treasure. One day he found soldiers instead of treasure.
They arrested him and exiled him to the *Kaala Pani* prison.

YOUNG NASIR

But Maulwi Sir said that they hanged him in Calcutta.

SHARIF QURESHI

Sod off!

YOUNG NASIR

Really, he did!

SHARIF QURESHI

Maulwi is a dumb ass. Sultana was a Qureshi, and only the second man in history to escape from the island prison.

YOUNG NASIR

Sultana dacoit?

SHARIF QURESHI

Yup.

YOUNG NASIR

Alive?

SHARIF QURESHI

And right here in Wasseypur. Still looting British trains.

Shahid Khan listens intently…

EXT. RAILWAY CROSSING - NIGHT

A small railway crossing with an old style wooden gate. A signal man is cooking his meal on an earthen pot. He hears a train approaching. He picks up a lantern and brandishes a green light at it. Just then a masked man atop a horse points his single barrel gun at the signal man. Signal man turns the green light into red.

CUT TO:

I/E. DESERTED RAILWAY (TRACK 1 /CROSSING/TRAIN) - NIGHT SUPER - WASSEYPUR 1941

From inside the train as the driver and his man put coal into the steam engine … Driver looks out … He can see the signal man holding the red flag …

He applies brakes on the train. The train stops and the man on the horse gallops towards the engine. He climbs on to the engine with his gun … the driver looks at him and is about to start again.

DRIVER

OH Lord!

SHAHID KHAN

We've removed the tracks, so don't bother going further, you'll die.

DRIVER 1

But we're carrying only grains, sir.

SHAHID KHAN

Hey, that's not a problem. Today your grain will be my treasure, buddy. I'll fill my belly instead of my pocket!

DRIVER 1

May we go?

SHAHID KHAN

Come on buddy, my bullocks are slow. So leave only when we're at a safe distance. Get it, old man? Now sit. Sit, asshole.

Shahid supervises.

SHAHID KHAN (CONT'D)

Stack them up ... take those.

CUT TO:

I/E. DESERTED RAILWAY TRACK 1 & TRAIN - NIGHT

A horse gallops upto the engine ... A different horse ... A different man (Sultana Daku) along with Ehsan...

SULTANA DAKU (to Ehsan)

Why has the train stopped? Let's open and check.

He approaches the driver and asks him.

SULTANA DAKU (to driver)

Hey, driver! Why've you stopped?

(O.S)

Boss, the train is looted.

SULTANA DAKU (to driver)

By whom?

DRIVER 1

Sultana Dacoit took everything.

The man uncovers his face ... His face resembles the sketch in the train (A wanted poster for Sultana Daku).

CUT TO:

EXT. KASAI MUHALLAH - DAY

SHARIF QURESHI

Who is pretending to be me?

EHSAN QURESHI

I wonder!

Shahid Khan walks by with his horse.

SHARIF QURESHI

What about Shahid Khan? He's the only one in this place who has a horse.

SHAHID KHAN (to Sharif)

Salaam!

SHARIF QURESHI (to Shahid)

Salaam!

Shahid Khan moves on and they continue talking

EHSAN QURESHI

He's a horse cart driver, right?

SHARIF QURESHI

He's not a horse cart driver anymore … Now he's a grain trader.

EXT. WHOLESALE MARKET - DAY

Ehsan Qureshi comes into the market on cart. The market has all the buyers crowded around Shahid's stall. Ehsan talks to one of the sellers in the market…

EHSAN QURESHI

How're you, brother? How's business?

SELLER

He's spoiled the whole market. His prices are two annas cheaper. We'll starve if we compete with that!

Ehsan looks at Shahid counting money and tucking it in his dhoti. A lot of sacks of grains stacked on top of one another. Shahid Khan sits behind them. Some grains are being weighed. His pregnant wife sits near him cooking on a clay stove. Shahid khan counts money.

BUYER

Brother Shahid, when's the baby expected?

Shahid continues to count the money.

SHAHID KHAN

In two months, rest is *Allah's* grace.

Ehsan inspects the grain sacks with precision. The East India Company symbol is visible on the sacks.

CUT TO:

EXT. KASAI MUHALLAH - DAY

Sharif Qureshi(Sultana Daku), Ehsan and few others sit around...

SHARIF (SULTANA DAKU)

The tracks go through the Qureshi colony. So rightfully Qureshis should get the first crack at the trains ... and not some *Pathan.*

He talks to an older man - Mukhtar.

MUKHTAR

Please understand that Shahid is also from this village. So solve this amicably without any bloodshed. He's your neighbor.

SHARIF QURESHI

But he's not a Qureshi.

CUT TO:

INT. SHAHID'S HOUSE - DAY

SHAHID KHAN

Relax! We'll apologise if we're caught.

YOUNG NASIR

What if they kill us?

SHAHID KHAN
The village headman won't allow it. I know him well.

EXT. WASSEYPUR ROAD 5 - DAY
Shahid walks down the street. He sees something. Stops.

It's a hand painted poster.

'WANTED SHAHID KHAN, DEAD OR ALIVE. REWARD 100 RUPEES'

He spits on it.

NASIR (V.O)
A dog always stays a dog. Shahid was like that. He knew that the whole town knew he was looting the trains but being rotten was in his stubborn blood. He continued playing with fire.

EXT. SHAHID'S HOUSE - DAY
Shahid with his men. His wife serves them tea in glasses.

SHAHID KHAN
You guys afraid?

SHAHID'S WIFE
Obviously. Sharif Qureshi is Sultana Dacoit.

SHAHID KHAN
Sultana died in the Andamans. The rest is a myth.

SHAHID'S MAN
You're forgetting he's a butcher!

SHAHID KHAN
Fuck them. These miserable butchers live on our Pathan scraps back home.
Silence.

SHAHID KHAN (CONT'D)
Tomorrow we'll strike the train away from the usual spot.

CUT TO:

EXT. RAILWAY TRACK 1 - NIGHT

Man struggling to take off the railway tracks. Shahid Khan is supervising. Shahid hears something and gestures everyone to keep quiet. Faint sound of horses can be heard.

SHAHID KHAN

Move quickly, we don't have time. The bastards have found us! Save yourselves!

Shahid fires from his single barrel, kills one of the attackers. Shahid tries to fill the gunpowder into the gun. Seeing them getting close he drops the powder and attacks with the gun. He hits out and then runs away on his horse.

SHARIF QURESHI

Kill each one of them! I want Shahid Khan dead.

I/E. SHAHID'S HUT - NIGHT

Shahid comes on his horse all alone. He drinks some water from the pot and then enters the house. Jameela (his wife) is lying on the bed.

SHAHID KHAN

How are you now?

JAMEELA

Better.

SHAHID KHAN

Rest.

NASIR (O.S)

Boss!

Shahid comes out of the house. Nasir is hurt.

SHAHID KHAN

Where are the others?

NASIR

It's just me. Others got killed.

Nasir is crying as he speaks. Shahid looks at him.

NASIR (CONT'D)
You said no one would die.

EXT. PANCHAYAT GROUND - DAY

Shahid sits on the ground with Nasir. Opposite to him are all the Qureshis. They sit in front of Mukhtar. Silence.

SHARIF QURESHI (SULTANA DAKU)
He should get out with his family and his men.

SHAHID KHAN
Okay, but how do I feed them, sir? And what's his problem anyway?

Sharif gets furious and takes his footwear off to beat Shahid.

SHARIF QURESHI (SULTANA DAKU)
Shameless bastard!! Motherfucker uses my name to loot and gives me attitude.

MUKHTAR
A bag of grain from each train will be given to you every week.

Shahid Khan thanks Mukhtar with a gesture and leaves. Sharif is furious.

SHARIF QURESHI
What the hell? Why are we being so generous?

CUT TO:

EXT. SHAHID KHAN'S HOUSE - DAY

A very pregnant wife of Shahid's climbs the horse. They leave. Nasir is with him…

NASIR (V.O)
Shahid Khan left the village. He knew the Qureshis would come after his family. We moved away to Dhanbad. Shahid's wife made him

swear on their child that he would earn an honest living.

Shahid digging coal in a coal mine.

INT. SHAHID KHAN'S HUT- DAY

Shahid's wife in labour. The midwife is worried. The child is not coming out.

MIDWIFE

Don't worry, dear … It's ok.

The second midwife goes and asks Nasir to call for Shahid.

MIDWIFE 2

The baby is stuck. Please call her husband.

I/E. VILLAGE ROAD 1 - EVE

Nasir runs on the unpaved road. It's raining heavily.

CUT TO:

EXT. COAL MINE 1- NIGHT

Some bouncers are outside the coal mine. A labourer comes and complaints about the water logging.

LABOURER 1

Sir, we should evacuate. The mine is getting water logged - we could all…

The Pehelwan hits the labourer.

PEHELWAN 1

Shut up! You've only worked 9 out of 12 hours.

LABOURER 1

We'll drown, sir.

PEHELWAN 1

Stop complaining, fucker! Get back to work … Now!

(hits him)

Nasir stops.

NASIR
Sir … sir…

PEHELWAN 1
What is it?

NASIR
Shahid Khan's wife is in labour.

PEHELWAN 1
So?

NASIR
He's urgently needed there.

PEHELWAN 1
Bugger off.

The labourer who is going down, hears him. Pehelwan hits Nasir who falls.

INT. COAL MINE 1 - NIGHT

Workers huddled together. Two workers are forcibly dragged to work. The Pehelwan shouts.

PEHELWAN 2
Nobody leaves before the shift is over. And if you stop, I'll peel your skin and hang you in the meat market.

Shahid looks up … continues to work.

LABOURER 1
Brother, do something.

Shahid continues to work.

The worker who heard Nasir comes to him.

LABOURER 2
Nasir had come to inform you that your baby's stuck in labour.

He looks at the labourer.

Pehelwan 2 (hits him).

PEHELWAN 2 (to the worker)
Stop gossiping … work!

Shahid stares at him.

PEHELWAN 2 (CONT'D)
Stop staring and work.

SHAHID KHAN
I have to go. My child is stuck in labour.

PEHELWAN 2
So? You're also stuck in 'labour', you dog!

SHAHID KHAN
I beg you, Sir.

PEHELWAN 2
Didn't you hear me, fucker?

Shahid takes his hand and surges him into the wall.

INT. SHAHID'S HUT - NIGHT
Jameela screams.

MIDWIFE
It will be ok, dear … relax

INT. COAL MINE 1 - NIGHT (CONT'D)
Shahid leaves and reaches the grill where Nasir is waiting for him. The Pehelwan stops him.

SHAHID KHAN
Open up.

PEHELWAN 1
Who do you think you are … the governor?

SHAHID KHAN
Listen you animal, I'm not going to take your shit like the others. I've been quietly working so far, so don't push me any more … or by God I will rip you apart and embalm you with coal. Open it!!

The Pehelwan stares at him. A man (Supervisor Ramadhir Singh) next to him watches Shahid staring at the Pehelwan. Ramadhir gestures at the Pehelwan to open the grill.

SHAHID KHAN (to Nasir)

How is she?

NASIR

Not good.

SHAHID KHAN

Why didn't you come earlier?

NASIR

I tried. They didn't let me in.

The grill is opened. Shahid and Nasir leave in heavy rains.

NASIR

It's been 6 hours. The baby hasn't come out

SHAHID KHAN

You didn't tell me for 6 fucking hours?

NASIR

I wanted to but the muscle man hit me.

SHAHID KHAN

Fucking weakling!

INT. VILLAGE- SHAHID'S HUT - NIGHT

Rains continue. Shahid reaches home. He stops. The midwife stands outside holding the kid. Shahid takes the kid. Emotional. He walks in. His wife lies there dead. He stares.

MIDWIFE 2

She couldn't make it as she lost a lot of blood … But she's left you with a beautiful boy.

EXT. VILLAGE ROAD 2 - DAY

Shahid is by his wife's grave along with Young Nasir. They have just buried her. Baby (Sardar

Khan) is held by Nasir who hands him over to Shahid.

INT. SHAHID HUT - NIGHT

NASIR (V.O)

We can't blame God for life and death. We may create life by will or accidentally, but death is always born out of human mistake. It wasn't the muscle man's fault for delaying me; it was mine in not fighting him. And my weakness did not go unpunished.

Nasir is seen offering Namaaz and then flagellating himself.

EXT. COAL MINE 1 - DAY

Heavy rains. All miners watch as Shahid beats the pehelwan. He smashes his head in with a stone and drags him to the corner.

ANOTHER PEHELWAN

Sir, Shahid Khan will kill our guard.

RAMADHIR SINGH

Who Shahid Khan?

EXT. COAL MINE 1 - DAY

Shahid Khan turns and looks at the supervisor (Ramadhir Singh) who just stares at him.

EXT. VILLAGE - NIGHT

Nehru's speech on Radio … "tryst with destiny".

FADE IN:

NASIR (V.O)

The real power struggle started post-independence. The new government gave the mines to their rich industrialist friends … who knew nothing of the business. Ramadhir profited from this. He was given the contract to run most of these mines. But contractors couldn't run mines by themselves. They needed muscle men.

Fireworks in the sky and SHAHID watches it with young SARDAR who is six years old.

Nehru's speech continues…

CUT TO:

EXT. COAL MINE 1 - DAY

Shahid walks with his son to the coal mines.

Young Sardar sits in a corner as Shahid walks into the cabin.

EXT. COAL MINES 1 - CABIN - DAY

Young Sardar gets down from where he is sitting and walks to the window. He peeps in. To see the moustached young Rajput (Ramadhir Singh) supervisor.

CUT TO:

INT. COAL MINES 1 - CABIN - DAY

Shahid Khan is sitting opposite Ramadhir.

RAMADHIR SINGH

Will you work for me?

SHAHID KHAN

I already am, sir.

RAMADHIR SINGH

I want you to be the muscle for me. You'll be set for life.

SHAHID KHAN

Yes sir.

(He nods)

RAMADHIR SINGH

See now these mines belong to me. All the coal that comes out is mine. So will the profit, or loss. But the workers think that in free India there will be less work and more wages. That's not true.

CUT TO:

EXT. COAL MINE 1 - DAY

[I/C] Hutments of workers destroyed. Huts are burnt and pulled apart. Shahid is supervising the destruction.

CUT TO:

RAMADHIR SINGH (V.O)

We need to increase production, which means finding new mines. Which means the worker's colony will have to go. We are not rich like English. We can either give them wages or a home, not both.

EXT. COAL MINE 1 - DAY

Heavy rains. All mine workers huddle up together outside the mine. Ramadhir Singh's car arrives. Shahid gets out. All labourers get up.

RAMADHIR SINGH

Why has the work halted?

Few workers step forward.

LABOURER 4

This is unfair, sir. Our homes have been destroyed.

RAMADHIR SINGH (folds his umbrella and looks at his watch.)

I am going inside and when I return the work should have begun.

(looks at SHAHID, he nods)

Ramadhir walks away.

SHAHID KHAN

Come on! Back to work.

LABOURER 4

Aren't you one of us, brother?

Shahid slaps him. He falls. Shahid pulls out his butcher knife.

SHAHID KHAN
Fuck off! Back to work!

They back out.

CUT TO:

I/E. COAL MINE 1 - DAY
Singh watches from the window. Rain continues.

CUT TO:

EXT. SHAHID'S HUT - NIGHT
Car moves on the road. It rains. Car stops outside Shahid's house. Ramadhir Singh gets out. Rain continues.

CUT TO:

I/E. SHAHID'S HUT - NIGHT
Shahid and his son eat as Nasir serves *roti* to them. Door is open.

NASIR
Boss?

SHAHID KHAN
Yeah...

NASIR
You think you're being fair to your worker friends?

SHAHID KHAN
There are no friends here. The white dogs left some bread, now the monkeys are fighting over it.

I/C

EXT. SHAHID'S HUT - NIGHT
Ramadhir enters the house. Closes his umbrella and puts it down.

SHAHID KHAN (O.S.)
You think Ramadhir got these mines from his

dad? Yesterday the British were our godfather, today it is Ramadhir.

He stops. Peeps into the corner.

CUT TO:

INT. SHAHID'S HUT - NIGHT

SHAHID KHAN

And tomorrow it'll be Shahid Khan.

CUT TO:

EXT. SHAHID'S HUT - NIGHT

Ramadhir Singh hears that. He leaves.

CUT TO:

INT. SHAHID'S HUT - NIGHT

Shahid finishes eating. Gives the plate to Nasir.

RAMADHIR'S DRIVER 1 (O.S.)

Shahid Khan!

A knock at the door.

NASIR

I'll get it.

RAMADHIR'S DRIVER 1 (O.S.)

Master wants to see Shahid Khan.

NASIR

Okay.

NASIR (to Shahid)

Ramadhir has called for you.

SHAHID KHAN

Why's he here now?

Shahid khan leaves.

CUT TO:

INT. RAMADHIR'S CAR - NIGHT

Shahid gets into Ramadhir's car. Ramadhir Singh hands Khan a bag.

RAMADHIR SINGH
You need to reach Banaras overnight.

SHAHID KHAN
Banaras?

RAMADHIR SINGH
The train leaves in 20 minutes. Your ticket has been booked.

SHAHID KHAN
But sir, I need to inform my son, Sardar.

RAMADHIR SINGH
I'll send word.

I/E. SHAHID'S HUT - NIGHT

Young Sardar notices an umbrella lying near the door. It's Ramadhir's. Nasir looks at the umbrella. Looks at young Sardar.

NASIR
Time for bed … Whose is it?

SARDAR KHAN
It was lying here.

NASIR
Here?

SARDAR KHAN
Yes.

NASIR
Show me.
Ramadhir Singh!

Nasir thinks for a while as though he has realized something. He goes in and starts packing clothes.

CUT TO:

I/E. SHAHID'S HUT - NIGHT

Ramadhir's car drives back in the rainy night. Stops outside the house. Ehsan Qureshi gets out with a butcher knife in hand. There is one man with him. He enters the house. It's empty. He looks around. No one.

EHSAN

Cowards ran away!

CUT TO:

INT. RAMADHIR'S HOUSE 1- DAY

Ehsan walks in.

EHSAN QURESHI

It's done.

RAMADHIR SINGH

And the kid?

EHSAN QURESHI

I killed him too.

RAMADHIR SINGH

What about the bodies?

EHSAN QURESHI

I chopped and buried them.

Ramadhir gestures him to leave.

CUT TO:

I/E. VARANASI HOTEL 1 - NIGHT

Shahid walks in the streets. Looks up. He sees an address. He enters. It's a hotel.

CUT TO:

INT. VARANASI HOTEL 1 - CORRIDOR ROOM - NIGHT

One man (Yadavji), young, around twenty one. Walks down the corridor. Stops outside the room. Knocks. The door opens. It's Shahid Khan.

SHAHID KHAN

Mr Yadav? Shahid Khan.

He shuts the door and sits on the chair unpacking his stuff.

SHAHID KHAN (CONT'D)
Boss has sent this money.

Yadav is fixing a gun. Shahid watches curiously. Takes out three four parts of a pistol. Slowly lays them all down. Puts it together. Shahid is mesmerized.

Yadav steps away.

SHAHID KHAN
That's a pistol, no? Can I try it?

Yadav shoots him. Shahid Khan falls back.

EXT. ROAD - BUS - DAY
Nasir and Young Sardar in a bus.

INT. SCHOOL - DAY
Sardar in school reads a poem.

SARDAR KHAN (V.O)
'She gurgles and mocks, and plays with rocks.'
'She flips and flops, she's made of dew drops …'
'… And makes only holy stops!' -
Asgar watches him. Raises his hand and shouts.

ASGAR
River Ganga!

NASIR (V.O)
I knew Shahid khan would never return. His son Sardar grew up with my nephew Asgar. One day he asked about his father.

EXT. RIVER - DAY
Shot of young Asgar & Young Sardar in a boat along with Nasir.

NASIR (V.O)
I told him that Ramadhir had him killed. And this killed Sardar's childhood. Revenge

became his sole obsession. And he shaved his head, swearing to grow his hair only after avenging his father.

Young Sardar gets his head shaved.

SUPER - 20 YEARS LATER

EXT- COAL MINING AREA- DAY

An older Nasir is watching over coal mines in a blast atop a mountain.

EXT: RAILWAY STATION - DAY

Sardar in a jeep outside railway station.

ASGAR

Girdi, Jharia, Dhanbad, Ranchi, Wasseypur. Where would you like to go?

SARDAR KHAN

Girdi, Jharia, Dhanbad, Ranchi, Wasseypur…

INT. WEDDING HALL - NIGHT

Sardar khan is getting married to Nagma Khatun. Asgar and Nasir are both present. A *maulwi* is reading out the vows.

MAULWI

Sardar Khan, Son of Shahid Khan, your marriage to Nagma Khatun, has been agreed to with a deposit of Rupees 501. Do you take her as your wife?

SARDAR KHAN

Yes, I do.

MAULWI

Do you take her as your wife?

SARDAR KHAN

Yes, I do.

In another room, Nagma is also taking her vows.

MAULWI

Do you take him as your husband?

Nagma doesn't respond.

INT. SARDAR'S HOUSE/ BEDROOM - NIGHT

Nagma in bed. She looks at Sardar Khan. He is drinking water. Nagma's hair is ruffled. They have made intense love.

SARDAR KHAN

Want some water?

Nagma shakes her head - no. A knock on the door. Sardar opens the door. It's Nasir, he leaves. Nagma alone in bed.

CUT TO:

INT. SARDAR'S HOUSE/ BEDROOM - DAY

Nagma starts to clean the house … clearing stuff. She opens her trunk, inside which is nothing but an umbrella … she picks it up.

SARDAR KHAN

He killed my father.

INT. SARDAR'S HOUSE/ BEDROOM - NIGHT

Sardar talks to Nagma. Sardar holds the umbrella in his hand.

SARDAR

My father left in his car to never return. He is emotional.

SARDAR (CONT'D)

My life has but one mission - Revenge. It hurts to see that dog prosper. I will end that bastard. I don't just want to kill him, I want to destroy him piece by piece, and he will know my name before I fuck him up. I'll slowly take away what's his and the motherfucker will die his own death.

Nagma holds him closer.

EXT. ELECTION AREA - DAY

Ramadhir giving speech next to C.S. C.S introduces him and Ramadhir touches his feet.

C.S

The honorable, Mr Ramadhir Singh!

RAMADHIR SINGH

My worker brothers, I give you my solemn word, that this time our reply to the opposition will not be verbal...

EXT. COAL MINES - DAY [MONTAGE]

Coal workers marching. Red flags. 'Jagjivan Ram Zindabad'. March past.

INT. UNION OFFICER'S CABIN - DAY

Ramadhir taking money from a union officer.

NASIR (V.O)

In 1952, India got its first Labour Minister. He started the Coal Welfare Association and the National Trade Union which allowed mine supervisors to pressurise mine owners. And Ramadhir Singh led this movement.

CUT TO:

[MONTAGE: ARCHIVAL FOOTAGE OF JAGJIVAN RAM, WORKERS PROTESTING, RAMADHIR LEADING UNION OF WORKERS, TAKING MONEY FROM OFFICERS OF BIHAR COLLIERY UNION]

EXT. COAL MINES - DAY

No money given. Workers getting beaten up.

INT. COAL MINES - DAY

Labourer putting thumb forward, signing thumb print to take salary (another office), Ramadhir's driver Ghanshyam is extorting money from the workers who are getting wages. A worker comes out and Ghanshyam snatches his money.

WORKER

My family will starve, sir.

NASIR (V.O)

Later, the same Trade Union became the mafia and began extortion in exchange for union membership. Union leaders started lending money and kept the worker's income as interest.

EXT. STREETS- DAY [MONTAGE]

Ramadhir in election Jeep. His son J.P. Singh next to him.

CUT TO:

EXT. STREETS - DAY

Ramadhir Singh wins the election.

CUT TO:

EXT. STREETS - DAY

Ramadhir Singh in a jeep garlanded.

NASIR (V.O)

Ramadhir Singh then jumped into politics and won the election and became the local worker's leader.

[MONTAGE: THE FLOODS THROUGH 1966-1972. NEWSPAPER CUT OUTS OF NATIONALIZATION OF COAL MINES AND THE FLOODS]

EXT. B.C.C.L. OFFICE - DAY

A small one floor building. That has a board declaring B.C.C.L. office. Ramadhir's son J.P. Singh has come to meet officer S.P. Sinha.

J.P. SINGH (O.S)

My father, Ramadhir Singh, has run mines for years.

CUT TO:

INT. B.C.C.L OFFICE - DAY

A Young man sits across an official…

J.P. SINGH

So Mr Sinha, we know how the contractors

steal coal. We can end this black marketing if you compensate us well.

S.P. Sinha looks on.

CUT TO:

INT. RAMADHIR SINGH'S HOUSE 2 - DAY

Inside the room 5-10 workers sitting along with J.P. Singh. An older Ramadhir Singh talks. He puts the coal on a weighing scale. The coal shows certain weight.

RAMADHIR SINGH

You see, coal is a very curious thing. Looks like stone, but lacks its density. However when you put it in water ...

(puts it in a bucket of water)

... it absorbs it ... and becomes heavier.

He holds it in water till the coal absorbs water.

CUT TO:

EXT. DHARAM KANTA - DAY

[I/C] A truck of coal drenched with water through pipes.

CUT TO:

INT. RAMADHIR SINGH'S HOUSE 1- DAY

Now the coal has settled at the bottom of the bucket. Ramadhir takes it out and puts it on the weighing scale. It has more than doubled in weight.

CUT TO:

EXT. DHARAM KANTA - DAY

A truck is weighed on the *dharam kanta*. Ehsan Qureshi and two people stand next to an official who gives receipt.

CHALLAN MAN (O.S.)

It weighs 16 tonne, sir.

EHSAN QURESHI (looking at the receipt)
16, eh?

Official writes the weight. Gives the receipt to Ehsan Qureshi. He leaves.

CUT TO:

INT. RAMADHIR SINGH'S HOUSE 1 - DAY
In a big house all workers sit on the ground as food is served to them. Hot littis are being fished out of a huge pan with boiling ghee. Ramadhir Singh serves. A very sickly labourer hides few littis in his pocket. He stops on being caught.

RAMADHIR SINGH
This nationalization of mines has been very unfair to you workers. Our own Union lends us money and keeps our wages as interest in the supervision of the Chief Officer. As long as Sinha is in that chair. We're surviving on dry weeds while he is frolicking in his garden.

I/C 72 INT. B.C.C.L OFFICE - CORRIDOR - DAY
J.P. Singh walks in furious. The peon tries to stop him, he is put against the wall.

PEON
You can't go in.

J.P. SINGH
Fuck you.

INT. B.C.C.L. OFFICE CABIN- DAY
S.P. Sinha looks up as JP Singh throws money on the table.

J.P. SINGH
Did I not tell you to compensate us equal to the others? Are we not supplying like we should?

S.P. SINHA

I'm sure you're sending it but it's not reaching. You guys think I'm an educated fool who only pushes pen in his office and know nothing about coal theft. I'm a son of this land, J.P. Singh. A Bihari. Like your father.

JP just stares.

CUT TO:

I/E. S.P. SINHA'S RESIDENCE-GARDEN - DAY

S.P. Sinha with his four year old in the garden. A car pulls up. Ramadhir Singh, J.P. Singh and two more people get out.

S.P.SINHA

Don't pluck them, son.

He notices Ramadhir and J.P. Singh approaching him with swords. He gets scared and runs inside the house leaving his child. The men chase him inside. We stay on the kid, as he looks at men carrying swords who disappear inside the house. They come out with a stained sword. Ramadhir swipes blood off the sword and puts a vermillion mark on the kid's head.

RAMADHIR SINGH

Your dad was a great man!

NASIR (V.O)

Under nationalization, Sinha had taken over Ramadhir's mines reducing him to a mere supervisor all over again. So the murder of a government officer in broad daylight created such a fear that it officially made Ramadhir Singh the first Godfather of Dhanbad.

CUT TO:

EXT. RED LIGHT AREA - NIGHT

Nagma walks down the street … a knife in hand …

NAGMA

Where's Sardar Khan? Did Sardar Khan come here?

She walks down furious and pregnant … people react to her … she comes inside a house and looks into various rooms. She reaches one room and she knocks furiously at the door.

SARDAR KHAN

Who is it? OH Nagma!

Nagma sees him with another woman and gets furious. Sardar jumps on the bed and uses the pillow as a shield. Nagma starts slashing the knife at him.

SARDAR KHAN

This BITCH told me she is you.

NAGMA KHATUN

But can't you see she's not Nagma, you bastard?

Sardar Khan jumps off the bed and takes the sex worker as a shield.

SARDAR KHAN

But I was half asleep … I didn't realise.

NAGMA KHATUN

So did you sleepwalk into her hole?

SARDAR KHAN

I was drunk, my dear … this bitch took advantage of me.

SARDAR KHAN (CONT'D)

Stop! She'll die!

NAGMA KHATUN

I don't care!

SARDAR KHAN

Murder is wrong.

NAGMA KHATUN

Fuck you!

SARDAR KHAN

It's a sin you don't understand.

NAGMA KHATUN

Move her out of the way! I'll deal with you later, bitch!

Sardar escapes from the back door. Nagma comes out running after Sardar.

NAGMA KHATUN (CONT'D)

Where are you running, coward? Wait till you come home, you asshole! You pimp! Whore fucker!

EXT. SARDAR'S HOUSE - NIGHT

Sardar now wearing clothes … carries a big fish … stops outside the house … a lot of crowd … Sardar looks at Nasir …

CUT TO:

INT. SARDAR'S HOUSE - NIGHT

Nagma in labour screaming … As Sardar enters … she looks at him. Picks up a glass by the table and throws it at him … He ducks and hits his head on something …

Nagma lying on the bed with the baby beside her.

CUT TO:

INT. SARDAR'S HOUSE - NIGHT

Sardar holding the child …

SARDAR KHAN

Oh my little boy! My little prince! Smile, my little prince!

Nagma comes to him with a glass of milk. With a gesture she asks for the baby. Sardar gives the baby away to her.

NAGMA KHATUN

'My little boy! My little prince!'

Sardar hands the baby to her. She leaves with the baby without saying a word.

SARDAR KHAN

Won't you forgive me even now?

INT. SARDAR'S HOUSE/ BEDROOM - NIGHT

A pregnant Nagma is folding her saree. Sardar is holding the saree from the other end on the bed … Sardar comes from behind and holds her…

NAGMA

What?

SARDAR KHAN

Nothing.

(Rubs himself against her … his smile is kind of sexual…)

NAGMA

That's a big, hard 'nothing'!

SARDAR KHAN

I know.

NAGMA

We can't have sex now.

SARDAR KHAN

Why not?

NAGMA

There's a baby inside, silly.

SARDAR KHAN

Let me say hello to him.

She hits him while laughing at the same time.

NAGMA

Shameless! Want to dirty your own child.

Nagma hits his crotch and Sardar sits down in pain. Nagma is laughing.

CUT TO:

INT. SARDAR'S HOUSE/ BEDROOM - DAY

A religious person sits Sardar, Nasir and Asgar in the courtyard...

MAULWI

Son, this is wrong. You should control your urges in such conditions.

ASGAR

So true.

Nagma comes with a glass of water for the priest.

NAGMA

He shouldn't have been born a man. God should've made him a horse in a brothel full of mares.

CUT TO:

INT/EXT. SARDAR'S HOUSE - NIGHT

Sardar and Nasir sit outside the house...

SARDAR KHAN (to Nasir)

I waited 9 months for my son Danish to come out. Then a month after, the first chance we got ... she got pregnant again.

ASGAR

Dinner is ready.

SARDAR KHAN

Yeah, coming.

(to Nasir)

How does one live without sex?

NASIR KHAN

I'm living fine.

SARDAR KHAN

Yours can't be called a life.

Nagma serves food to all of them ... Sardar, Asgar and Nasir sitting close to each other.

NAGMA

Go fuck whoever you want. Just don't bring them home or I'll chop them and bathe before you enter my home.

He looks at her.

SARDAR KHAN

What is she talking about?

NAGMA KHATUN

Eat. Fucking needs energy. Or you'll embarrass me outside.

Sardar is angry.

EXT. DHANBAD ROAD 1 - DAY

Large crowd on the streets. J.P. Singh on a jeep with his father next to him. Both are garlanded. It's a campaign … with the farmers *hal* (plough) as a sign.

Announcement

To the left, to the right, all sing
J.P. Singh! The country's King!
Best character, social worker…
all sing … J.P. Singh!

INT. OFFICE - NIGHT

J.P. Singh at a new petrol pump.

ASGAR

We just need fuel for the jeep and a monthly stipend, sir?

J.P. SINGH

You can take fuel from our gas station.

ASGAR

Can the jeep do private gigs too?

J.P. Singh nods.

CUT TO:

EXT. PETROL PUMP - DAY

Asgar filling out petrol in a canister.

ASGAR (to the pump attendant)

Fill the tank, and this jerrycan too.

NASIR (V.O)

Asgar got a driving contract from J.P. Singh … and started black marketing the free petrol … while Sardar became the jeep driver.

EXT. SARDAR'S HOUSE - DAY

A small nondescript colony.

A jeep comes to a halt. Sardar Khan & Asgar get out…

CUT TO:

INT. SARDAR'S HOUSE - DAY

Sardar Khan brings a newspaper. He shows it to Nasir. Asgar is sitting. He reads it out.

… *As soon as he became an MLA, J.P. Singh has opened five petrol pumps, his house has turned into the Singh Mansion and he has begun claiming title-less lands.*

Nagma serves the food to him and Nasir. Sardar is now 33 years old.

Sardar puts the paper down.

SARDAR KHAN

Did you read this, Uncle?

NASIR (smiles)

I know more than the newspapers. 'J.P. Singh Sanctions 5 Petrol Pumps' These are being fronted by Ramadhir's family members.

NAGMA KHATUN

Please eat something.

Looks Up …

SARDAR KHAN

Asgar, time to pay them a visit.

(Nasir continues eating)

Sardar, Nasir and Asgar leave ... While Nagma sits back wondering.

CUT TO:

EXT/INT. PETROL PUMP 1 - DAY

A newly painted petrol pump.

Sardar Khan's jeep comes into the pump. Sardar, Asgar and Nasir get off the jeep. Attendant comes forward with a pipe to fill petrol.

ASGAR

Fill her up!

They all cover themselves with their shawls. Sardar walks towards the office along with Nasir. The attendant can't find where to fill in the petrol.

ATTENDANT

The fuel tank is on the other side, sir. Please, turn the jeep.

Sardar talks to the accountant at the counter.

SARDAR KHAN

Approximately how many trucks come here daily?

PUMP MAN

About 500.

SARDAR KHAN

Wow! Really?

PUMP MAN

YES.

SARDAR KHAN (to his man, Asgar)

Hey, they fill 500 trucks daily! Holy shit!

While he is saying that, Sardar takes a knife out. Asgar takes out a sword from his jeep and threatens the attendant.

PETROL PUMP ATTENDANT

What are you doing, Sir?

ASGAR

Fuck off! (scares him away)

Nasir strangles the clerk and asks for the key of the safe.

NASIR

Where's the key?

CLERK (Scared)

This is Ramadhir Singh's station.

Sardar comes in, picks out the key from the clerk's pocket and opens the safe. A truck comes in for petrol … sees Asgar holding up a sword. Driver looks at him.

ASGAR

You lucky dog! Petrol's free today - go for it.

Truck moves on. Asgar laughs.

Sardar takes out all the money from the safe and wraps it in his cloth. Nasir hits the clerk with the telephone.

SARDAR KHAN

Did you kill him?

NASEER

I'm not sure.

They all head to the jeep.

SARDAR

Start the jeep.

All three of them get into the jeep and escape.

CUT TO:

EXT. COAL MINE - DAY

A coal mine with dynamites blowing up the mountains. Sardar driving some men. He gets them to a large machine.

Ramadhir escorts the men out of the machine. Sardar looks at him from distance and Ramadhir notices him back.

I/E. JEEP - DAY

Sardar is driving the officials out of the mine in his jeep.

OFFICIAL 1

We've rented the last 2 bogies of the good's train. We will take care of loading and unloading the iron scrap. Please take care of the paper work.

Sardar listens to the conversation quietly.

I/E. RAILWAY PLATFORM - NIGHT

Nasir and Asgar walk up to a man sitting on a bench on a railway platform. Asgar limps while Nasir consoles him.

NASIR

Ok … easy … slow … careful. Sit here.

They sit next to the man on the bench.

NASIR (CONT'D)

Hello, sir. Greetings.

TRAIN GUARD

Hello!

NASIR

You're the guard of the good's train, right?

(TO ASGAR)

Easy.

CUT TO:

I/E. GOODS TRAIN - NIGHT

A goods' train crosses a station. The same guard we saw earlier is now in the Guards cabin of the running goods' train. He hangs out of his cabin as if waiting for something. Another guard at the passing railway station waits with a wire ring in his hand, which he hands to the train guard as the train crosses him. The train guard comes back inside the bogey. As he reaches inside, Asgar puts a knife on his neck.

ASGAR

Don't move or I'll chop you.

(TO NASIR)

Uncle, show the guard the signal to stop the train.

Nasir takes the lamp and brandishes it in order to be seen by Sardar who is waiting for them at an isolated location.

After identifying the train, Sardar hollers at his men.

SARDAR KHAN

Alright boys, that's our train. Come on. Move it.

Sardar walks ahead as the men unload the scrap.

I/E. PETROL PUMP 2 - DAY

Nasir comes near the petrol pump office window.

NASIR (to the clerk)

Can you please open the door? I need some water.

The clerk opens the door. Sardar, Asgar and Nasir get in. Asgar strangles the clerk with a cloth. Sardar opens the safe and takes out all the money. Nasir goes and drinks water from the pot.

SARDAR
Let's go!

CUT TO:

I/C

EXT. PLOT WITHOUT A FENCE - DAY
Sardar drives JP and his men back. JP instructs his men in the car while Sardar listens.

J.P. SINGH
Speak to the owner of the land. If he doesn't yield … push him off the cliff.

EXT. SARDAR'S HOUSE - DAY
Sardar, Asgar and Nasir are making a plan. They're having fun. They drive into sunset.

EXT. PLOT WITH A FENCE - DAY
Ramadhir and JP are driven to a plot with barbed wire fence. Ghanshyam is driving the car. They stop.

J.P. SINGH
Are you sure this is the place?

GHANSHYAM
Yes sir, but someone's forced their way in.

J.P. SINGH
Who?

Ghanshyam is silent.

J.P. SINGH (CONT'D)
Who is encroaching?

GHANSHYAM
Sardar Khan.

J.P. SINGH
Who Sardar Khan?

GHANSHYAM
Your jeep driver … who ferries our men to and fro.

J.P. SINGH
When the fuck did he become a gangster?
Ramadhir observes workers working on the barbed wire fence.

RAMADHIR SINGH
Get him to our office.

GHANSHYAM
He won't come.

J.P. SINGH
Why?

GHANSHYAM
Because when I asked him … he said, 'You come to my office if you want to talk.'

J.P. SINGH
Does he know I can squash him right now? Has he forgotten he lives off my scraps?

RAMADHIR SINGH
JP!

J.P. SINGH
He's forgotten I can fuck his fucking … Father, I'll fuck him up so bad he'll…

Ramadhir cuts him abruptly.

RAMADHIR SINGH
JP! If a worm wants to be a lion, let him. If you engage with him you will make him your equal.

J.P. SINGH
So what should I do?

RAMADHIR SINGH
He is using illegal method, you've got the legal way. Isn't Dhanbad police station in your command?

J.P. Singh nods.

J.P. SINGH

Hmm...

RAMADHIR SINGH

Invite the Superintendent over for dinner. Then we'll put a barbed wire up that worm's ass and fly him like a kite on this very land.

INT. SARDAR'S HOUSE - DAY

Sardar is in the bathroom getting ready. Sardar comes out of the bath. Nagma is in the kitchen burning coal.

Nagma directs some burning coal fumes around Nasir and Sardar as a way to ward off evil.

NASIR

That's enough!

Sardar carries Ramadhir's umbrella and leaves along with Nasir and Asgar.

NASIR (CONT'D)

(To Nagma who is directing fumes at Asgar now) The evil eye is already upon us ... your burnt chillies can't do shit.

Sardar greets his neighbour before getting into the Jeep.

SARDAR KHAN

Hello!

I/E. POLICE STATION - DAY

Sardar, Asgar and Nasir arrive at the police station. Ramadhir and JP are having tea outside. Sardar takes out the umbrella and flaunts it. Ramadhir recognizes his umbrella.

NASIR (V.O)

Ramadhir didn't know Sardar as Shahid's son. But he would never forget his umbrella. Back then, people could forget their name but never their possessions.

INT. POLICE STATION 1 - DAY

Sardar sits across from the SP with JP. Silence.

SARDAR

If you're saying this is your land, then prove it.

J.P. SINGH

We've bought it. It's ours. So stop this illegal encroachment or else...!

SARDAR KHAN

Spare me your legal jargon, Mr Minister. *(Asgar hands Sardar a paper, he slams it in front of JP)* Here's the proof that I have paid 10 rupees for this land.

JP looks at it. Laughs.

J.P. SINGH

10 bucks? Think you can get away with this...? *(looks at the SP)* You worthless mother fucker ...

Sardar slaps him.

SARDAR

Oh JP! JP!

Everyone is shocked.

SARDAR KHAN

(to the SP) It would be wise to remain seated, sir. *(turns to JP)* Remember Mr Minister, even the biggest balls are subservient to the dick!

SP Moves.

Do you know who I am, fucker? Actually you don't know who I am, Mr Minister. Why don't you ask your dad about me when you're wiping his arse at home.

Silent standoff.

SARDAR KHAN

Sir… *(SP looks)*

What's the penalty for slapping a minister? I do hope it's not more than being jailed.

SP keeps sitting, unable to say a word.

Asgar hits JP on his head.

ASGAR

Even I feel like going in.

JP hits back. Ramadhir leaves angrily. JP and Ghanshyam follow. JP complains.

J.P. SINGH

Father! Why didn't you say anything…

Ramadhir gestures him to shut up angrily and ushers Ghanshyam to start the car.

RAMADHIR SINGH

Start the car.

CUT TO:

EXT. RAMADHIR'S HOUSE 2 - DAY

Ramadhir beats J.P. Singh in front of people.

RAMADHIR SINGH

Stupid dickhead prides himself on being a minister … but can't even do a basic background check. I should kill you…

J.P. SINGH

But how was I supposed to know…

RAMADHIR SINGH

Everyone watch your minister getting thrashed … was nursing a fucking snake…

RAMADHIR'S WIFE

Please stop!

RAMADHIR SINGH

Quiet or I'll chop you up. Your womb created this worthless punk. Fucking 'minister'. You should be a janitor.

RAMADHIR'S WIFE

It's ok, son.

INT. POLICE STATION 1 - DAY

Sardar Khan brought into the prison. He walks on as people stare.

SARDAR KHAN

We kicked the minister's lilly ass in the police station.

ASGAR

Under his daddy's nose.

SARDAR KHAN

My name is Sardar Khan. Make sure the whole town knows.

CUT TO:

INT. RAMADHIR SINGH'S HOUSE 2 - DAY

Ghanshyam escorts Ehsan Qureshi into the house.

EHSAN

Salaam sir.

RAMADHIR SINGH

How are you, Ehsan? Come on in.

Ehsan sits down. Ramadhir asks him to sit on the couch, by his side.

RAMADHIR SINGH (CONT'D)

Sit by my side, you're not my servant. I had a frightening nightmare last night. Remember Shahid Khan? My chief muscleman?

Ehsan tries to recollect.

EHSAN QURESHI

Was he in your nightmare?

RAMADHIR SINGH

Not him … his son. His son's ghost. The one you killed and buried. Where did you bury him?

Ehsan is clueless and shocked. He doesn't answer.

RAMADHIR SINGH (CONT'D)
Where did you bury him?

Ehsan is speechless.

RAMADHIR SINGH (CONT'D)
You remember, right?

Ehsan nods in a yes.

EHSAN QURESHI
I buried him right there…

RAMADHIR SINGH
Do one thing for me, dig that grave and bring me his remains.
Thing is, my priest thinks the boy's soul is haunting me … for revenge.

EHSAN QURESHI
As you say sir.

Ramadhir slaps him.

RAMADHIR SINGH
Mother fucker! At least speak the truth now, mother fucker! Or I'll kill you and fucking bury you.

EHSAN QURESHI
Forgive my lie, sir. They ran away before I reached.

RAMADHIR SINGH
You have no idea what a big disaster your lie is about to cause.

Ehsan stares.

INT- POLICE STATION - JAIL - DAY
Sardar introduces Pappu to Asgar as the bomb maker.

ASGAR
Brother, this is Pappu from Punjab. A bomb expert.

SARDAR KHAN
You'll make bombs for me?

PAPPU
Sure.

SARDAR KHAN
What will you need?

PAPPU
Potassium.

SARDAR KHAN
And?

PAPPU
Sulphur.

SARDAR KHAN
And?

PAPPU
Iron powder.

SARDAR- KHAN
Is that it?

PAPPU
Sure.

CUT TO:

INT. SARDAR'S HOUSE - DAY
Nagma puts the masala (bomb ingredients) in the tiffin … She gives the tiffin to young Danish. Danish takes the tiffin … walks to Nasir…

NASIR
Where to?

YOUNG DANISH
Food for my father.

NASIR
Open the box.

Danish opens the tiffin.

Nagma hits him on his head.

NAGMA KHATUN
What did I teach you?

YOUNG DANISH
Don't hit me.

NAGMA KHATUN
Then do it with attitude.

Danish looks at Nasir.

NASIR
Where?

DANISH
I've brought food for my father.

NAGMA
(hits him) Stop whimpering, you wuss! Are you my son, or some 2 penny whore's runt?

Young Faizal watching.

CUT TO:

INT. POLICE STATION 1/ PRISON - DAY

Danish has come to deliver the tiffin to Sardar Khan. At the gate he is stopped by the cop.

YOUNG DANISH
I am Sardar Khan's son. I've brought him food.

JAILOR
What is it?

DANISH
Food.

JAILOR
Let me check.

DANISH

Why? Do you want to saute the pulses with your fingers now?

Cop stares at him...

INT. POLICE STATION 1 - CELL - DAY

Sardar and Asgar are opening the tiffin box. They find nails in one of the boxes in it.

ASGAR

And what is this?

SARDAR

Broken glass and nails.

They look into the next box which has iron powder in it.

ASGAR

Ah! Spices for the bomb.

EXT. DHANBAD JAIL - NIGHT

Prison inmates are singing a song. Asgar joins them wearing a saree. He starts dancing with a midget. Meanwhile Sardar is making the bomb with Pappu in a different place in the jail. The song can be heard.

SARDAR KHAN

How long will it take?

PAPPU

I'm making a bomb, not tea.

SARDAR KHAN

Dude, I don't want to be here till Ramadan.

Sardar goes and checks if all the cops are away. Song continues.

SARDAR KHAN

Hurry up!

PAPPU

If I don't wind it tightly it won't explode.

SARDAR KHAN

If you don't hurry up the Inspector will blow it in our asshole.

Sardar is impatient. He notices something.

SARDAR KHAN (CONT'D)

He's coming!

Asgar comes out of the cell and strangles a cop with his saree. Sardar and Pappu join him with the bombs.

ASGAR

Pappu, come on.

SARDAR

Come on...

ASGAR

Let's go.

They shoot at a cop pursuing them. They hurl a bomb at one of the walls. Nothing happens. They hurl another bomb. With the loud sound and shudder, the jailor wakes up. He runs outside. The jailor, cop and other policemen look through the broken down wall. They shoot but everyone has fled the place.

The song continues.

CUT TO:

Shot of a newspaper of '21 prisoners flee Dhanbad prison'.

CUT TO:

EXT. QAMAR MAKHDOOMI'S HOUSE - NIGHT

Qamar, Sardar, Asgar sit together and eat. Durga is serving. As she serves Sardar stares at her intensely, then he looks at her cleavage. She *(Durga)* starts to shiver and drops the gravy...

QAMAR MAKHDOOMI

Another epileptic fit?

SHAMSHAD

An older woman comes and shoos her off.

Older woman starts to serve…

QAMAR

I wonder why she gets these 'fits' only around new guests. She's run away from Bengal. These Bengali men don't teach their women about modesty. She shamelessly sashays around uncovered. If the butchers see her they'll feast on her alive.

ASGAR

Why's she here?

QAMAR

Sultan, the head butcher, wanted to pimp her. I saved her and brought her here. But she's a remarkable chef!

ASGAR

True!

Sardar gets up.

SARDAR KHAN

Where's the washroom?

CUT TO:

EXT. QAMAR MAKHDOOMI'S HOUSE - DAY

Sardar Khan wakes up. Asgar is still asleep. He looks down and finds a beautiful woman washing clothes by the well. He comes down and watches her while brushing his teeth with a twig. The woman, Durga, is shy and aware of Sardar watching her. They meet mid way. Sardar watches her from head to toe and then holds her hand.

SARDAR KHAN

Which family do you belong to? Have you heard of me?

She doesn't say a thing.

SARDAR
Are you mute? Are you married?

She shakes her head - no.

SARDAR KHAN (CONT'D)
So ripe … and so unmarried.

SARDAR KHAN (CONT'D)
Won't you look at me? Let me help you!

Takes the bucket from her hands. She lets go. He holds her cheeks. She starts shivering.

SARDAR KHAN (CONT'D)
Why are you shivering? Have you not been touched yet?

She runs away.

CUT TO:

EXT. QAMAR MAKHDOOMI'S HOUSE - DAY

Sardar is bathing near the well near the fields. Durga tiptoes and watches him bathe. Another old song plays in the background. She comes close to take her bucket but gets scared with Sardar's gaze.

SARDAR KHAN
Take it.

She runs away without taking the bucket.

CUT TO:

EXT. RAILWAY TRACKS 2 - DAY

Asgar and Sardar walking on the tracks.

SARDAR KHAN
See, Allah wants us to marry 4 times. I can't disobey him! He must have some logic for us marrying 4 times. Afterall, 4 households get taken care of.

Asgar is silent and looking at Sardar.

SARDAR KHAN (CONT'D)
The problem is you moralists … self-centred and selfish!

ASGAR (sarcastically)
That's right! I'm the selfish son of a bitch!

CUT TO:

I/E. SARDAR'S HOUSE - NIGHT

Nagma Khatun sleeps with her children. A loud knock on the door. She gets up.

NAGMA KHATUN
Danish. Danish.

He sleeps, she kicks him. He wakes up, falls down and then gets up again.

DANISH
Why are you kicking me?

NAGMA KHATUN
See who's banging on the door.

DANISH
Can't even sleep in peace…

He gets up. Walks to the door and opens it.

DANISH (CONT'D)
Don't you know the fucking time?
It's the police.

INSPECTOR
Is Sardar Khan home?

DANISH
He's in jail.

INSPECTOR
Let me check.

DANISH
I said he's in prison…

Inspector puts him aside. Comes in. Nagma coming into the hall.

NAGMA
What the hell do you want? This is my home, not your mom's garden.

INSPECTOR
Where's Sardar Khan?

NAGMA
Why, is he one of the fugitives?

INSPECTOR
Who else is at home?

NAGMA
Just my kids. Come back, in the morning.

INSPECTOR
Let me check.

NAGMA
Hey, fuck off come back at a decent hour in the morning. Or I'll chop you up.

Inspector retreats.

The door is slammed on them.

INT. SARDAR'S HOUSE - NIGHT
Nagma turns to Danish.

NAGMA
Go to bed. I'll take care of these bastards.

CUT TO:

(CONT'D) EXT. QAMAR MAKHDOOMI'S TUBE WELL - DAY
Durga is washing Sardar's clothes. Sardar is sitting by her side and watching her. Asgar is sitting over by a corner.

EXT. QAMAR MAKHDOOMI'S HOUSE-ROOF - NIGHT
Sardar on the roof tossing and turning.

SARDAR KHAN (O.S)
You know, I have just the thing for your 'epilepsy'.

He sees her approaching him where he is sleeping … He pretends to close his eyes. She comes slowly next to him and gets into his quilt. He opens his eyes and turns to her staring at her. He gets on top of her. She stares at him. He is shivering with excitement.

DURGA

Ahhhh…

Her hands disappear between the two and she knows exactly what to do. He thrusts into her and she yells. He puts his hand on her mouth. He picks a pillow and puts it on her mouth and continues.

INT. SARDAR'S HOUSE - DAY

A baby (Young Perpendicular) is crying. Out in the courtyard, Asgar and Nasir sit head down. Deathly silence.

NAGMA KHATUN

What's her name?

ASGAR

Durga.

NAGMA

She's a Hindu?

Nagma is angry. Something falls. She looks.

Young Faizal is stealing money from the kitchen. He drops the can full of flour. Nagma comes into the kitchen with the sound. She starts beating him.

NAGMA KHATUN

Now what? What happened? Stupid boy! Why didn't you call me?

Faizal picks up the money that fell in the flour. She notices him picking it.

NAGMA KHATUN (CONT'D)

Open your hands. What are you hiding? This is not your dad's money.

FAIZAL KHAN
Why are you beating me?

NAGMA KHATUN
What else can I do?

Faizal runs out. She sits there picking up the flour. Nasir comes and sees all this. He sits there. Nagma is crying.

NAGMA KHATUN (CONT'D)
Why don't you talk to Sardar?

NASIR
How can I? I'm a mere servant … his father was my master. Even though I've raised Sardar like my son.
But you're right - he's a man!

NAGMA KHATUN
Then why don't you fuck around? You're a man too.

Nagma leaves angry.

CUT TO:

INT. DURGA'S HOUSE - NIGHT
Sardar and Durga make love. Asgar sits in the outside room. He can hear lovemaking noises. He turns up the radio volume.

CUT TO:

EXT. SARDAR'S HOUSE - ROAD 12 - DAY
Young Faizal sits angry on the road side. He looks at an ice-cream vendor selling ice cream from a wooden box … old style ice candies … A boy come sits next to him … he is Young Fazlu…

YOUNG FAZLU
Want a free ice cream?

Young Faizal looks at him.

FAZLU (CONT'D)(to Faizal)
Grab one for me too.

Fazlu goes. Takes the ice cream wallah's cycle and pushes it … it rolls and drops … ice cream wallah runs after young Fazlu … Fazlu goes to the wagon and runs away with it. The ice-cream vendor chases him. Fazlu suddenly drops the wagon. Ice-creams fall out of it. Fazlu runs. The vendor follows him. Seeing the opportunity, Faisal goes to the wagon and picks up two ice-cream bars and runs in the opposite direction.

CUT TO:

EXT. RAY TALKIES - DAY

Young Faizal stands outside Ray Talkies with young Fazlu, licking his ice cream. Young Mohsina is watching.

FAZLU

You'll never have to pay for anything as long as I'm around. Next time I'll get you the red one.

FAIZAL

Who's that girl?

Young Mohsina is requesting the usher to let her in to the theatre.

MOHSINA

Please let me watch the film, sir.

CUT TO:

EXT. VILLAGE STREET - DAY

A *burqa* clad woman gets abducted from the street. The same woman is discovered in the fields by a man from the village.

NASIR KHAN (V.O)

Qureshis had always ruled over Wasseypur. Then it was Sultana the dacoit, now it was Sultan the butcher. The non-Qureshi women were regularly picked up and dishonoured by the butchers. And this fear made all the non-Qureshi Muslims voiceless.

Montage

EXT. VILLAGE STREET - EARLY MORNING

A man comes to poop by the side of the road. As he squats, he notices a dead body.

CUT TO

EXT. WASSEYPUR HOUSE 1 - DAY

A lot of crowd outside a house … a crowd of mourners.

A dead body lies there. Blood seeps on to the sheet covering him. Qamar Makhdoomi sits quietly as the woman cry. The women are seated on one side, near the corpse, while the men are on the other side.

CUT TO:

I/E. KASAI MOHALLAH - DAY

Kasais busy with their work. One of them looks at Qamar Makhdoomi walking towards them.

NASIR KHAN (V.O)

Their leader and Sardar's host in Wasseypur, Qamar Makhdoomi decided to speak for them. But the butchers mocked him.

BADOOR QURESHI

Salaam, sir. What brings your holiness here? When are you planning to share Durga with us?

All laugh.

QAMAR MAKHDOOMI

I'd like to speak to Sultan.

A slap of meat comes flying and goes above his head.

BADOOR QURESHI

It's free. Keep it.

Qamar looks in the direction of where it came from. Ehsan is smiling and Sultan is smiling too as he slices through his meat.

I/E.

INT. DURGA'S HOUSE - DAY

Qamar Makhdoomi sits with Sardar. Asgar is also there.

QAMAR MAKHDOOMI

Sultan is Sultana dacoit's nephew, raised by Ehsan Qureshi. He could butcher an entire buffalo alone when he was 12 and now he butchers 60 a day. So, everyone fears him. These Qureshis are a menace! We've tried everything, begging, pleading … but to no avail. But people know you stood up to Ramadhir. They also know whose son you are. The butchers will take you seriously. I'd bought a house in the neighbourhood but Sultan's men have encroached there. They use it for gambling, drinking and raping kidnapped women.

EXT. FAIZAL'S HOUSE (NASEERUDDIN'S HOUSE) - NIGHT

Evening. A house. Lower floor is lit from within.

CUT TO:

INT. FAIZAL'S HOUSE (NASEERUDDIN'S HOUSE) - NIGHT

Five men drinking. Playing cards. One roasts kebabs on a clay stove. A small little thing rolls inside and goes under the table. They stop playing. One of them looks underneath trying to figure out what it is.

CUT TO:

I/E. FAIZAL'S HOUSE (NASEERUDDIN'S HOUSE) - NIGHT

A loud sound flash of light and smoke. One wounded man having lost the palm of his hands comes out screaming. Sardar Khan emerges from the shadows with a sword, with one swipe kills him.

I/E. QAMAR MAKHDOOMI'S HOUSE - DAY

Hot onion *pakodas* are getting fried. Sardar eats some *pakodas* with tea … Asgar sits too … as a girl sits across Qamar Makhdoomi …

GIRL

I can't even walk to college anymore. The pehelwan stalks me everywhere. I've never seen a man look at a woman like that.

Qamar closes his eyes. Sardar is ogling Durga's back, who is making pakodas in the kitchen while listening to the girl.

QAMAR MAKHDOOMI

He's J.P.'s muscle man. We must kill him within Wasseypur.

ASGAR

It doesn't matter where we whack him, J.P. will send the police after us.

Sardar is staring at Durga all through this conversation. Durga is in the kitchen, cooking with her back visible.

EXT. ROAD 4/MARKET PLACE - DAY

A big man is shopping for his ration. He walks out of the shop. He walks down the road.

Sardar joins him.

SARDAR KHAN

What's up, buddy?

LAXMAN

Fuck off, asshole.

Sardar takes out an ice pick from an ice slab. He stabs him. A jeep comes. Asgar gets down. Laxman hits back at Sardar but Sardar is light on his feet, he evades. Laxman drops his ration. Sardar stabs him again.

SARDAR KHAN

Asshole. Asshole. Asshole.

Laxman is hurt and he attacks Sardar. Sardar stabs him repeatedly. Asgar blinds Laxman with a shawl. Laxman runs away. Sardar and Asgar follow him in a jeep. They knock him down.

SARDAR KHAN (CONT'D)

Is he dead? Fucker's not dead yet?

He is half-dead. Sardar comes out of the jeep and stabs the ice pick until he is dead.

NASIR (V.O)

J.P.'s muscleman was a feared wrestler in Wasseypur. And he was a Hindu. Sardar killed him and threw his chopped body in the Slaughter House run by Qureshis. Knowing the Qureshis' animosity with Qamar Makhdoomi and Sardar Khan, the Qureshis could've easily given Sardar to the cops. But they didn't. Even Sultan the Butcher stayed silent. It was now the 80s. And Wasseypur was integrated into Dhanbad where Sardar led a double life. One home with Durga in Wasseypur, where Qureshis were the enemy. And one with Nagma in the city of Dhanbad, where Ramadhir was the enemy. But Wasseypur's advantage was that the police feared the Qureshis and stayed away.

CUT TO:

EXT. SARDAR KHAN'S GODOWN - DAY

Sardar Khan & Qamar Makhdoomi are standing looking at Asgar who is chopping up Laxman's leg.

EXT. KASAI MOHALLAH - DAY

A police officer at the meat shop. Looks around … Few local men avoid … All in silence … Officer looks around … Looking at the meat … He sits down … looks around.

CUT TO:

EXT. KASAI MOHALLAH - MEAT SHOP - DAY

All the meat refuse is being checked. Police officer bends down and picks a finger from the refuse behind him … He reacts. He looks back … It is Sultan walking towards him with a butcher knife. Sultan picks the cop up, taking him by surprise and puts him against the wall with the knife on the cop's throat …

SULTAN

Are you new here? What brings you here? Don't you know this is Wasseypur? Run along!

COP

I believe that Sardar killed a man from Dhanbad and disposed the body here.

SULTAN

So arrest him when he steps out into the city. In Wasseypur even a pigeon flies with only one wing because it needs the other one to cover its ass. Now fuck off! Hey, leave that finger.

COP

It's … evidence …

Police officer looks at Sultan… Sultan looks at him. Cop looks at it and throws it back with the refuse.

CUT TO:

INT. SARDAR KHAN'S GODOWN - DAY

Asgar and Sardar are getting guns made. The gun expert is making country guns.

SARDAR KHAN

We need to make a pistol.

GUN EXPERT

Sure.

SARDAR KHAN

I've got some bicycle parts.

GUN EXPERT

That won't help. Cycle tubes are weak and will burst open like a flower.

SARDAR KHAN

Really?

We see the details of gun making during this conversation.

SARDAR KHAN (CONT'D)

So what do we use then?

GUN EXPERT

Truck steering.

Nasir, Asgar and other Sardar men steal steering wheels from trucks from a truck parking area.

SARDAR KHAN

How many?

GUN EXPERT

One gun will need a foot long pipe.

SARDAR KHAN

What's the range of the gun?

GUN EXPERT

We can make 2 kinds of guns. Country or Long range.

SARDAR KHAN
From what distance can I kill a man?

GUN EXPERT
20 feet. With a long range

SARDAR KHAN
Death within 20 feet!

CUT TO:

EXT. KASAI MOHALLAH - DAY

Sardar is following a Qureshi walking into a lane. He calls him and shoots at him.

SARDAR KHAN
Hey, Qureshi! You fucking …

The gun backfires and hurts Sardar. Sardar runs after the Qureshi. Asgar comes from the other side and shoots at the Qureshi.

SARDAR KHAN (CONT'D)
Catch him.

ASGAR
HEY!

SARDAR KHAN (CONT'D)
Can't you run faster?!

Asgar and Sardar chase the Qureshi but he escapes.

CUT TO:

INT. GUN WORKSHOP - DAY

Sardar and Asgar throw the gun at the gun expert.

SARDAR KHAN
This is shit! The kick backs are horrid … and when I aim at the ground, it shoots the fucking sky.

ASGAR
Think we're dumb fucks?

CUT TO:

EXT. QUERESHI BUTCHER MARKET - DAY

The market is bustling with activity. An old man is singing prayers. Kids playing while the market is busy with meat hanging everywhere. Asgar walks in and hurls something at Badoor who is chopping meat. It's bomb powder. The bombing attempt has failed.

Badoor, Ehsan and all the Qureshis run after him. Asgar manages to flee the place.

BADOOR QURESHI

Wait, mother fucker! Grab him!

EXT. QURESHI BUTCHER MARKET - DAY

The town is abuzz with Moharram. It's that time of the year when Muslims punish themselves to as 'the day of grief'. All butchers are out to offer prayers. Sardar and his men come in to the market. They kill each and everyone around. They bomb the whole market and leave it piling debris. Ehsan comes out and asks one of his men.

EHSAN QURESHI

Who was it? Who was it asshole?

Sultan arrives at the place. Ehsan explains.

EHSAN QURESHI (CONT'D)

Everyone was off for Muharram. I was sick and asleep upstairs. I heard a sudden blast of sorts, ran out, and wherever I saw it was just …

EXT. STREETS - NIGHT

Sardar is driving through a street busy with festivities.

NASIR KHAN (V.O)

Sardar's power was on the rise in Wasseypur. And he was so blind in his ambition … that he ignored Nagma and the kids back in the city.

INTERMISSION

EXT. SARDAR'S HOUSE - NIGHT

Nasir is sleeping in the hall. Nagma comes.

NAGMA KHATUN

Shall I turn off the lights?

NASIR

I'll turn them out later.

A pregnant Nagma enters her bedroom. The two kids are sleeping. Sardar is sleeping on their side. She then lies down on bed. He again puts his hand on her stomach.

SARDAR KHAN

Is it kicking?

NAGMA

Yes.

SARDAR KHAN

Still kicking?

NAGMA

No.

He then suggestively moves his hands towards her breasts. She grabs it and puts it back on the stomach.

NAGMA (CONT'D)

J.P. Singh and his father seem awfully quiet.

SARDAR KHAN

Not really it's the silence before the storm. A landlord is like a mongoose. They always time their attack.

His hands slide again. She again grabs it and puts it back on her stomach.

SARDAR KHAN (CONT'D)

Why not?

NAGMA

Doctor's orders.

SARDAR KHAN

They are fools. You spread your legs. I'll do the rest.

NAGMA

Great medical advice.

SARDAR KHAN

So what do I do?

NAGMA

What you always do.

He gets up from bed. Goes out. She stays in bed. Not bothered.

Sardar gets angry and leaves the bedroom. He goes to the verandah, has a glass of water and looks pissed. He comes back to her.

SARDAR KHAN

You bloat like a balloon just to keep me away.

Nasir is listening to all this in the hall.

NAGMA

That's right! God came down and fucked me.

SARDAR KHAN

My mother didn't have so many kids.

NAGMA

So you're compensating?

Sardar looks at her.

SARDAR KHAN

No, you love squirting them out.

NAGMA

So what should I do? You're never home. At least the brats stay at home.

SARDAR KHAN
What if I get another woman?

NAGMA
Like I don't know about the Bengali bimbo.

He looks at her, silent.

NAGMA (CONT'D)
Has she become a balloon too?

He stares at her.

NAGMA (CONT'D)
What are you staring at?

He walks out angry. She just breathes out. Not bothered. He walks out through Nasir's room. Nasir pretends to sleep. Sardar shakes him up and tells him.

SARDAR KHAN
Uncle, I'm leaving.

He goes out, wakes up his henchmen sleeping on the cot outside and asks for the jeep keys.

SARDAR KHAN (CONT'D)
Give me the keys.

Nasir comes out after Sardar, worried.

NASIR
But where are you going?

Sardar doesn't bother to respond. Nasir watches him leave with his two henchmen.

EXT. DURGA'S HOUSE - NIGHT

He stops outside a house. Gets down. Goes upto the door. Knocks.

MALE VOICE
Who is it?

SARDAR KHAN
Sardar.

Door opens. It's Asgar. Sardar looks at him nods.

ASGAR

Where were you, brother? Sis-in-law is in such pain.

He walks in. He peeps into the room.

SARDAR KHAN

Durga. What happened, dear? Does it hurt a lot?

She is crying. She starts beating him.

DURGA

Just leave me alone. Good God! Leave me alone.

SARDAR KHAN

Enough! Want to kill me or what? What's wrong?

DURGA

What have you done to me? You've turned me into a cow.

SARDAR KHAN

Please don't say that.

DURGA

I don't want to become a child vending machine like Nagma.

SARDAR KHAN

I completely agree.

DURGA

What is this then?

(pointing at a very pregnant stomach)

SARDAR KHAN

It's love dear. It is my love.

EXT. SARDAR'S HOUSE - DAY

Young Danish and Faizal are sitting in front of the door. Danish looks towards the gate.

YOUNG DANISH
Faizal!

Young Faizal looks.

Sardar drives to the house. He gets off the jeep and greets the neighbor like usual.

SARDAR KHAN
Hello, Mr Yadav.

He meets Danish and Faizal at the door.

SARDAR KHAN
Where's your mother?

DANISH
She's still unconscious.

SARDAR KHAN
Is it a girl or boy?

DANISH
Boy.

SARDAR KHAN
Then smile son. Why so sad?

He pulls out Faizal's cheeks. The kids start smiling.

SARDAR KHAN (CONT'D)
Want some money?

They nod. Sardar gives them money.

SARDAR KHAN (CONT'D)
Share it.

He turns and goes back.

FAIZAL KHAN
Won't you see mummy?

SARDAR KHAN
No, let her rest. But tell her I wore a new shirt.

Sardar leaves. The kids just stand there.

INT. SARDAR'S HOUSE - DAY

Nagma and Faizal have worn *burqas*. Nagma is making Danish wear a burqa.

DANISH

I don't want to wear this.

NAGMA

Quiet!

Nagma slaps him.

NAGMA

He's worn it too. So stop blushing!

EXT. MARKET AREA - DAY

Durga and Sardar are buying utensils. They are having a good time, romancing slyly. Nagma and the kids watch them from a distance. Faizal can't watch this anymore and he runs away.

INT. SARDAR'S HOUSE - DAY

Nagma is sitting in the backyard. Faizal is crying.

NAGMA KHATUN

I can't afford your school. Your dad has stopped supporting us. Go, work and earn some money.

Nagma continues with her work. Faizal looks sad.

EXT. SMALL LANE - DAY

Faizal is angry and he has a huge rock in his hand. He is walking in to narrow lanes. Fazlu catches up with him.

FAZLU

Faizal! At least tell me where you're going?

Faizal doesn't answer.

FAZLU (CONT'D)

Who are you going to hit?

Faizal is not answering. They both continue and reach Durga's house.

EXT. DURGA'S HOUSE - DAY

Faizal hurls rocks at Durga's door.

FAZLU

Whose house is it?
Can I also throw some?

Fazlu joins Faizal at hurling rocks at the door. Durga opens the door. She keeps screaming at the kids in *Bengali*.

DURGA

Bloody brats, you better not let me catch you … I'll stick this spoon up your ass. You pricks!

CUT TO:

INT. TRAIN COMPARTMENT - DAY

Faizal and Danish are cleaning trains to earn some money.

CUT TO:

EXT. TRAIN STATION - DAY

Danish and Faizal are walking out of the station after work.

FAIZAL KHAN

How much did we earn?

DANISH

Twenty bucks.

FAIZAL KHAN

That's it?

DANISH

Yes.

FAIZAL KHAN

Gimme ten bucks?

DANISH

All of it will go straight to mom, alright?

Danish and Faizal are stopped by Ramadhir Singh. Ramadhir Singh is in a car, almost waiting for them.

RAMADHIR SINGH

Danish.

Danish comes close to the car

RAMADHIR SINGH (CONT'D)

Recognize me?

DANISH

Uh...

RAMADHIR SINGH

I'm Minister Ramadhir. Come, I'll drop you home.

CUT TO:

INT. RAMADHIR'S CAR - DAY

Ramadhir and Danish are sitting at the back. Faizal is in the front.

RAMADHIR SINGH

How long since your dad left?

(Danish is quiet)

A year? Or more? He spends millions on his mistress and her son. And you two are forced to clean toilets in trains. Doesn't it make your blood boil?

Danish nods in a yes. Ramadhir counts some money and gives it to Danish while Faizal is watching all this.

RAMADHIR SINGH

Take these thousand rupees. Give it to your mother, tell her that Ramadhir Singh is with her.

INT. SARDAR'S HOUSE - DAY

Nagma is doing the dishes in the backyard. Danish

and Faizal come to her. Danish hands over the money to Nagma.

YOUNG DANISH

Mother …

NAGMA KHATUN

Where did you get this money?

DANISH

From Ramadhir Singh. He asked us to come by if we need more.

NAGMA KHATUN

And you took it like a beggar? Is your dad dead?

She slaps him continuously.

DANISH (crying)

Then where is he? Why doesn't he send money?

Nagma gets up and starts hitting him with a broom.

NAGMA KHATUN

So what do you want to do? You want to kill him and make me a widow? Your brother an orphan? So what if he doesn't come home? Don't you get food? Don't you bear his name and respect?

Nasir comes in to rescue Danish.

NASIR KHAN

Why are you hitting him?

NAGMA KHATUN

Ramadhir gave him money and this asshole took it.

NASIR KHAN

Just stop it.

NAGMA KHATUN

Move or I'll beat you too!

In rage, Nagma takes a bucket and throws it.

CUT TO:

INT. SARDAR'S HOUSE - DAY
Nagma is putting medication on Danish's bruised back. Faizal comes in.

DANISH
Enough, mummy. It's not hurting. Stop mummy. - Shut up.

NAGMA KHATUN (weeping)
Shut-up!

Faizal comes and hugs his mother from the back.

INT. SARDAR'S HOUSE - NIGHT
Nagma is sobbing and Nasir is trying to console her. Faizal wakes up from his sleep and goes toward the hall to have water. He goes to check her mother. From the ajar door he sees, Nagma and Nasir getting intimate. He bangs at the door and runs away. Nagma tries to stop him but he runs away.

NAGMA KHATUN
Faizal! Wait son! Let me explain.

CUT TO:

INT. SARDAR'S HOUSE - NIGHT
Nasir flagellates himself in his room.

NASIR KHAN (V.O)
Faizal disappeared for many nights. And he wasn't the same when he returned. The episode affected him so much that he stopped growing physically. His skin started to grow darker. He began to look older than his friends and his elder brother. Even doctors couldn't explain this. And then he took to drugs. And none of us mentioned that night ever again. We could never look each other in the eye

again. What he didn't know was that he had saved us from committing a sin.

MONTAGE: FAIZAL WANDERING HOPELESSLY. FAIZAL SMOKING UP WITH FAZLU. FAIZAL AND DANISH CLIMBING HILL, FAIZAL RETURNS HOME BY JUMPING INTO THE HOUSE WHILE NAGMA AND NASIR LOOK AT HIM IN SILENCE.

EXT. WASSEYPUR ROAD 1 - NIGHT

SUPER - 1985

A bunch of boys are singing out loud in a jeep. They are drinking too. Asgar watches them pass by. The boys see a girl walking on the road.

BOYS IN THE JEEP

Hide the bottle. There's hot girl coming our way!

A drunk boy gets off the jeep and comes near her and teases her.

INT. QAMAR MAKHDOOMI'S HOUSE - DAY

Asgar and Sardar are in the courtyard. The abducted girl's father is mourning. Qamar is sitting by his side.

ASGAR

Some drunk boys in a jeep … they abducted his daughter.

QAMAR MAKHDOOMI

Must be Ramadhir's men.

SARDAR KHAN

What time is it?

CUT TO:

EXT. WASSEYPUR ROAD 1 - DAY

Sardar and Asgar get on a cinema wagon. The wagon is used for film promotions. This time it is for the Hindi film 'Kasam Paida Karne Wale Ki'. A song from the film is playing on the mike and one guy dressed like Mithun Chakravarty (hero of the film) dances on the song. Sardar gets on the mike.

SARDAR KHAN

May I have your kind attention! I inform you with a heavy heart that last evening a Wasseypur girl was abducted. If she doesn't return home safely in the next 3 hours then we will bomb this entire area and turn into a graveyard. And I promise to make Minister Ramadhir and his family do a naked cabaret on the streets. Thanks for listening! Song please.

Song and dance begins again.

I/E. RAMADHIR SINGH'S HOUSE 2 - DAY

Ramadhir listens to the announcement while on the phone. He goes out to look at Sardar Khan ridiculing him on the announcement. He comes back in with J.P.

RAMADHIR SINGH (to J.P.)

Shut the damn door. How much more will you humiliate me, son? Find out who picked up that girl immediately.

J.P. SINGH

Yes, father.

J.P. Singh walks out. Some people come and ask him for help. They touch his feet.

J.P SINGH (CONT'D)

It's fine!

(to Ghanshyam)

Get the car!

(to the people)

Hey! Get out of here!

CUT TO:

EXT. WASSEYPUR ROAD 1 - DAY

J.P. Singh and his men go out to find out about the abducted girl. They stop a passerby.

J.P. SINGH

Sir … are you from this colony?

MAN ON THE STREET

Yes.

J.P. SINGH

Was any girl abducted from here?

MAN ON THE STREET

Yes, Mr Khan's daughter.

They drive around to find the boys who abducted the girl. They stop by at the petrol pump.

EXT. PETROL PUMP - DAY

GHANSHYAM

Some drunk boys kidnapped a Wasseypur girl. Any idea who they were?

PUMP ATTENDANT

Was it Mohsin?

Ghanshyam looks at J.P. Seeking affirmation

GHANSHYAM

Mohsin?

CUT TO:

INT. ABANDONED BUILDING - DAY

J.P. and his men come to an abandoned place. The abducted girl is about to hit the boys with a brick. She hides as she hears the sound of Jeep. J.P. comes in and looks at the drunk boys.

J.P SINGH

Wake the motherfuckers up!

His men start beating them.

CUT TO:

INT. RAMADHIR SINGH'S HOUSE 2 - NIGHT

RAMADHIR SINGH (on the phone)

Don't they ever fucking think? Have they forgotten how Sardar chopped up our muscleman?

CUT TO:

INT. ABANDONED BUILDING - NIGHT

J.P. comes back with a gun.

DRUNK BOY 2 (O.S)

We were so drunk and horny, sir … we just had to pick her up!

J.P. shoots the boys. Two shots. We don't see whom he shoots.

J.P. SINGH

Take the bodies and return the girl respectfully.

GHANSHYAM

Okay.

CUT TO:

I/E. QAMAR MAKHDOOMI'S HOUSE - NIGHT

Asgar and Sardar come to Qamar's house. The abducted girl's father is weeping. Lot of crowd has assembled around the place. Two of the drunk men's dead bodies are laid out.

SARDAR KHAN

What's up, Sir?

ASGAR

They've sent only 2 bodies but the girl says there were 4 men.

I/E. DRUNK BOY'S HOUSE - DAY

Asgar and Sardar arrive at the drunk boy's place. Sardar is trying to kick the door open. It won't open. Asgar interrupts.

SARDAR KHAN

Open, mother fucker!

ASGAR

Relax! It opens the other way.

They enter the house.

SARDAR KHAN

Where are they? Ah! They're partying while we were searching everywhere. Who among you is a Muslim?

One of them points at the other drunk man. Sardar shakes hands with the Muslim man.

SARDAR KHAN (CONT'D)

So am I. Salaam!

Asgar takes the other man out.

ASGAR

Come with me.

DRUNK MAN

Brother … please … brother … sir …

Asgar takes a knife and starts chopping the man.

SARDAR KHAN

Come on now, it's over. What's done is done. Let's go. Don't drink so much, man. You'll fall sick! Feeling sick, are you? Come on, look. Don't you dare close your eyes.

Sardar takes him in the other room and makes him see the massacre.

SARDAR KHAN (CONT'D)

Hey, chop his dick. Saw that?

The drunk man is horrified but Sardar puts his hand on his mouth and makes him watch the whole thing.

INT. DRUNK BOY'S HOUSE - DAY

Ramadhir and J.P. have come to inspect the place.

A police officer, Gopal Singh gets them to witness. Ramadhir and J.P. watching in horror.

GOPAL SINGH

They have chopped the whole body and made it disappear. They haven't even left a toe behind.

Ramadhir and J.P. are speechless. They leave the place. J.P. tries to speak to him.

J.P. SINGH

Father …

Ramadhir asks him to leave with a gesture.

CUT TO:

INT. QAMAR MAKHDOOMI'S HOUSE - DAY

Qamar Makhdoomi is getting the abducted girl married to the drunk man.

QAMAR MAKHDOOMI

Your marriage to Sabrina has been agreed upon … with a deposit of 1 Lac rupees. Do you take her as your wife?

The drunk man is beaten up badly. He can barely speak. Asgar responds.

ASGAR

He does.

QAMAR MAKHDOOMI

He needs to agree.

Asgar beats the man.

ASGAR

Speak, bastard.

QAMAR MAKHDOOMI

Do you take her as your wife?

DRUNK MAN

I do.

CUT TO:

I/E. A TEMPLE - DAY

Ramadhir and C.S. come to visit a temple. Ramadhir touches his feet when he arrives.

CUT TO:

INT. QAMAR MAKDOOMI'S HOUSE - DAY

Sardar Khan calls Ramadhir. Qamar Makdoomi and Asgar watch.

SARDAR KHAN

The priest has decreed one million as the deposit. Who will pay?

CUT TO:

INT. RAMADHIR SINGH'S OFFICE - DAY

Ramadhir puts some money in a briefcase and gestures to J.P. Singh to deliver it.

CUT TO:

INT. RAMADHIR SINGH'S HOUSE 2 - DAY

C.S. guides Ramadhir.

C.S.

To fight Muslims, you need Muslims. The kind that the other Muslims fear. The butchers!

CUT TO:

INT. RAMADHIR SINGH'S OFFICE - DAY

Ramadhir picks up the phone and dials it.

RAMADHIR SINGH (on the phone)

Ehsan Qureshi.

CUT TO:

I/E. RAMADHIR SINGH'S HOUSE 2 - DAY

Sultan enters the courtyard. Ehsan gestures him to come in.

SULTAN

Where to, uncle?

EHSAN QURESHI
Inside

EXT. RAMADHIR SINGH'S HOUSE 2- DAY
They walk in. Ehsan introduces Sultan to Ramadhir.

EHSAN QURESHI (CONT'D)
Sir, this is Sultan.

Sultan touches Ramadhir's feet and sits down.

RAMADHIR SINGH
Sit next to me, son. Don't be shy.

RAMADHIR SINGH
All good?

SULTAN
Yes, sir.

Sultan is quite pleased. He looks around the house.

RAMADHIR SINGH
I heard what happened in Wasseypur.
Ramadhir's wife Suman walks in to the hall.

SUMAN
Won't you all have lunch?

RAMADHIR SINGH
Of course! Can't you see Sultan's here!

Suman is unsure but nods.

SUMAN
Of course …!

Sultan touches her feet.

SUMAN (CONT'D)
Live long! So should I lay out the supper?

RAMADHIR SINGH
Absolutely.

SUMAN
In the meat eating plates?

Ramadhir nods in a yes and continues talking to Sultan.

RAMADHIR SINGH
How many died?

SULTAN
Around 12. We can't fight bombs with swords and choppers.

Suman is asking the house help to get the china-ware instead of the regular ones.

RAMADHIR SINGH
Sardar is nothing compared to his dad Shahid. He used to work for me.
His fear made grown men soil their pants.
Sardar is not even the size of his father's pubic hair.
I'll give you all the ammunition, you ready your crew. They have bombs, just finish the bastards. Shoot them in the asses.

SULTAN
Yes, sir.

RAMADHIR SINGH
Can you do it?

SULTAN
Yes sir, we need the automatic guns.

RAMADHIR SINGH
Consider it done.
(to J.P.)
Learn from him. He just sits around warming his chair. Now go help mommy.

CUT TO:

EXT. COAL MINES 4 - DAY

Some workers steal some coal and load it on their heads and go.

SUPER - 1989

NASIR KHAN (V.O)

By now coal theft was a petty job. Everyone including coal workers were doing it.

CUT TO:

INT. COAL MINE - DAY

Some workers get inside a mine with torches on them. They get in further to show that some logs of wood are supporting the ceiling of the mine at one place.

NASIR KHAN (V.O)

The big money was in getting contracts.

Ext. Wood-cutting factory.

Logs of wood are unloaded from a truck. It is then cut with an automated axe-machine.

NASIR KHAN (V.O)

Like contracts for logging hollow mines or contracts for filling defunct mines with sand.

CUT TO:

EXT. COAL MINE AREA - DAY

Nasir gets off a truck at a coal depot. He goes to the payment counter. A B.C.C.L officer sits looking at the truck. Nasir puts the invoice. Officer looks down at it. It has 32 trucks written on it.

B.C.C.L OFFICER

But here it says 32 trucks.

NASIR KHAN

Of course there are 32 trucks.

B.C.C.L Officer

(looks around)

Where?

NASIR KHAN
Right here.

B.C.C.L OFFICER
That's just one truck.

NASIR KHAN
That's the 32nd one.

Officer looks at Nasir.

B.C.C.L OFFICER
Sir. The mine needs to be filled completely or the land will cave in.

NASIR KHAN
Superb. Then we can build open cast mining.

NASIR KHAN (V.O) (CONT'D)
Contracts went to those who could wrangle them.

EXT. RIVERBANK - DAY
Some tractors loaded with sand leave a river bank.

SUPER - 1990

NASIR KHAN (V.O)
We quit coal and started stealing sand off the river bank.

EXT. COAL MINE - DAY
Nasir drives a truck.

NASIR KHAN (V.O)
Sardar got the contract to fill the defunct mines in my name. And Sardar became the new Godfather of Wasseypur …

I/E. SOME HOUSE - DAY
Sardar and his accomplice get into a house. We hear gunshots inside the house. They come out.

NASIR KHAN (V.O)
… by systematically pushing the Qureshis out

of there … and started trading iron scrap illegally along with Asgar.

EXT. WASSEYPUR - DAY

A shot of Wasseypur city from a rooftop.

CUT TO:

EXT. SCRAPYARD - DAY

Some people loading scrap on to trucks.

NASIR KHAN (V.O)

Coal was now a mere chapter in the history of Dhanbad Mafia.

CUT TO:

EXT. WASSEYPUR STREET - DAY

Sardar and Asgar are walking by.

SARDAR KHAN

They're selling the old machines of the paint factory.

ASGAR

Yeah, I heard.

From across the street they see Nasir sitting with a grown up Danish.

SARDAR KHAN

Asgar?

ASGAR

Yes?

SARDAR KHAN

My boy's all grown up! Come here.

He gestures at Danish to come near. Danish and Nasir come to them.

DANISH

Salaam, father!

SARDAR KHAN

Walekum Salaam! Will you work with us?

DANISH
Yes.

SARDAR KHAN
Shall we employ him, Uncle?

NASIR KHAN
Sure. What will you put him in?

SARDAR KHAN
Steal or kill.

CUT TO:

I/E. WASSEYPUR ROADS - DAY
Danish is actively taking part in the iron scrap stealing business. He supervises an army of kids to get scrap off the trains, load them on themselves, ferry them into the workshop and get it processed. Badoor Qureshi watches the kids carry stolen iron scrap in one of the lanes.

INT. SARDAR'S SCRAP FACTORY - DAY
Sardar is sipping tea while Danish is handling the kids who are excited about their pay.

DANISH
Shut up and form a queue.

Asgar and Sardar come out.

SARDAR KHAN
Danish! How's your mother?

DANISH
She's well.

SARDAR KHAN
And Faizal and the little one?

DANISH
Father, may I ask you something?

SARDAR KHAN
Sure.

DANISH

Why don't you come home?

SARDAR KHAN

I'd like to son, but your mother scares me. Ramadhir can't touch me, but your mom can rip out my liver and fry it.

Sardar Khan opens the gate as he says this. From across the road Sultan shoots at him. Danish pushes Sardar in order to save him. Sultan is on a motorbike with someone. They run off.

DANISH

Father!!

SARDAR KHAN

Get a pistol! Get it fast.

Asgar fires back at Sultan but the gun backfires.

ASGAR

Damn it!

SARDAR KHAN

Get a damn pistol!

He sees Sultan fleeing.

SARDAR KHAN (CONT'D)

Why doesn't anyone keep a fucking pistol? Fucking idiots …

He realizes Danish is hurt.

SARDAR KHAN (CONT'D)

Danish? he's been shot!

DANISH

I am okay, father!

SARDAR KHAN

Get the jeep. Take him to the hospital.

DANISH

I'm fine.

SARDAR KHAN
You're not fine! You're not fine!

Sardar keeps slapping Danish.

ASGAR
Pick him up.

They all pick him up.

DANISH
I'm really fine.

SARDAR KHAN
You're really not, son.

Danish is taken into the Jeep. Sardar can't find the keys.

SARDAR KHAN
Where's the key? Who the fuck is warming the key in his ass?

ASGAR
You had it.

CUT TO:

INT. ISMAT NURSING HOME - DAY

Sardar and his men get Danish to the hospital. Sardar is furious.

SARDAR KHAN (to the doctor)
Doctor, my son's got two bullets in him.

DOCTOR
Where is the patient?

SARDAR KHAN
Right here.

Danish is standing over by him.

DOCTOR
But he looks fine.

SARDAR KHAN
I'll fuck your mother. Let's go.

Sardar gets the doctor at gun point.

DOCTOR
This is wrong.

Sardar drags him in the operation room. It's a dark room.

SARDAR KHAN
Asgar, switch on the lights.

Asgar switches on the light.

SARDAR KHAN (CONT'D)
Put him on the stretcher. Wait son!!! He could die trying to lie down himself. Take his shirt off …

Suddenly the light in the room goes off.

SARDAR KHAN (CONT'D)
Now what?

ASGAR
The power's out.

SARDAR KHAN
Fuck it. Start operating.

DOCTOR
Nothing can happen in the dark.

SARDAR KHAN
But lots can happen in your arse.

DOCTOR
Sardar, I don't have a tubelight in my ass. This could definitely kill your son.

SARDAR KHAN
Then don't make a mistake, motherfucker.

CUT TO:

INT. ISMAT NURSING HOME - DAY

The hospital is lit up with candles. Nagma comes to see Danish.

NAGMA KHATUN
Where's Danish?

NASIR KHAN
Inside, getting bandaged.

NAGMA KHATUN
How's he?

NASIR KHAN
See for yourself.

NAGMA KHATUN
Where?

NASIR KHAN
Go straight.

Nagma walks inside. She sees Danish being bandaged by the doctor and surrounded by Sardar and other men holding up torches.

Nagma and Sardar sit together outside the clinic waiting. They are both emotional. Sardar holds Nagma's hand.

CUT TO:

EXT. WASSEYPUR BRIDGE - DAY
Sardar and Asgar ambush Ramadhir's car in the middle of the bridge. Sardar comes to Ramadhir's car and speaks to his driver.

SARDAR KHAN
Move it!

Sardar gets into the car and drives.

CUT TO:

I/E. OLD GARAGE - DAY
Sardar gets Ramadhir to a garage.

SARDAR KHAN
Do you need an invitation card to step out, Mr Minister?

Ramadhir comes out of the car. Sardar walks toward the garage owner.

SARDAR KHAN (CONT'D)
See that car there?

GARAGE OWNER
Yes.

SARDAR KHAN
Dismantle every part.

GARAGE OWNER
Ok.

SARDAR KHAN (to Ramadhir)
We're only dismantling it but if anything were to happen to my son … I'd pump so many bullets in it that your driver would be rich just by selling the shells.

(to Asgar)
Are you enjoying this?
Why don't you sniff and tell us what the minister had for breakfast?

Asgar pretends to put his hand at Ramadhir's ass and then smells his finger.

ASGAR
His Wife's beating.

SARDAR KHAN
Shameful.

Sardar laughs …

CUT TO:

INT. DURGA'S HOUSE - DAY
Sardar is in the kitchen with Durga. She's chopping vegetables.

DURGA
I'm not going to respond to this.

SARDAR KHAN

But we can all be together. You on one floor, Nagma on the other. Okay, separate kitchen if you like.

Durga becomes furious. She leaves the kitchen and comes near her son Definite. Sardar keeps calling out to her.

SARDAR KHAN (CONT'D)

Durga. Hey Durga!

DURGA (to Definite)

Do you want your father?

She goes back to where Sardar is standing.

DURGA

How about we divide you too. One leg for me, one for her. One ass cheek for me … and we split your dick too. Piss from your mouth.

Sardar slaps her. Durga just leaves him and shuts the door.

SARDAR KHAN

Open up, Bengal Tigress!

DURGA

Get out!

SARDAR KHAN

Won't come with me?

DURGA

Never!

SARDAR KHAN

Fair enough. I'll come back later.

Definite asks Durga.

DEFINITE

Where has father gone?

DURGA

To hell … and to give away what's yours.

CUT TO:

INT. RAY TALKIES - DAY

A grown up Faizal Khan is watching a film with Fazlu. Amitabh Bachchan's scene from *Trishul* plays on screen. Amitabh blasting the mines with his beedi and walking. Followed by his dialogue *'jis aadmi ne aapne maa ko roj teel teel marte dekha, usse maut se kya dar … '* ['For someone who's seen his mother die on a daily basis, why would he ever fear death.'] Faizal looks at a girl in the front row who's hooting with excitement. She is Mohsina.

MOHSINA

Live long, Bachchan!

She is whistling. The film is over and everyone comes out. Mohsina goes to the usher along with her friends.

MOHSINA (CONT'D)

Sir, can't we see another show? Please let us in, sir … Why not? You know I come here daily. Can I go in?

USHER

Ticket?

MOHSINA

I don't have it. Please let me in.

Faizal turns back to see her. He is reminded of his childhood.

FAZLU

Faizal, want to eat baked dumplings?

FAIZAL KHAN

Yup.

CUT TO:

EXT. FAIZAL'S HOUSE - DAY

Faizal and Fazlu are walking back home after watching the film.

FAZLU

Come with me. Why are you going back to Sanjeev Kumar's house??

(Reference to Trishul - Sanjeev Kumar is the actor who plays the hero's father)

FAIZAL KHAN

Till Waheeda Rehman is alive, Sanjeev Kumar is everything!

(Reference to Trishul - Waheeda Rehman is the actress playing the hero's mother)

CUT TO:

INT. FAIZAL'S HOUSE - DAY

Sardar is having tea with Danish and the rest of the family. Nagma is cleaning with a vacuum cleaner.

SARDAR KHAN

These country pistols are lousy.

DANISH

What?

SARDAR KHAN (to Nagma)

Stop it, will you?

NAGMA KHATUN

I need to work.

SARDAR KHAN

We're talking about work too.

NAGMA KHATUN

It's a big house. Go elsewhere.

SARDAR KHAN

Stop it, dear!

NAGMA KHATUN

Talk elsewhere dear.

SARDAR KHAN

Please stop!

NAGMA KHATUN
Please talk elsewhere!

SARDAR KHAN
What are you doing?

NAGMA
I'm cleaning the house.

They move out of the hall.

DANISH
So, what were you saying father?

SARDAR KHAN
No one knows you in the city of Banaras. I know a gun seller there. Meet him. He is selling 6 second hand guns for a mere 2 lacs ... when a single gun costs about 1.5 lacs anywhere else.

DANISH
Why're they so cheap?

Faizal is watching all this and he interrupts.

FAIZAL KHAN
Can I go instead? Brother hasn't healed yet. And no one knows me in that city either.

CUT TO:

I/E. TRAIN - DAY

Faizal is on his way to Banaras, smoking up.

CUT TO:

I/E. BANARAS HOTEL - DAY

Faizal gets out of Varanasi railway station. He asks for directions and walks through Banaras streets. He arrives at the same hotel where his grandfather had come years ago. He checks in. Mr Yadav comes to see him. There is a knock at the door.

FAIZAL KHAN
Door's open.

Mr Yadav comes in. Keeps his bag on the table. Shuts all the windows and opens the last window. He takes the guns out of the bag and lays them all out on the table. Faizal gives him the money. Mr Yadav takes it and leaves. Faizal looks at the gun and fancies them. He picks one up and makes a mark on it with his key 'F.K.'. He brandishes the pistol at the mirror and shoots in the style of heroes in old Hindi films.

CUT TO:

INT. TRAIN COMPARTMENT - DAY

Faizal is looking at this guy who looks like Amitabh Bachchan. The cops come for an inspection in to the train.

COP

Hey?

FAIZAL KHAN

What?

COP

Where are you going?

FAIZAL KHAN

Home.

COP

Where's home?

FAIZAL KHAN

Why?

COP

Answer me, wise ass. Where's home?

FAIZAL KHAN

Dhanbad.

COP

Any bags?

FAIZAL KHAN

Just one.

COP
Where is it?

FAIZAL KHAN
Here.

COP
Hey, check his bag.

The constable checks his bag and finds guns in them.

COP (CONT'D)
What's this? What's all this? He's carrying an entire armory with him.

The cops take away Faizal. The Amitabh Bachchan look-alike watches.

CUT TO:

EXT. BANK - DAY
Sardar is having tea with his men. He sees Fazlu and his men looting a bank. Sardar is surprised.

CUT TO:

INT. FAIZAL'S HOUSE - DAY
Nagma is taking care of a new refrigerator. Sardar comes in and sits down.

SARDAR KHAN
Street kids are looting banks in broad daylight. Everyone's got a damn gun these days.

Nagma is engrossed with the fridge. Asgar and Nasir join her.

SARDAR KHAN (CONT'D)
Faizal's friends are openly looting banks now. Any fucker's got a damn gun these days. Everyone thinks he's a dacoit. Not like the good ol' times when there was just Ramadhir and I locked in battle.

Asgar and Nasir are still engrossed with the refrigerator.

ASGAR

It helps cool your head.

NASIR KHAN

No, it freezes the head, if you have one.

Sardar continues to talk to Danish.

SARDAR KHAN

Enough bloodshed! Let's change business.

DANISH

Like?

SARDAR KHAN

Extortion.

Nasir joins Sardar and Danish.

NASIR

What?

SARDAR KHAN

Extortion. People respect me. They will happily pay up. There's a lot of demand for fish today … so we'll politely tell the fishermen. 'We'll sell the fish from now!'

DANISH

In that case there's a pond on the outskirts of the town that belongs to the priests. Call them, they won't refuse you.

NASIR KHAN

Who talks business on the phone?

SARDAR KHAN

Why don't you live inside that fridge, silly woman? I'll sell you with the fridge

Nagma and Asgar are still engrossed in the fridge.

EXT. TOPCHANCHI POND - DAY

Danish is supervising the fishing business.

DANISH

You see all this fish being caught, it's now ours. We've bought this pond, you see. So if a single fish is stolen, I will drown you right here. Understood?

INT. FISH MARKET - DAY

Asgar extorts money from the fishermen in the market.

EXT. MARKET AREA - DAY

Asgar collects 'hafta' (extortion money) from some shopkeepers.

SHOPKEEPER

Walekum salaam, brother Asgar!

ASGAR

And how are you today?

SHOPKEEPER

Here take it…

INT. JEWELER'S SHOP - DAY

Danish is at a Jewellery shop, collecting some payment from the owner. Shama Parveen and Mohsina have come to buy jewels. Danish is attracted to Shama. He speaks to the jeweler.

JEWELER

She's butcher Sultan's sister, Shama Parveen.

CUT TO:

I/E. MASJID - DAY

Badoor Qureshi has just come out a prayer at the Mosque.

SUPER - BADOOR QURESHI

Danish approaches him to talk.

DANISH

Badoor uncle, hey, uncle.

BADOOR QURESHI

Hey, don't make me abuse you right after my prayers.

DANISH

Abuse me if you wish, sir. But I feel this war should end.

BADOOR QURESHI

It is your father who started it all.

DANISH

Technically, your grandfather drove mine out of the village …

DANISH (CONT'D)

… but isn't this history a vicious circle we need to break? Shouldn't we just unite?

Badoor looks at him.

BADOOR QURESHI

What do you mean?

DANISH

Uncle, we pray to the same God, even practice the same profession. 'Make love, not war.' Isn't that what the wise say?

BADOOR QURESHI

Will your father agree?

CUT TO:

INT. SULTAN'S HOUSE - SHAMA'S ROOM - DAY

Girls are singing and dancing - all dressed up. It appears to be an occasion. Mohsina is among them.

CUT TO:

INT. SULTAN'S HOUSE - SULTAN'S ROOM - DAY

Sultan is locked inside his room. He's trying to open it desperately. He knocks from inside and looks out through the window calling for help.

SULTAN
Open the fucking door!

A woman passes in front of the locked room with a tray full of cold-drinks. She ignores Sultans pleas.

SULTAN (CONT'D)
This is wrong Uncle. You will all pay. Bastards!! Open the fucking door!
Sultan is angry and keeps screaming from inside the locked room.

CUT TO:

INT. SULTAN'S HOUSE - LIVING ROOM - DAY
Danish's engagement in progress. Sweets are being served. Sardar, Danish, Qamar Makhdoomi, Nasir, Asgar, Ehsan Qureshi etc., are sitting there.

INT. SULTAN'S HOUSE - SHAMA'S ROOM - DAY
Girls continue to dance and enjoy. Nagma conducts engagement ceremony for Shama by covering Shama's head with a red dupatta.

CUT TO:

INT. SULTAN'S HOUSE - SULTAN'S ROOM - DAY
Sultan screams.

SULTAN
Uncle, this stupid "truce" is going to cost us dearly.

He finds his gun but notices that there are no bullets in it.

SULTAN (CONT'D)
They've taken the fucking bullets!! This is wrong, uncle!!

CUT TO:

INT. SULTAN'S HOUSE - LIVING ROOM - DAY
Everyone's busy celebrating. Sultan's voice can

be heard softly from the other room over all the noise and music. Badoor stands in a corner watching all this and also listening to Sultan's threats. Sweets making rounds. Sardar offers them to someone.

SARDAR KHAN

Please eat something...

Nasir is also cautious of Sultan's screams from the other room. He looks at Qamar Makhdoomi who also has ears for Sultan's threats.

CUT TO:

INT. BANARAS JAIL. MEETING AREA - DAY

Danish has come to meet Faizal. They talk through the partition. Faizal has a beard.

DANISH

I'm getting married next month. I'm just waiting for you to get released. By the way we've quit the bloody business, and started fish business. It's actually pretty good.

Faizal is looking elsewhere, as if not interested.

DANISH (CONT'D)

Where are you lost man? I'll come to get you before my wedding ... understood?

Faizal is still looking somewhere else.

FAIZAL KHAN

I'll come by myself.

CUT TO:

EXT. BANARAS JAIL - DAY

Faizal walks out of the jail. He has a beard.

CUT TO:

EXT. BANARAS STREETS - NIGHT

Faizal walks through Banaras streets. He drinks lassi from a shop. He takes a ride on a cycle rickshaw. Smokes. Looks at shops, mannequins, etc.

CUT TO:

EXT. BANARAS. GANGA GHAT - DAY

Faizal gets a shave and checks out his reflection in a mirror.

CUT TO:

I/E. BANARAS HOTEL - DAY

An older Yadavji walks through the corridors of the same hotel we've seen before. He gets in to a room. Faizal is inside.

FAIZAL KHAN

Hello, Mr Yadav! Come on in.

Yadav Ji has come in with a bag. He takes out guns from the bags and spreads them out on a table, as before. Faizal picks up one of the guns and notices his initials (F.K.) still scratched on it. He realises it is the same gun that he bought earlier and was taken from him by the cops.

FAIZAL KHAN (CONT'D)

Have you got the bullets?

Yadav Ji puts a box of bullets in front of him. Faizal takes a bullet and loads the gun.

FAIZAL KHAN (CONT'D)

I met your old friends in jail. When dad sent me with the money last time I didn't quite get the deal. Why would anyone sell this expensive shit so cheap? Because this is … oh! Your money's over there but I get it now these are made in your father's gun factory.

Yadav Ji looks at him with fear. Faizal points in the other direction. Yadav Ji checks the money and puts it in his bag all the while looking at Faizal.

FAIZAL KHAN (CONT'D)
Mr Yadav … Bam!

Yadav looks at him. Faizal pretends to shoot Yadav Ji, mockingly, and laughs. Yadav Ji steps out of the room. Faizal cocks the gun and calls out to him again.

FAIZAL KHAN (CONT'D)
Mr Yadav …

Yadav Ji looks back, knowing that he's going to be shot. Faizal shoots him for real this time. He drags Yadav Ji's body inside the room, packs up the guns and money.

CUT TO:

INT. TRAIN TOILET - DAY

Faizal hides the bag with guns and money in the train toilet, in the false ceiling above, next to the water tank. There's a knock on the toilet door.

FAIZAL KHAN
Let a man shit in peace.

Voice from outside:

I need to go too.

Faizal is busy tightening screws of the false ceiling.

FAIZAL KHAN
Go to the next cubicle.

Knocking persists.

FAIZAL KHAN (CONT'D)
Just shit in the next toilet.

Voice from outside:

Fine. I'll stop the train for
your royal shit.

Faizal is now done. He throws the screw driver through the toilet hole and opens the door. It's a cop outside, the same cop who had arrested Faizal earlier. The cop checks the toilet and then follows Faizal in the compartment.

CUT TO:

INT. TRAIN COMPARTMENT - DAY

Faizal is arranging another bag on his seat. The cop approaches him.

COP

What's the rush, buddy? Where are you going?

FAIZAL KHAN

Home.

COP

And where's home?

FAIZAL KHAN

Dhanbad.

COP

Your name?

FAIZAL KHAN

Faizal Khan.

COP

Is this your bag?

Faizal nods.

COP (CONT'D)

Open it.

Faizal hands him the bag. Cop checks it from inside thoroughly. He takes out all the clothes.

COP (CONT'D)

What's with the new clothes?

FAIZAL KHAN

Your buddies in jail didn't return my bag.

COP
Really?

COP (CONT'D)
Whose bag is that?

SOMEONE
Mine.

COP
Put it back.

FAIZAL KHAN
You've ruined the ironing.

COP (to Faizal)
I'm on to you wise ass! We will meet again.

Faizal smiles.

There's a group of young college boys (hippie style) singing a song. Faizal listens to the song and enjoys. He also notices that there's a man by the door of the train bogey who's keeping a watch at him. Faizal walks up to the other door of the train, leans out and writes something on the train wall outside. Faizal watches the boys sing and enjoy.

CUT TO:

EXT. DHANBAD RAILWAY STATION - DAY
Faizal comes out of the station. Fazlu is waiting for him. They meet and leave. The other man from the train follows them.

CUT TO:

EXT. DHANBAD STREETS - DAY
Faizal and Fazlu are on a cycle rickshaw. The other man from the train is following them on another cycle rickshaw. Fazlu keeps a watch on the other man.

CUT TO:

EXT. RAMADHIR SINGH'S HOUSE 2 - DAY

A caravan of many Ambassador cars pass through Dhanbad streets. The car with the red light on top of it enters Ramadhir's bungalow compound. Lots of people are waiting for a meeting with the minister. Sultan is waiting there with Jabbar and Ali inside the bungalow premises. Ramadhir gets out of the car. Sultan touches Ramadhir's feet. Ramadhir ignores him and walks inside. Ehsan Qureshi also gets out of the car. He also ignores Sultan and walks ahead. Sultan feels dejected.

SULTAN

Didn't he see me?

ALI

Maybe it was tough through the dark glasses …

CUT TO:

INT. RAMADHIR SINGH'S HOUSE 2 -
LIVING ROOM - DAY

Ramadhir is reading from a wedding card invitation. Ehsan Qureshi ushers Sultan inside the room. Sultan stares at him but he looks down.

RAMADHIR SINGH

"No real friends here, no lovers even,
For only marriages are truly made in heaven."
What a thought!

Sultan touches Ramadhir's feet and waits for his response.

SULTAN

Have I displeased you, sir?

Ramadhir throws the wedding card on the table.

RAMADHIR SINGH

Are you trying to play politics with me by aligning with my enemy?

You and Sardar are now becoming family!
That's why he's still alive.
Now you will all celebrate … eat yummy food!
'I do' indeed. Well, I don't!

EXT. RAMADHIR SINGH'S HOUSE 2 - DAY

Sultan walks out with Ehsan, Ali and Jabbar. They're all quiet and serious. Suddenly Sultan takes out his slipper, picks it up. Ehsan notices this and starts running. Sultan chases him with his slipper in hand, catches up to him and starts hitting him with the slipper. The other two control him.

JABBAR

What happened, Sultan?

ALI

Stop man.

EHSAN QURESHI

Hey, Sultan … Stop. Why are you hitting me?
You're hurting me. What could I do? He saw
the invitation card and lost it.

CUT TO:

INT. SULTAN'S HOUSE - DAY

Shama is sitting all ready for the wedding. Mohsina and Nagma sit next to her among other ladies. They are putting the sehra on Shama's head. Other ladies are singing.

NAGMA

Don't fool around now. Tie it properly.

Sultan enters the house with Ali and Jabbar. People are arranging furniture and decorations in the house. Badoor is supervising it.

SULTAN

Where's that senile fucker?

BADOOR

No please fix that chandelier properly.

SULTAN

Decorating, are we? But why are you dressed in a mournful white?
Shouldn't you be in a skirt? Hey get him a chick's skirt someone.
You can even dance and be the entertainment today. Get the fucking skirt I say.

Badoor tries to calm him down.

BADOOR QURESHI

Son, Ramadhir is taking advantage of a family feud. Wasseypur is not even his concern.

Sultan stares at him.

SULTAN

Aren't you ashamed? You're Sultana Daku's son, his direct offspring.
The British shat at his mention. This miserable fuck has got his face, not his balls!

Despite being ridiculed, Badoor tries to explain to Sultan.

BADOOR QURESHI

I understand your anger but fighting here is futile. We should maintain decorum.

SULTAN

There's no 'we'. Count me out. I believe in loyalty. Why don't you become Sardar's nautch girl?

BADOOR QURESHI

Watch your mouth, Sultan.

SULTAN

Don't teach me manners! Where's my sister?

Badoor tries to stop him, but he pushes him out of the way.

SULTAN (CONT'D)
Move. Where is she?

BADOOR QURESHI
Sultan, wait!

Badoor goes after him. Sultan goes towards Shama's room. Badoor stops at the living room where the wedding ceremony of Danish is going on. The priest is conducting the vows. Sardar, Asgar and other men watch.

MAULVI
Danish Khan. Son of Sardar Khan. Your marriage to Shama Parveen, has been agreed upon with a depoist of Rupees 51,000. Do you take her as your wife?

DANISH
I do.

Sardar and other people congratulate each other.

SARDAR KHAN
Wonderful! Congratulations!

Faizal is also present there, but appears lost.

CUT TO:

Sultan enters the women's room where Shama and other women are waiting for the ceremony. The women stop singing as Sultan enters the room. Sultan goes up to Shama and whispers in her ear.

SULTAN
Shama! I speak to you as your older brother, you better say 'no' or I'll shoot you.

Nagma who's sitting next to her, has heard all this. Sultan leaves.

CUT TO:

INT. SULTAN'S HOUSE - NIGHT
Wedding is through. Reception party is on. A

singer performs on stage. He's a man but sings both in male and female voices. Guests enjoy the song. Sardar, Nasir, Asgar, Nagma, Danish, Shama, all enjoy and dance. Money being thrown. Sultan watches all this angrily from his room on the first floor. Ehsan gestures to him to stay in control and not do anything. Faizal walks to the other tent where food is being served. He notices Mohsina there, serving food. He starts dreaming a romance, but soon comes back to reality. There's a spark between the two.

CUT TO:

EXT. DHABA - NIGHT
Sultan is getting drunk at a *dhaba* with his friends. He is not happy.

CUT TO:

INT. SARDAR'S HOUSE. DANISH'S BEDROOM - NIGHT
It's Danish and Shama's wedding night. Shama is sitting with her head down, shy. Danish is smiling at her.

DANISH
Please look at me. See how I'm bursting with joy!

DANISH (CONT'D)
What's wrong?

SHAMA PARVEEN
You've saved a lot of lives by marrying me. My parents must be blessing you right now.

DANISH
Then why are you crying?

SHAMA PARVEEN
Because I am happy.

DANISH
You're happy?

She nods.

DANISH (CONT'D)

Do you know that I did this only to be with you?
I fell in love with you and knew Shama Praveen would be my bride.

SHAMA PARVEEN

It's Par-veen, not Pra-veen!

DANISH

Shama … Pra-veen

SHAMA PARVEEN

It's Par-veen!!

DANISH

Look, an orange doesn't turn into an apple just because you call it an apple.
Golden, sweetly fragrant, and juicy on the inside!

CUT TO:

EXT. A POND - DAY

Faisal and Mohsina walk next to a pond. They're on a date. It's a quiet, romantic place. Mohsina sits on a bench and asks Faizal to sit too.

MOHSINA

Please sit.

He sits next to her.

MOHSINA (CONT'D)

It's so green here!

Faizal is looking at Mohsina.

FAIZAL KHAN

Oh, it's pretty lush. The pond, that is.

MOHSINA

I love the color green. I wore new clothes today.

FAIZAL KHAN

I like the red nail polish too.

MOHSINA
I like red as well.

FAIZAL KHAN
But you just said green.

MOHSINA
I like both.

They're both quiet. It's an awkward moment. Faizal puts his hand on hers. She notices this.

MOHSINA (CONT'D)
What? What is this?

MOHSINA (CONT'D)
Stop smiling and speak! Is this decent, shouldn't you ask?

FAIZAL KHAN
I just thought ...

MOHSINA
Thought what? You thought you can do as you please, touch me...?

FAIZAL KHAN
No, I just felt ...

MOHSINA
Felt what? That you'll feel me up? Should you not ask for permission? Don't you ask before you enter someone's house?

Faisal is upset. He gets up from there. Mohsina stops him. Changes her tone.

MOHSINA (CONT'D)
Where are you going?

FAIZAL KHAN
Nothing, I ... just ...

MOHSINA
Please sit.

He sits back.

FAIZAL KHAN

I'm sorry for the mistake.

MOHSINA

That's ok. I'm not angry. But you should ask.

He holds her hand again.

FAIZAL KHAN

Sorry.

MOHSINA

I'll never stop you if you ask first.

FAIZAL KHAN

Next time I'll surely ask.

MOHSINA

Ok, now stop crying.

CUT TO:

EXT. TOPCHANCHI POND - DAY

Fisherman are busy at work. Asgar, Sardar and Danish are there. Danish walks up to Sardar.

DANISH

Father, the nets are full of fish. Shall we call it a day?

SARDAR KHAN

Why?

DANISH

I Just…had some important work.

SARDAR KHAN

With your bride? Go…just don't turn into a sissy because of her.

Danish smiles. Fazlu and Sultan are watching Sardar from a distance. They are sitting in a jeep on the other side of the pond. Fazlu fills in Sultan with information on Sardar.

FAZLU

They've taken over all the ponds.

Sardar kisses off Danish.

FAZLU

He's here every morning and leaves in the evening.

Fazlu and Sultan drive away. They look at Sardar's Ambassador car on their way.

CUT TO:

EXT. DHANBAD RAILWAY STATION - DAY

Faizal goes back to the railway station. There's a train on the platform. He looks for a certain bogey. He then notices, 'F.K.' scratched on a bogey and gets in it. He withdraws his bag with guns and money from the train toilet. The train starts to move. He gets out of the slow moving train.

CUT TO:

EXT. FAZLU'S TERRACE - NIGHT

Fazlu and Faizal are chatting with the other man from the train who was chasing Faizal earlier. They're smoking.

FAZLU

How long have you been working?

POLICEMAN

5 years.

FAZLU

Why did you become a cop? There was a time when film heroes became policemen … for revenge? Now they're smarter, they become villains to wreck more havoc.

FAIZAL KHAN

'When you shoot, shoot. Don't talk!'

FAZLU

Get it, Mr Superintendent?

POLICEMAN
You are funny sir.

FAZLU (to faizal)
Are you leaving already?

FAIZAL KHAN
I've to go 'cos dad's leaving for work and brother refuses to leave the bedroom.

FAZLU
Chill man.

FAIZAL KHAN
Gotta go, man.

FAZLU
Don't be daddy's little slave. He's got bodyguards now.

FAIZAL KHAN
There's no one tomorrow, man.

FAZLU
Chill! I'll drop you home. Smoke up, brother.

CUT TO:

Later, they're all sleeping on the terrace. Fazlu gets up and quietly goes downstairs to the phone. He speaks on phone to someone.

FAZLU (CONT'D)
Hello! The 'doctor' is sans 'stethoscope' tomorrow.

CUT TO:

INT. SARDAR'S HOUSE - DAY
Its early morning, Sardar walks down from his room and calls out for Danish.

SARDAR KHAN
Danish. Danish!
Nagma is working in the kitchen. She answers.

NAGMA KHATUN
He slept late.

SARDAR KHAN
Faizal?

NAGMA KHATUN
His friend called - Faizal slept there last night.

SARDAR KHAN
Nasir?

NAGMA KHATUN
He's still sleeping.

SARDAR KHAN
Asgar??

NAGMA KHATUN
He's gone out.

SARDAR KHAN
Are you the resident BBC?

NAGMA KHATUN
No, you're the grumpy early bird!

SARDAR KHAN
And what's my name?

NAGMA KHATUN
Sardar khan.

SARDAR KHAN
Glad you remember it. Now chop onions. I'll return by evening.

NAGMA KHATUN
Okay.

CUT TO:

EXT. STREETS - DAY

Sardar drives through streets.

CUT TO:

I/E. DURGA'S HOUSE - DAY

Sardar parks his car outside Durga's house. He walks up to the door and knocks it.

SARDAR KHAN

It's me.

Durga's son (Definite) comes out. Durga stands behind the curtain and looks from there.

DEFINITE

Father, salaam!

SARDAR KHAN

Bless you, son. And listen tell your mother I was here. Here's 10 grand, ask if you need more. May I leave now?

He hands over a bundle of money to Definite, kisses him and leaves.

SARDAR KHAN (CONT'D)

Goodbye!

DEFINITE

Goodbye!

Durga calls Definite in when Sardar is gone.

DURGA

Definite, come here.

She takes the money from him and goes and picks up the phone receiver which was on hold.

DURGA (CONT'D)

(on phone) He just left.

CUT TO:

EXT. STREETS - DAY

Sardar drives.

CUT TO:

EXT. PETROL PUMP - DAY

He stops his car at a petrol pump. He gestures to the pump attendant to fill his car's tank. He sits waiting. Suddenly he notices four men including Sultan, driving on two motor bikes towards his car. They take out guns and shoot at him. Sardar ducks to protect himself. Many shots are fired at the car. Some people at the nearby tea stall hide and watch. The attackers start to leave on their motorbikes. One of the attackers is caught by a man and pulled back from the bike. This attacker is beaten and captured. The others escape. Sardar comes out of his car. He's injured and hit on the forehead. He drops himself on a cart that's passing through. Cart moves away from the camera. The gun falls down from Sardar's hand, indicating he dies on it. The cart's wheel goes over the gun, triggering it.

All in slow Motion.

SARDAR KHAN (V.O)

My life has but one mission - Revenge. It hurts to see that dog prosper. I don't just want to kill him ... I want to destroy him piece by piece. And he will know my name before I fuck him over.

END OF PART 1

TO BE CONTINUED......

CREDITS ROLL ON BLACK.

GANGS OF WASSEYPUR

PART II

FADE IN:

FLASHBACK FROM PART 1

INT. DURGA'S HOUSE - DAY

Sardar is at the door with young Definite.

SARDAR

Can I go now?

Without waiting for a response, he kisses young Definite on the forehead and bids farewell.

SARDAR (CONT'D)

See you later. Khuda Hafiz.

YOUNG DEFINITE

See you later. Khuda Hafiz.

Sardar leaves. Durga calls young Definite inside.

DURGA

Definite … come here.

She takes money from him and calls someone.

DURGA (CONT'D)

(on the phone) He just left.

CUT TO:

EXT. PETROL PUMP - DAY

(Snippets from end of Part 1) Sardar is in his car, waiting for petrol to be filled. Four guys on two bikes come up and fire at him. Sardar gets hit. One of the assailants gets caught by some passersby present at the scene. The remaining three escape.

FLASHBACK ENDS.

CUT TO:

EXT. FAZLU'S TERRACE - MORNING

Fazlu comes up to where Faizal and another guy are sleeping. He shakes Faizal up.

FAZLU

Faizal … hey Faizal … someone has killed your father.

Faizal slowly wakes up.

FAZLU (CONT'D)

Someone has killed your father.

It sinks in. Faizal runs down the terrace.

CUT TO:

EXT. FAIZAL'S HOUSE - DAY

Danish, Nasir and Asgar rush out of the house, followed by Nagma, Shama and Nagma's sister.

NAGMA

Danish … Danish, son!

Danish chides her.

DANISH

Mom, you go back.

Shama and Asgar dissuade Nagma.

SHAMA PARVEEN

Wait mom!

ASGAR

You wait at home. Nothing has happened.

Danish pushes Nagma back.

DANISH

Nothing will happen to dad. Shama, take her inside.

NAGMA

Let me go with you, son.

As they are rushing out, Faizal walks towards them. Danish is upset at seeing Faizal here and grabs him.

DANISH (CONT'D)

What're you doing here? You didn't go with dad?

FAIZAL

I fell asleep.

Danish starts hitting him.

DANISH

Fell asleep? Fell asleep? Asshole! Must be lying stoned on Fazlu's terrace.

FAIZAL

Like you're always lying on top of sis-in-law in the bedroom.

Asgar somehow stops the fight.

ASGAR

Enough!

NAGMA

Hurry up!

They all run towards the jeep.

CUT TO:

EXT. PETROL PUMP - DAY

There's a big crowd at the petrol pump. They're all looking at something.

SOMEONE (O.S)

We were having tea at the tea stall. That's when Mr Sardar Khan's car came in.
Danish, Asgar, Nasir and Faizal get off the jeep and run towards the chaos.

SOMEONE (O.S) (CONT'D)

We know him. He keeps coming here. Suddenly there was loud noise of firing. We saw that few guys on the motorcycle...

Danish and gang barge in the middle of the gathered crowd. Danish sees his father's dead body and grabs the police officer standing there.

DANISH

Father! Who killed him? Who killed my dad?
One guy from the crowd points Danish to the police jeep parked there.

SOMEONE

Sir, they have caught one of the shooters.
Danish runs to the back of the jeep and pulls the arrested guy out.

DANISH

Get out Mother fucker!

He's seething with anger and starts beating him, while Asgar and Nasir hold the police officer back.

POLICE OFFICER 1

Look you can't.

ASGAR

I said stand back!

NASIR

Stay back.

DANISH

Speak, bastard! Speak. Die, bastard.

Danish tries to force the arrested guy to say something, and then suddenly shoots at him. All this while Faizal stands back, looking confused.

DANISH

Hey Faizal, let's take father's body home.
The police officer intervenes.

POLICE OFFICER 1

Listen, let the police do their procedures.

Danish shoves him away.

DANISH

This is our father. His body will go straight home. It will not go through any legal procedures. Understand?

Asgar, Nasir and Faizal lift Sardar's body. Danish joins in.

DANISH (CONT'D)

Lift it ... Uncle, give a hand here...

CUT TO:

EXT/ INT. FAIZAL'S HOUSE - DAY

Funeral procession of Sardar goes on in the house. Lots of people have gathered to pay their respects among police security. Fazlu is there too. A live band performs and their lead singer sings a sad song. Inside the house family is in mourning. Nagma is shattered, Shama consoles her. Faizal watches everything quietly. Faizal and Mohsina steal a look at each other. Nasir watches them. They all lift the dead body and carry it away for burial.

CUT TO:

EXT. RAMADHIR HOUSE - GARDEN - DAY

Ramadhir is meeting with a senior bureaucrat and the police officer, who was earlier seen investigating Sardar's murder.

BUREAUCRAT

This will now be a good year, Mr Singh. The officers feel at peace for the first time in twelve years.

POLICE OFFICER 1

I fear it won't last long. We had one Sardar Khan, but he has four sons from him...

Ramadhir intervenes.

RAMADHIR SINGH

Five.

They can't understand.

BUREAUCRAT
Sorry?

RAMADHIR SINGH
Five. Four from the first wife and one from the second. The second one is a cook at my place.

A young boy (around 8 years old) serves them snacks. Ramadhir puts an arm at his shoulder.

RAMADHIR SINGH (CONT'D)
He is Sardar Khan's fifth son.

Ramadhir asks the boy.

RAMADHIR SINGH (CONT'D)
What's your name?

The boy responds.

DEFINITE
Definite.

RAMADHIR SINGH
Why Definite?

DEFINITE
Because I have a definite ambition in life.

RAMADHIR SINGH
What's your ambition?

DEFINITE
Sardar Khan's death.

RAMADHIR SINGH
But Sardar Khan is dead.

The boy looks confused. Ramadhir laughs.

CUT TO:

INT. FAIZAL'S HOUSE - NIGHT
Shama is in the kitchen with other women of the house. Rest of the family is having dinner. Nagma is sitting around and staring into space.

SHAMA PARVEEN
How many chapattis are done?

NAGMA' SISTER
Eight or ten...

SHAMA PARVEEN
Can we hurry up a bit? They're all waiting. I'll serve some dal till then.

Shama serves dal to Danish.

DANISH
That's enough.

Nagma comments.

NAGMA
How do you all manage to digest your food?

They all seem taken aback. Danish stops eating and leaves the table.

CUT TO:

INT. FAIZAL'S HOUSE - DANISH'S ROOM - NIGHT
Danish is sitting alone in dark. Shama walks in and switches on the light. Danish wipes his tears.

SHAMA PARVEEN
Even I belong to Sultan bhaijaan's family.

DANISH
You belong to my family.

SHAMA PARVEEN
And my parents?

DANISH
They are my parents too.

SHAMA PARVEEN
But how do we deal with what mom just said?

Danish puts a finger to her lip.

CUT TO:

INT. FAZLU'S HOUSE - NIGHT

Fazlu is giving pep talk to Faizal. A phone rings in the background.

FAZLU

You were the one who boasted that, you'll kill Sanjeev Kumar and piss on him. Now that someone else has killed him, you're burning…

Fazlu is interrupted by his mother's shout from the inside room.

FAZLU'S MOTHER (O.S.)

Fazlu … Saggir bhaijaan's call for you…

FAZLU

Yes, coming mom…

Fazlu hands over the pot to Faizal and gets up.

FAZLU (CONT'D)

Go to hell!

Faizal sits thinking.

CUT TO:

INT. FAIZAL'S HOUSE - NIGHT

Danish is advising Faizal. Asgar is also there.

DANISH

You'll be in trouble if you don't stay alert. Fazlu got you to smoke pot and get stoned. He himself called Sultan to inform him that Sardar is travelling alone.

ASGAR

Sultan was on the motorcycle himself. Saggir was also there with him and another guy.

DANISH

And you're so dumb … you were happily hanging out with Fazlu. Look Faizal, you've learn to cheat a cheater.

CUT BACK TO:

INT. FAZLU'S HOUSE - NIGHT

Faizal sits thinking. Fazlu can be heard on the phone in another room.

FAZLU

At Rajhans Mansion? Tomorrow morning? No, no, I can't make it.

Fazlu can be heard disconnecting the phone. Faizal is sitting the same place. He has Danish's voice in his mind.

DANISH (V.O.)

If you don't have the guts for it, say so.

CUT TO:

INT. RAJHANS MANSION - DAY

Danish and Asgar look for someone in Rajhans mansion. They check each shop. Asgar peeps into one shop and dismisses someone.

ASGAR

Nah!

They don't find who they're looking for.

DANISH

Not here.

ASGAR

Faizal had said he'll be here. At 11.

DANISH

What time is it?

Asgar looks upto the sky. Danish suddenly notices Saggir and shoots at him. Saggir falls. Danish pumps another bullet into him, then takes out a dagger and stabs his eye. Asgar hurries him.

ASGAR

Let's leave son.

Danish looks for something around the dead body.

ASGAR (CONT'D)

What are you doing? Hurry up. People will start gathering, let's go.

Danish walks away from the body, still looking for something. Asgar notices a passerby looking and fires in the air to scare him.

CUT TO:

INT. FAIZAL'S HOUSE - DAY

Nagma is picking lice from her youngest son's hair. Danish's son is sitting around.

NAGMA

Stay away from long haired girls. Look, this one's so fat!

Danish and Asgar come in. Danish asks the kids to go away.

DANISH

Boys, go to your rooms.

He gives the bullets to Nagma. Nagma gets serious. Danish asks the maid for Shama.

DANISH

Where is Shama?

Maid points upstairs. Danish leaves.

CUT TO:

INT. FAIZAL'S HOUSE - BATHROOM - DAY

Danish is having a bath. Shama sits at the bathroom door.

SHAMA PARVEEN

Can I ask something?

DANISH

Go ahead.

SHAMA PARVEEN

Can't you leave all this and pay attention to your family more?

Danish does not look too pleased.

CUT TO:

INT. FAIZAL'S HOUSE - DANISH'S BEDROOM - DAY

Danish is getting into clothes. Shama hands him fresh clothes. Danish appears upset.

DANISH

Begging for your brother's life? Huh?

SHAMA PARVEEN

No, yours.

DANISH

Shama Parveen, don't interfere in my work.

Danish leaves.

CUT TO:

EXT. STREETS - DAY

Danish and Asgar driving in a jeep.

ASGAR

What will you do now?

CUT TO:

INT. POLICE STATION - DAY

Danish walks into the police station and sits in front of a police inspector.

DANISH

I've come to surrender … for stealing wood.

CUT TO:

INT. JAIL - DAY

A cop is taking Danish inside a jail. He holds Danish by a rope tied to his hand. Danish asks him to hold the rope a bit loosely.

DANISH

Relax there, will you?

CUT TO:

INT. COURT - DAY

Someone announces in a packed courtroom.

(O.S.)

Bring in Danish Khan.

Danish is brought to stand in the witness box.

CUT TO:

(I/C)

EXT. COURT - DAY

It's a usual busy day outside a court. Sultan drives into the court compound on a scooter. Fazlu is his pillion.

SULTAN

Faizal … Police??

FAZLU

There are cops here.

SULTAN

Fuck them.

CUT BACK TO:

INT. COURT - DAY

Danish is answering questions of the prosecutor.

DANISH

I couldn't control my anger, so I had threatened him … to kill him. But that day, I wasn't there in Rajhans mansion at all.

PROSECUTOR

Why did you surrender then?

DANISH

I had stopped a train and unloaded wood from it. Someone said it's illegal and that I should go to the police before police catches you.

JUDGE (O.S.)

Do you have any other witness?

PROSECUTOR

No, your honour.

JUDGE

You are released with a fine of Rs. 500. If the fine is not paid, then 15 days imprisonment.

CUT TO:

EXT. COURT - DAY

As Danish walks out free with his colleague, he is shot by Sultan and Fazlu. Fazlu scares people off by firing in the air.

FAZLU

Bastards! Run you bastards!

They escape.

CUT TO:

EXT. RAILWAY TRACKS - DAY

Faizal takes a drag from chillum. A train passes by, Faizal opens his eyes.

CUT TO:

EXT. FAIZAL'S HOUSE - DAY

A lot of crowd has gathered. Faizal walks in. Guddu informs him about Danish's death. Same old band is performing a song. Asgar sees Faizal and takes him inside. He asks Guddu to wait outside, but Faizal takes him along when he goes inside.

CUT TO:

INT. FAIZAL'S HOUSE - DAY

Danish's body is lying on the floor. Covered. Shama Parveen is heartbroken, but not crying. Mohsina is trying to console her. Faizal comes and stands, soaks in everything. He drinks some water from an earthen pot. Qamar Makhdoomi, Badoor Quereshi and Ehsan Quereshi stand in a corner. Faizal asks Asgar something, probably about his mother Nagma. Asgar signals that she is upstairs. Faizal goes upstairs.

CUT TO:

INT. FAIZAL'S HOUSE - NAGMA'S ROOM - DAY

As Faizal walks to Nagma's room, she can be heard talking to someone.

NAGMA

I don't think he can do anything. His life is in pot. To lose your son that young … Danish was my first child.

Nagma is with Nasir. Faizal comes inside and stands. She sees him.

NASIR

Calm down. I understand your…

NAGMA (CONT'D)

Faizal, when will your blood boil at all this? You were dead stoned when your father was murdered. Now your brother's been killed in broad daylight! When on earth will you take to arms? When will you stop wasting your life with your druggy friends, and avenge your father's and brother's deaths?

Faizal just stares.

NAGMA (CONT'D)

Look at your stoned eyes … red…

Nasir tries to pacify her.

NASIR

Oh Nagma…

NAGMA

If all your fingers are good for stuffing your mouth with food, then I might as well feed you with my hands…

NASIR

Oh Nagma...

Nagma goes on insulting Faizal.

NAGMA

Why are you staring at me?

She goes and picks up a knife, comes to him.

NAGMA (CONT'D)

Give I'll chop them off.

Nasir intervenes.

NASIR

Nagma, have you gone mad? Have you gone mad?

NAGMA

Yes, let me chop all the ten fingers off.

Faizal holds her hands to stop her, while Nagma goes on.

FAIZAL

Old woman, you will cut your own fingers.

NAGMA

Yes, cut them. Get your hands off me bastard.

Nasir intervenes again.

NASIR

This is madness Nagma!

FAIZAL

Old woman...

NASIR

Are you mad!

Faizal doesn't like Nasir interfering.

FAIZAL

Shut up! (to Nasir) Please don't interfere.

Nagma starts crying.

FAIZAL (CONT'D)

I swear on you, this son of yours will avenge everybody - father, grandfather, brother. Don't cry my old lady.

Faizal pulls her close and holds her.

NAGMA

Old lady can't see all her sons vanish before her…

CUT TO:

INT. FAIZAL OFFICE - DAY

Faizal sits with Nasir and Asgar. He keeps filling his chillum.

ASGAR

Faizal, staying stoned all the time won't make you forget Danish's death.

FAIZAL

Who wants to forget it, uncle?

NASIR

It's been a month since we buried him.

FAIZAL

I know that.

ASGAR

If you know, then what are you doing about it?

FAIZAL

The same thing that you are … counting days…

CUT TO:

EXT. STREETS - DAY

Fazlu in a jeep. Garlands around his neck. A victory rally.

(V.O.)

Long live Wasseypur's new youth leader - Fazlu Ahmed!

The cheers continue. Fazlu stands waving at people. Faizal watches this from his office balcony. He pulls at his chillum.

CUT TO:

INT. FAIZAL'S OFFICE - NIGHT

Faizal comes in from the balcony, smoking chillum. Nasir watches him as he takes out a dagger from a cupboard.

NASIR

Where are you going?

FAIZAL

Fazlu has won the election today.

Nasir stares at him.

NASIR

Take someone along...

FAIZAL

He's a friend of mine. I will go by myself to congratulate him.

CUT TO:

INT. FAIZAL KHAN'S HOUSE - NAGMA'S ROOM - NIGHT

Nagma is sitting with Shama Parveen. Her plate of food lies untouched.

NAGMA

Eat something. What happened?

She looks at the door. Faizal enters. He comes and kisses his mother on the forehead and leaves.

NAGMA (CONT'D)

When will you stop blaming yourself?

Shama Parveen doesn't say anything, just cries.

CUT TO:

INT. FAZLU'S HOUSE - NIGHT

Chitrahaar (a program of Hindi film songs) is on.

The whole house overflows with people. Drinks floating around. Fazlu's friends are hailing him.

FRIENDS

(singing in unison) Long live Fazlu!

Fazlu is clearly enjoying it.

FAZLU

Shut up, bastards!

Someone calls.

FAIZAL

Fazlu…Fazlu…

It's Faizal. Fazlu reacts happily.

FAZLU

Hey Faizal … hey, my friend's here.

Fazlu gets up and makes way in the crowd to come out.

FAZLU (CONT'D)

Get off the way … Hey Faizal … where were you brother? I've won the election. There's celebration at home. Where were you?

CUT TO:

EXT. MANDIR - NIGHT

Faizal and Fazlu are sitting in a temple ground … smoking chillum.

FAIZAL

At home everyone looks down at me. When I step out, everyone laughs at me … bastards!

FAZLU

Why?

FAIZAL

Because all the fuckers say that Faizal sacrificed his father and brother in the name of friendship. My old woman says that if I wasn't born, there wouldn't be any mourning at Sardar Khan's house.

FAZLU

How do you mean?

FAIZAL

I mean, just light it.

Fazlu takes the chillum. Faizal lights it. Fazlu pulls. Fazlu coughs.

FAZLU

Fuck - it's loaded!

Faizal stares at him.

FAZLU (CONT'D)

Why're you staring at me?

FAIZAL

I used to think that I'm a Bachchan born into Sanjeev Kumar family. But then it turns out that I'm actually Shashi Kapoor … Someone else is the Bachchan…

Fazlu starts laughing.

FAZLU

Who?

FAIZAL

You motherfucker!

Just then Faizal pulls out the Khanjar (Dagger) and slashes Fazlu's neck. Fazlu collapses. Faizal pulls him down and slashes at his neck till he cuts the head off.

CUT TO:

EXT. FAZLU'S HOUSE - NIGHT

Fazlu's mother hurries out of her room as the door is knocked.

FAZLU'S MOTHER

Coming … coming…

She opens the door. Fazlu's head hangs outside the door in a transparent polythene bag. She screams and faints.

CUT TO:

MONTAGE BEGINS ON MUSIC.

INT. CLASSROOM - DAY
Young Faizal is narrating a poem in class.

CUT TO:

INT. FAIZAL'S OFFICE - NIGHT
Bundles of money kept on a table in front of Faizal. Someone hands him a chillum and he smokes from it.

NASIR (V.O)
After butchering Fazlu in broad daylight, Faizal's power and influence shot up astronomically. The ruthless manner in which he got rid of Fazlu made people fear him...

EXT. SOMEPLACE - DAY
Iron scrap is being unloaded and moved.

NASIR (V.O.)
All those in the illegal trade of stolen iron were scared.

CUT TO:

EXT. SCRAP YARD - DAY
Few traders sit and discuss business. Iron scrap is being weighed on a machine. Another trader joins them.

NASIR (V.O.)
The situation became such that every one of those iron smugglers became his cronies ... Irrespective of where the iron was cut.

CUT BACK TO:

INT. FAIZAL'S OFFICE - NIGHT
Faizal takes another drag.

NASIR (V.O.)

…or sold…all of it happened under Faizal Khan's supervision…And even the police was well aware of this.

CUT TO:

INT. POLICE STATION - DAY

Asgar walks into the police station. Asgar openly puts some money on the table. Cop pockets it. Music.

NASIR (V.O.)

… at every police station, there was an arrangement…

CUT TO:

EXT. RAILWAY SCRAP YARD - DAY

Faizal hands over some money to a cop. The cop pockets it. Faizal leaves … Music.

NASIR (V.O.)

And so all policemen would happily turn a blind eye to all this illegal trade…

CUT BACK TO:

INT. FAIZAL'S OFFICE - NIGHT

Faizal is laughing. He's sitting with a few people, including Guddu and the same trader we saw in the scrapyard scene. They all smoke up.

CUT TO:

EXT. FAIZAL GODOWN - DAY

A big godown saying FK Traders. Decorated. It's just opened. Faizal's family including Nagma are there for the occasion. Drums are being played. Sweets distributed … Celebration. Music. Faizal Khan walks greeting the crowd.

NASIR (V.O.)

After that, he set up an Iron Godown (Warehouse) on twenty *kattas* (6000 square metres) of land, and his business became stable...

CUT TO:

EXT. MOHSINA'S HOUSE - NIGHT

Faizal walks up to Mohsina's house. He climbs the pipe to get into Mohsina's balcony.

CUT TO:

INT. MOHSINA'S HOUSE - MOHSINA'S ROOM - NIGHT

Mohsina is watching a sensuous song, *Bharo maang meri bharo,* on TV. She's lying on the bed and totally into the song. Faizal comes into the room and sits next to her, without distracting her. He eyes her cleavage.

MOHSINA

This song is very ... you know?

FAIZAL

You're also very ... you know?

MOHSINA

Huh?

Mohsina doesn't pay attention to what he says.

FAIZAL

I want to ask your permission for something.

MOHSINA

What?

FAIZAL

You won't mind, right?

FAIZAL

I want to have sex with you.

Now he has her attention.

MOHSINA

Do you want a bashing?

She gets up and begins to shove him away.

MOHSINA (CONT'D)
Come'on … it's enough … get out now.

FAIZAL
But you said you won't mind.

She pushes him out to the balcony, from where he came.

MOHSINA
Yeah right! Come'on. Get out now. Or I'll start yelling and call everyone.

FAIZAL
Ok … ok.

Faizal leaves.

CUT TO:

EXT. STATIONERY SHOP - DAY

Mohsina is looking at books to buy. Faizal is standing behind her, reading from a list of movies running in cinemas.

FAIZAL
Dilwale Dulhaniya Le Jayenge?

MOHSINA
Seen it four times.

FAIZAL
Hum Aapke Hain Kaun?

MOHSINA
It's gone already.

FAIZAL
Rangeela?

MOHSINA
Seen it.

FAIZAL
Karan Arjun?

No response from Mohsina. Faizal jumps at the opportunity.

FAIZAL (CONT'D)
Come on … Let's go for Karan Arjun.

She asks the shop guy for another book.

MOHSINA
Show me that.

FAIZAL
It has both Shahrukh and Salman.

She shakes her head in negative.

MOHSINA
You'll hold my hand.

FAIZAL
I won't.

MOHSINA
You won't pinch my cheeks?

FAIZAL
Swear on my mother, I won't touch them.

MOHSINA
And you won't grope my lap to 'look for popcorn'?

FAIZAL
Swear on my mother, I won't look for it.

MOHSINA
No? Will you try to sit close to me?

FAIZAL
Swear on my mother, I won't.

MOHSINA
Then why don't you go with your mother only. You don't need me.

Faizal is shocked. She gives the books to the shopkeeper and wraps up her shopping.

MOHSINA (CONT'D)
Here … And give me two pencils also.

CUT TO:

INT. FAIZAL KHAN'S HOUSE - DAY

As Faizal is leaving for work his mother fusses around.

NAGMA

Take someone along with you. What if someone attacks you from behind?

FAIZAL

Old woman, in this line of work, there are a couple of things you can't trust: First, the fear within you, and second - anyone else's association. Death is certain. I have only one life. Either Allah (Almighty) will take it or the Mohalla (neighbourhood).

NAGMA

God Forbid!

Wears his clothes. Walks to her.

FAIZAL (CONT'D)

The guy who orphaned me - Fazlu. I used to trust him more than myself. But what came of it? Anyway, let it be.

Nagma looks at him go.

CUT TO:

INT. HOTEL IN BENARAS - DAY

Faizal smokes pot while two guys display some guns to Guddu.

VENDOR 1

You just have to press this button once, all bullets will pour out.

Guddu is convinced and mentions his gun shopping list.

GUDDU

I want 15 pieces of these and 12 of those.

VENDOR 2
Is that all?

GUDDU
Yes, boss wants just these many.

Vendor 1's pager goes off and he takes it out to check the message. Faizal notices this.

FAIZAL
What's that?

VENDOR 1
Pager.

FAIZAL
What does it do?

VENDOR 1
You send a message through it. It's like you call someone from your home land-line and tell him that I've to give this message. So he sends a written message.

FAIZAL
Who do you give the message to?

VENDOR 1
I have the message, so I have to send the message.

FAIZAL
Who gives it?

VENDOR 1
Whoever has some work?

FAIZAL
No, but who gives it?

VENDOR 1
Anyone - my family, my friends.

CUT TO:

EXT. FAIZAL'S OFFICE - DAY
Faizal walks out of the office in style, with a pager hanging on his waist. Music.

CUT TO:

EXT/ INT. MOHSINA'S HOUSE - DAY

Faizal arrives in his jeep outside Mohsina's house. Mohsina's younger sister sees him and goes in to tell Mohsina. Mohsina comes running out to the balcony. Faizal steps out of his jeep oozing lots of forced style - almost comic. Mohsina throws him a flying kiss. They flirt with each other. Faizal walks towards the house. Mohsina rushes inside her room to add make up. When she steps out of her room she notices that Faizal is sitting down with her parents, entertaining them with his new pager. Snacks are being served. Mohsina is surprised. She dances with joy and then joins everyone. All look happy. Faizal leaves. Music.

CUT TO:

EXT. GANGA - BOAT - NIGHT

Faizal and Guddu travel in a boat with a consignment of guns.

CUT TO:

INT. FAIZAL'S GODOWN - DAY

Some Faizal men sit together drinking and talking. Faizal is standing a little away, smoking, listening to Nawed.

NAWED (O.S.)

Merely holding a gun doesn't make you a Don.

Faizal is stoned.

NAWED (CONT'D)

Killing Sultan and Ramadhir Singh is no child's play. You need guts to do that. And how many has Faizal killed anyway? Just Fazlu … that too by conning him with friendship. For now people seem afraid, but that fear will soon evaporate.

Faizal gets up. Comes around in front of Nawed.

NAWED (CONT'D)

What say, brother… Am I wrong? Check this out. Brother, any clue what day of the week it is today?

Faizal shoots him point blank. Nawed falls down dead. Faizal puts his gun in and walks out … All stare after him … Music.

CUT TO:

INT. RAMADHIR HOUSE - DAY

Faizal and Ramadhir are sitting face to face and talking.

FAIZAL

I've sworn on my mother that I'll lay your dead body at her feet.

RAMADHIR SINGH

Why?

FAIZAL

Because you've killed my father.

RAMADHIR SINGH

If I hadn't killed him, he would have killed me.

FAIZAL

Because you killed his father.

RAMADHIR SINGH

Yes. But he would have killed me too. That's where everything began in the first place … Faizal, I have no animosity towards you, or your father, or your brother. I killed them, so that I could stay alive. Tell me who wants to die without a reason?

Faizal appears amused … he is thinking.

FAIZAL

What do you want?

RAMADHIR SINGH

I won't come in your way. You rule Wasseypur …do whatever you want … mint as much money as you want. The Dhanbad government will be with you. If our men make any mistakes, you can shoot us. But if you make a mistake, then we'll also have to take the necessary steps. You shouldn't mind then.

CUT TO:

EXT. STREETS - LASSI SHOP - DAY

Sultan and JP are having lassi at a street corner shop.

SULTAN

Your father has joined hands with those people, and now expects us to forget about everything? That bastard chopped Fazlu into pieces … you expect me to forget it?

J.P. SINGH

So you also killed his brother and father. Didn't you? Didn't you? My father has declared that there should be no attack on Faizal now.

SULTAN

What if he attacks us?

J.P. SINGH

Then handle it … but don't involve us.

CUT TO:

INT. FAIZAL'S GODOWN - DAY

A door opens. A man silhouetted at the door. He puts on the light. It's Faizal. Another man tied on a charpoy. Faizal shuts the door. Comes and sits on a chair next to the charpoy … He notices that the tied man has pissed in his pants. He checks under his pants.

FAIZAL

Have you crapped also? (adds calmly) Where is Khalid?

Man looks at Faizal. Cloth in mouth.

CUT TO:

INT. SOMEPLACE - DAY

Khalid beats up a man by banging his head on a wall.

FREEZE FRAME

NASIR (V.O.)

Khalid - Sultan's main henchman.

CUT TO:

EXT. PETROL PUMP/ROAD - DAY

Repeat scene

Sardar Khan is shot at by Sultan and his men including Khalid.

Freeze frame-on the Khalid escaping.

NASIR (V.O.)

He unleashes mayhem when he's accompanied by his men. But when alone he wouldn't even venture out of his house.

CUT BACK TO:

INT. FAIZAL'S GODOWN - DAY

Unfreeze - The man tied on the charpoy.

FAIZAL

How much does he give you? A few morsels and leftover meat? Work with me, and you'll get a whole goat every month.

Man stares. Faizal takes out the gun.

FAIZAL (CONT'D)

Now tell me, where do I shoot you?

Faizal puts the gun up his ass.

FAIZAL (CONT'D)
In the ass? In the intestines? Or…

Puts it on his chin and takes it away after holding it for a bit.

FAIZAL (CONT'D)
Should I let you go?

The man is scared. He replies inaudibly through the cloth tied on his mouth.

MAN
Let me go.

Faizal can't understand him.

FAIZAL
What?

MAN
Let me go.

FAIZAL
Let you go? Okay. You will inform us about all his whereabouts. And if you try to deceive me … I'll bury you wherever I find you standing.

CUT TO:

EXT. LAKE - DAY

Faizal and Mohsina are sitting on the bank of a lake. Romantic spot. Serious conversation. Faizal confesses.

FAIZAL
I smoke pot, hash. I've killed Fazlu … and a few more. I've done time in a jail too. You also tell me whatever you've done.

Mohsina whispers something in Faizal's ears. Faizal is surprised at hearing this.

CUT TO:

EXT. MOHSINA'S HOUSE - DAY

Preparations for wedding are on. Decoration lights are being put up...Gifts and sweets being brought in ... lots of people.

CUT TO:

INT. MOHSINA'S HOUSE - DAY

Lots of women sit together singing and dancing. It's Mohsina's haldi ceremony. Nagma is leading the singing and other women do chorus. Shama and Mohsina dance with other girls. Towards the end of the song, Nagma gets emotional. Shama consoles her.

CUT TO:

INT. MOHSINA'S HOUSE - LIVING ROOM - DAY

Wedding of Faizal and Mohsina in progress. Qazi conducts the ceremony first with Faizal.

PRIEST

... Masood Hamid, 1st witness - Nizamuddin, Main Road Jhariya Dhanbad, 2nd witness - Mukhtar Ansari - Naipar, Ramzanpur, Dhanbad. I registrar Priest, I offer you the hand of Mohsina Hamid, daughter of Masood Hamid, for an alimony of Rs. 11,151, in front of all these people present here. Do you accept it?

FAIZAL

Yes.

PRIEST

Do you accept it?

FAIZAL

Yes.

PRIEST

Do you accept it?

FAIZAL

Yes.

CUT TO:

INT. MOHSINA'S HOUSE - MOHSINA'S ROOM - DAY

Qazi now conducts the ceremony with Mohsina in the women's room.

PRIEST

I'm about to execute your marriage to Faizal Khan, son of Sardar Khan. Do I have your permission for it?

MOHSINA

Yes.

PRIEST

Do I have your permission for it?

MOHSINA

Yes.

PRIEST

Do I have your permission for it?

MOHSINA

Yes.

Everyone including Nagma, Shama and other women congratulate her on the wedding.

CUT TO:

INT. FAIZAL'S HOUSE - NAGMA'S BEDROOM - NIGHT

Bed post shakes vigorously. Love making noises. Loud orgasmic moans of Mohsina can be heard. A painting falls of the wall.

NAGMA

What broke?

CUT TO:

INT. FAIZAL'S HOUSE - NASIR'S ROOM - NIGHT

Nasir is up on his bed, listening to sounds from Faizal's and Nagma's rooms. Nagma screams out her advice to Faizal.

NAGMA (O.S.)

Either go off to sleep or lay the mattress on the floor.

CUT TO:

EXT. FAIZAL'S HOUSE - FAIZAL'S BEDROOM - NIGHT

Faizal comes out of his bedroom and goes down to drink water from the kitchen. Nasir watches him drink water and go back to his room. Nasir goes back to his meditation.

CUT TO:

INT. FAIZAL'S HOUSE - NASIR'S ROOM - NIGHT

Nasir flagellates himself with a whip. He intensifies his whipping as he hears more love-making sounds from Faizal's room.

CUT TO:

INT. FAIZAL'S HOUSE - NAGMA'S BEDROOM - NIGHT

To shut off the love making sounds, Nagma puts her hands on her ears and tries to go to sleep.

CUT TO:

INT. FAIZAL'S HOUSE - FAIZAL'S BEDROOM - DAY

Nasir knocks on Faizal's door. Faizal opens the door

NASIR

Some guy is here with news of Khalid.

FAIZAL (O.S.)

Where is my pistol?

MOHSINA (O.S.)

In your pants … (laughs)

MOHSINA (CONT'D)

Where are you going?

Faizal cocks his pistol. As he comes out of the room, Mohsina follows him out. Nagma's voice can be heard in the background from the lower floor.

She's giving advice to the maid about drying clothes.

NAGMA (O.S.)

Get it? You've to wash coloured clothes separate from white clothes ... if they're cotton. Georgette can be mixed.

Mohsina says hello to Nagma.

MOHSINA

Hello mom!

Faizal climbs down to the lower floor and walks towards Nagma.

NAGMA

See, you can see all the ironing marks here. And does it look white to you?

Faizal kisses her on the forehead and leaves. Nagma calls after him.

NAGMA (O.S.) (CONT'D)

Faizal?

CUT TO:

EXT. FAIZAL KHAN'S OFFICE - DAY

Faizal walks towards his office ... Nasir with him...

NASIR

Faizal ... An enemy ... he's come to our place. Doesn't seem right to me...

FAIZAL

You take care of the house and mom. Let me handle the work...

ASGAR

Faizal, he's a close aide of Khalid's...

FAIZAL

Was a close aide ... now he's mine ... You go look after the house.

Nasir doesn't like it, still follows Faizal.

CUT TO:

INT. FAIZAL'S OFFICE - DAY

Faizal and his men enter the room. The Man is sitting with Asgar. Asgar holds a gun on him...

FAIZAL

Where is Khalid?

MAN

He's stepped out alone for breakfast at Mooli crossing. His family has gone on Pilgrimage, so eats out often.

Faizal wears his glasses and checks his pistol. He walks out. His other men follow him, but he asks them not to.

FAIZAL

I don't want anyone following me ... In case I don't return, finish him off.

He walks out. Nasir looks.

CUT TO:

EXT. DHABA - DAY

Khalid has his tea alone ... Faizal's jeep stops outside. There's a barber with him. Faizal gets off and asks the barber to get off.

FAIZAL

Step out ... come, come.

Faizal walks up to Khalid. Followed by the barber. He fires in the air to scare the other customers off.

FAIZAL

Everyone run along ... c'mon.

Others run away.

FAIZAL (CONT'D)

Hey, asshole, how's it going?

KHALID

Forgive me Faizal brother.

Khalid starts pleading with Faizal. Faizal asks the barber to shave his head.

FAIZAL

Shave him bald.

Khalid stops the barber and continues pleading with Faizal.

KHALID

(to the barber) Stop. (to Faizal) I'll get you Sultan.

FAIZAL

What a complete two-faced bastard you are. I'll get Sultan myself.

KHALID

Faizal brother, look, we are both muslims. Even Allah forgets one mistake.

Faizal puts a gun on his head.

FAIZAL

C'mon. Shave him.

The barber scared … Hands shaking … Starts to shave off his hair … Faizal watches amused. Looks at shaved Khalid … Smiles … Takes off his glasses…

FAIZAL

Wear these.

KHALID

Forgive me please.

FAIZAL

Wear them.

Khalid wears them.

FAIZAL (CONT'D)

You look exactly like *Shakaal*.

He shoots him.

CUT TO:

EXT. DHABA - DAY

Lots of people and policemen stand at the spot where Khalid was killed. Sultan, Ali and Jabbar are at a phone booth at the same dhaba. Sultan's on the phone.

SULTAN

That bastard Faizal shaved and shot him, and we should twiddle our thumbs? What? Don't keep mumbling about your father. Go and speak to him.

CUT TO:

INT. RAMADHIR OFFICE - DAY

JP walks into Ramadhir's cabin. Ramadhir is in a meeting with some bureaucrats.

RAMADHIR SINGH

It's a highway. All the way from Patna to Kolkata. Will cross the Ganga river. Its tender will be out soon.

JP interrupts.

J.P. SINGH

Papa.

Ramadhir listens. JP hesitates, but speaks.

J.P. SINGH (CONT'D)

Sultan called.

Ramadhir gets irritated.

RAMADHIR SINGH

You go out and arrange for some tea or snacks.

CUT TO:

INT. RAMADHIR OFFICE - ANOTHER ROOM - DAY

JP is drinking tea with some friends. Ramadhir walks in.

RAMADHIR SINGH
What's going on here? Musical chairs? Get out!

The friends disappear. JP begins to explain.

J.P. SINGH
Papa, we're just…

RAMADHIR SINGH
I've told you a thousand times that don't bring up a goon's name in front of other people.

JP explains.

J.P. SINGH
Faizal's shot the guy who killed Sardar Khan.

RAMADHIR SINGH
So why is that a problem?

J.P. SINGH
But he was our man Papa!

RAMADHIR SINGH
Not ours. Sultan's man. And Sultan is not our man any more.

J.P. SINGH
But he still works for…

RAMADHIR SINGH
You … stick your sentiments up your arse. You while away all your time in petty politics with your good-for-nothing friends. Instead you should go to your elected region, motivate people there … Where were you last night by the way?

J.P. SINGH
I'd gone for a movie.

RAMADHIR SINGH
Which movie?

J.P. SINGH

Dilwale Dulhaniya Le Jaayenge.

RAMADHIR SINGH

Son, I don't think you have it in you. You're good for nothing.

CUT TO:

EXT. FAIZAL OFFICE - DAY

Faizal gets of his Jeep with a goat and walks towards his office. Asgar and Guddu watch from the balcony. Faizal blows a whistle. Guddu runs down. Faizal puts the goat in the Guddu's hand.

FAIZAL

Here...Give him the whole goat ... and let him go.

Faizal walks towards his house.

CUT TO:

EXT. FAIZAL'S HOUSE - DAY

As Faizal walks into the house, Perpendicular - his younger brother walks out. He is in school uniform with a school bag on his shoulder. We follow Perpendicular.

NASIR (V.O.)

Babu Khan alias Babua alias Perpendicular. The youngest brother... He was fourteen years old but crime was child's play to him...

As Perpendicular gets away from the house, he takes out a blade from his pocket and puts it in his mouth.

CUT TO:

EXT. RIVER BANK - DAY

Perpendicular and Tangent (his friend) are sitting on an iron slab at an isolated spot on a river bank. Guddu is giving instructions to them on how to use a blade for attack.

GUDDU

You see this blade. If you use it sideways, nothing will happen. So always hold it like this and use it perpendicularly. Do you know what's perpendicular?

PERPENDICULAR

Yes.

GUDDU

What?

Perpendicular responds with demonstration.

PERPENDICULAR

Like this iron slab, I'm perpendicular to it.

GUDDU

If you have a dead body, then the blade must have been perpendicular. If you just have slit skin, then it was tangent.

Guddu hands the blade to Perpendicular.

GUDDU (CONT'D)

Take it and go. Tell me later what happened.

CUT TO:

INT. FAIZAL'S HOUSE - PERPENDICULAR'S ROOM - DAY

Perpendicular is playing with the blade in his mouth in front of a mirror.

NASIR (V.O.)

People were not as terrorized by Faizal khan as by Perpendicular… A fourteen year old kid who dabbled with a blade in his mouth…

CUT TO:

INT. PERPENDICULAR CLASSROOM - DAY

A teacher questions Tangent while holding him by his hair. Just then Perpendicular comes up and slashes the teacher's neck in front of other kids. Blood flows out. Both Perpendicular and Tangent run away…

NASIR (V.O.)

All he knew was that if you placed that blade against human flesh, there will be blood.

CUT TO:

EXT. RIVER BANK - DAY

Perpendicular and Tangent come to meet Guddu. Perpendicular happily reports.

PERPENDICULAR

I hit perpendicular, he hit tangent.

CUT TO:

EXT. STREET - DAY

Perpendicular running in alleys. Cops chase him and fire at him. Perpendicular dodges the bullets…

NASIR (V.O.)

He had many run ins with the police … and escaped unscathed every time…

CUT TO:

EXT. SCHOOL GROUND - DAY

Perpendicular with his friends,

PERPENDICULAR

They were shooting incessantly… One bullet grazed my ear… Boom!

CUT TO:

EXT. STREET - DAY

Perpendicular bends down as a bullet passes next to his ear.

CUT TO:

EXT. SCHOOL GROUND - DAY

Perpendicular with friends.

PERPENDICULAR

But they couldn't catch me…

CUT TO:

EXT. STREET - DAY

Perpendicular keeps running. Cops keep chasing.

CUT TO:

Perpendicular hides behind sacks of vegetables. Cops have guns on his head. He looks up... surrender in his eyes.

NASIR (V.O.)

No evidence was found against him. Nor did anyone ever testify, to escape the wrath of Faizal Khan.

INT. POLICE STATION - DAY

Perpendicular is handcuffed. He sits on the ground with his hands tied to a chair. A jeweller is standing in front of the police inspector. He looks at Perpendicular and shakes his head in a No.

JEWELLER

It isn't him.

The Police Inspector looks at Perpendicular with anger.

NASIR (V.O.)

So he always managed to get off...

CUT TO:

INT. FAIZAL'S HOUSE - PERPENDICULAR'S ROOM - DAY

Continuation of earlier shot. Perpendicular plays with the blade in his mouth and gun in his hand.

EXT. FAIZAL'S HOUSE/STREET - DAY

Perpendicular comes out of the house. Continuation of beginning shot. Tangent joins him. They walk on.

NASIR (V.O.)

His best friend was Tangent. But Tangent, who did everything together with Perpendicular, was the first to flee in case of imminent danger.

CUT TO:

INT/EXT. STREET/JEWELRY SHOP - DAY

They walk down the street to a jewelry shop. Both have guns in their hands. They take off their slippers and get into the shop. The jeweller is busy with a customer. The jeweller looks up. Perpendicular holds a gun on him…

PERPENDICULAR

My name is Perpendicular … and Faizal Khan is my elder brother. We've come to rob your shop. Don't call the police, or we'll shoot you.

Perpendicular looks at the perplexed customer and asks him to leave.

PERPENDICULAR (CONT'D)

Are you finished uncle?

The customer nods a yes.

PERPENDICULAR (CONT'D)

Go on then. Hurry up!

The customer leaves. Perpendicular asks the jeweller to open the cupboards with jewellery on display. Both he and Tangent now cover their faces with handkerchiefs.

PERPENDICULAR (CONT'D)

Give me the keys. Come'on, open it. Fast. We should mask up now, or they'll identify us. Here … give me the keys. Open it … quickly!

CUT TO:

Lots of empty Jewellery boxes are lying around.

They throw the last box down and exit the shop. Tangent puts on his slippers, but Perpendicular stops him.

PERPENDICULAR (CONT'D)
That slipper is mine.

Tangent goes for the other set of slippers and Perpendicular wears his own. Perpendicular hands over the loot to Tangent.

PERPENDICULAR (CONT'D)
Go hide it in my room...

They both leave in opposite directions.

CUT TO:

EXT. STREET - DAY
Perpendicular turns a corner. He walks down. Sees the customer from the jewellery shop on a motorbike with a police inspector. The customer points to Perpendicular. Perpendicular smiles and shows his arm to convey up yours.

INT. FAIZAL'S HOUSE - PERPENDICULAR'S ROOM. DAY
Perpendicular is getting out of his school clothes.

NASIR (V.O.)
Perpendicular got caught. And the Jeweller said -

CUT TO:

INT. POLICE STATION - DAY
Same shot in Police Station.

JEWELLER
It wasn't him.

CUT TO:

EXT. STREET - DAY
Perpendicular and Tangent walk free. They do and dance jig.

NASIR (V.O.)
Perpendicular was released.

CUT TO:

EXT. FAIZAL'S HOUSE - DAY
Nagma, her sister and Mohsina are sitting with the Jeweller on the porch, looking at some jewellery. Perpendicular enters home. His mother calls him.

NAGMA
Babua!

Perpendicular looks.

NAGMA (CONT'D)
Come here...

Nagma points to the jeweller and asks Perpendicular.

NAGMA (CONT'D)
What is he saying?

JEWELLER
Sir, that stuff you took from the shop today, the shop keys went along with it. If it can be found...

Perpendicular looks at him angrily. He looks at Nagma when she asks him.

NAGMA
What did you get from the shop?

Perpendicular does not respond. Turns and leaves. The Jeweller covers up for him.

JEWELLER
No problem, he's just a kid. Mistakes happen.

CUT TO:

INT. FAIZAL'S HOUSE - PERPENDICULAR'S ROOM - DAY
Perpendicular enters his bedroom. Pulls up the bed. Jewels lying there. Spreads it. Finds the key.

CUT TO:

EXT. FAIZAL'S HOUSE - DAY

Mohsina tries a necklace. Nagma praises it.

NAGMA (O.S.)

It's nice. Very nice.

Perpendicular drops the key in his hand. Jeweller looks.

MOHSINA

Beautiful, isn't it?

Phone rings in the background. Nagma talks to the Jeweller while Perpendicular goes inside the house.

NAGMA (O.S.)

You send the receipt in Faizal's office.

CUT TO:

INT. FAIZAL'S HOUSE - LIVING ROOM - DAY

Nasir on the phone. It's a call for Perpendicular. Nasir shouts for him.

NASIR

Babua... Babua...

Perpendicular walks to the phone. Takes it from Nasir.

PERPENDICULAR

Hello...

INTERCUT

EXT. PCO - DAY

Definite on the phone in a shop.

DEFINITE

How're we buddy?

BACK TO:

INT. FAIZAL'S HOUSE - DAY

PERPENDICULAR

Yeah, what?

INTERCUT

EXT. PCO - DAY

DEFINITE

Wanna make five grand?

BACK TO:

INT. FAIZAL'S HOUSE - DAY

Perpendicular thinks. Nasir sits behind repairing an old clock.

(V.O.) NASIR

Times had changed. Wasseypur had changed.

CUT TO:

EXT. BRIDGE - DAY

Perpendicular and Tangent arrive near a bridge, on Perpendicular's bike.

(V.O.) NASIR

It was no longer the time when there was just one Ramadhir Singh and one Sardar Khan. Now every one of them wanted to be a Sardar Khan or a Sultan...

Definite with some friends ... Definite turns in slow motion.

(V.O.) NASIR (CONT'D)

Definite. His mother had handed him a country pistol right when he was a little kid...

CUT TO:

INT. DURGA'S HOUSE - DAY

A young kid (young Definite) ready for school. Durga walks to him with a gun. Opens the bag. Puts it inside.

DURGA

Where is that matchbox you stole from me?

The kid responds with a lot of attitude.

YOUNG DEFINITE

If I had a matchbox, I'd have put the world on fire.

Durga smiles.

DURGA

Okay, go now.

Kid leaves.

YOUNG DEFINITE

Okay.

DURGA

And don't pick a fight with anybody!

CUT TO:

INT. CINEMA HALL - DAY

Young Definite is in a cinema hall watching a scene from *Maine Pyaar Kiya* - a Salman Khan film.

NASIR (V.O.)

Every guy took himself to be his own neighborhood's Sanjay Dutt, or Salman Khan. Better still, Definite was Durga's son … Sardar's own blood.

A scene from the film plays. In the scene the hero (Salman Khan) and the heroine are being ridiculed by a Villain.

CUT TO:

INT. BARBERSHOP - DAY

Few boys get haircuts the Salman Khan style. Definite is one of them.

NASIR (V.O.)

Faizal and Perpendicular were of the same bloodline … and there were new ones born everyday … The most dangerous of them was Definite…

Definite takes the comb from the barber and styles himself like Salman Khan. The cheesy dialogues of the villian from the 'Maine Pyar Kiya' scene play on his mind.

CUT TO:

INT. SOME ROOM - DAY

Definite puts on his trousers. He's with a girl who's not seen.

GIRL (O.S.)

What're you doing, Definite? I'm your friend.

DEFINITE

A girl and a boy are never friends.

GIRL (O.S.)

This was Mohnish Behl's dialogue, right?

DEFINITE

So?

CUT TO:

INT. DURGA'S HOUSE - DAY

Definite is busy with something. Durga incites Definite.

DURGA

While you're busy playing with cats and dogs, Faizal Khan is gobbling up your father's entire wealth.

DEFINITE

I don't want any part of that bastard father's territory. I want to rule the whole of Dhanbad.

CUT TO:

EXT. WASSEYPUR STREET - DAY

A snake charmer on streets. He blows on his flute as the snake sits up … Crowd surrounds him.

Definite makes his way through the crowd. He looks at them and asks the snake Charmer,

DEFINITE

Which snake is this?

SNAKE CHARMER

It's a cobra … Snake Cobra!

DEFINITE

How do you hold it?

The snake charmer holds its tail lightly and then releases it.

SNAKE CHARMER

Snake Cobra!

DEFINITE

Really?

Definite suddenly grabs the snake and runs. Everyone protests.

CROWD

Hey!

SNAKE CHARMER

Hey! My snake…

CUT TO:

INT. FAIZAL OFFICE - DAY

Faizal Khan sits in his office. The snake charmer sits in front of him. Asgar, Nasir, Guddu, Mohsina are all present.

ASGAR

He's your brother after-all. He's always been muddled … That woman who was killed in the Hindu colony after Ramzan last year … That was his handiwork…

GUDDU

He used to love her daughter. The two of them would screw around everyday … on the terrace, or in the yard. When the mother found out, she sent her daughter away to her uncle's, in Calcutta. Definite threatened to kill the mother if she didn't bring her daughter back. When the mother threw him out of the house, he got enraged … took a rod and bashed her to death.

Faizal just listens.

CUT TO:

EXT. PAAN SHOP - DAY

Definite comes to a paan shop with a snake wrapped around his hand. He asks the shopkeeper for a paan, while showing off the snake.

DEFINITE

Make a paan uncle… and make it good, or I'll unleash it in your lungi. Get it?

shopkeeper

Yes, I get it.

DEFINITE

Do you?

The shopkeeper gets working on the paan. Definite's friend comes rushing to him.

DEFINITE'S FRIEND

Hey Definite.

Definite turns.

DEFINITE'S FRIEND (CONT'D)

People are looking for you.

DEFINITE

Who's issued a warrant against *me*?

DEFINITE'S FRIEND

Faizal bhai has issued a warrant for you, understand? Now hurry up…

Definite looks pleased with the information. He asks the paanwaala to put a paan in his mouth.

DEFINITE

Give me that paan … fast.

Definite's friend puts a paan in his mouth. They start walking.

DEFINITE (CONT'D)

Do you understand? Do you know what this 'warrant' means? My time has begun.

Definite's friend asks about the snake.

DEFINITE'S FRIEND

Where did you get this?

CUT TO:

INT. FAIZAL'S OFFICE - DAY

A busy office. Definite walks in with the snake. He greets Asgar.

DEFINITE

Salaam Uncle!

Guddu notices him from the inside room where he is sitting with Faizal, Mohsina, Nasir and the snake charmer.

(O.S.) GUDDU

Definite's here…

Faizal looks as Definite walks in … snake in his hands. He wears the snake around his neck.

DEFINITE

Salaam-wallekum brother!

Faizal is amused…

FAIZAL

Do that again…

Definite doesn't understand.

DEFINITE

Salaam-wallekum!

FAIZAL
Do that again...

DEFINITE
Salaam-wallekum!

FAIZAL
Stupid, what you just did... throwing it around like a muffler...

Definite relaxes.

DEFINITE
Oh that!

He takes the snake back in his hands and wears it in his neck again. Mohsina laughs.

FAIZAL
Is it dead?

DEFINITE
No, it's alive...

FAIZAL
Why'd you run away with it?

DEFINITE
Just like that. It looked sexy...

FAIZAL
Sexy?

DEFINITE
Sure.

FAIZAL
Return it.

Definite returns it.

DEFINITE
Brother, I've been wanting to talk to you...

Faizal finishes his cigarette and gets up.

FAIZAL

Later. This shit shouldn't happen again. Let's go Mohsina.

Mohsina wraps up her makeup.

MOHSINA

Okay.

Faizal walks away. She follows. Definite keeps sitting there.

CUT TO:

EXT. BRIDGE - DAY

Back to scene on the bridge between Definite and Perpendicular.

PERPENDICULAR

What do we do?

Definite takes off his sunglasses. There is big chasm between the two sides of a broken bridge. Definite and Perpendicular look at it.

DEFINITE

It's ten feet. I've measured it.

PERPENDICULAR

You'll actually fly the bike across?

DEFINITE

Of course. You think I've randomly come up with the bet?

PERPENDICULAR

Have you done it before?

DEFINITE'S FRIEND

Many a times.

Perpendicular looks down. He sees goats grazing down below.

PERPENDICULAR

If a goat is crushed, I get to eat it.

DEFINITE
You can shove the hooves up your ass too. First decide who goes first.

PERPENDICULAR
Let's toss a coin.

Takes out a coin. Tosses it in the air.

DEFINITE
Choose.

PERPENDICULAR
Heads.

Coin falls. Definite loses.

PERPENDICULAR (CONT'D)
I win.

Perpendicular tries to pocket the coin. Definite snatches it from him.

DEFINITE
Hey, give the coin here.

PERPENDICULAR
Take it. You go first.

DEFINITE
But I have another condition. You won't copy my technique…

PERPENDICULAR
Cool. Go now.

Perpendicular makes fun of him.

PERPENDICULAR (CONT'D)
Technique, is it?

DEFINITE
I'll show you moron.

PERPENDICULAR
Yeah right! Fucker!

Definite starts preparing. He puts two wooden planks against the wall on the edge, to drive up the bike.

PERPENDICULAR (CONT'D)
What's he doing?

DEFINITE'S FRIEND
He is a master at this. He's done it a million times. He'll hit 80 on speed, take the bike up the plank and fly straight across the hill. What will you do?

Perpendicular changes his mind.

PERPENDICULAR
Wait, just listen.

DEFINITE
What?

PERPENDICULAR
Aye … I won the toss, didn't I? I've change my mind. I'll go first.

DEFINITE
That's not fair!

PERPENDICULAR
I'm *Perpendicular*. Everything I do is fair.

DEFINITE
You know the technique now. You're throwing your weight around because of your brother…

PERPENDICULAR
Why are you dragging my brother in this? Pass me the keys. Give it!

Definite hands over the keys and in the process drops some money.

DEFINITE
Take it asshole.

Perpendicular goes for the money. Definite stops him.

DEFINITE (CONT'D)
Leave the money. Give it back.

PERPENDICULAR
Take it. Tramp!

Perpendicular gets on the bike.

PERPENDICULAR (CONT'D)
Which key is it?

He puts the key in and starts the bike. Revs it up and drives from a distance. Full speed. He rides … Climbs onto the elevation … Goes up and down … Falls into the ditch … Definite laughs…

DEFINITE
Asshole!

PERPENDICULAR (O.S.)
Bloody mother fucker! You tricked me, bastard! I'll break into your house and bash you up!

CUT TO:

INT. FAIZAL'S OFFICE - DAY
Faizal slaps Definite.

DEFINITE
You shouldn't have slapped me, brother.

FAIZAL
Very fond of playing a hero, are you?

Faizal stares.

DEFINITE
I respect you a lot because you're my brother and you don't fear anybody. You should also respect me, because I don't even fear you…

Faizal stares at him. Relaxes. Faizal walks around sits down on his chair.

FAIZAL
Sit.

Definite sits down.

SUPER - 2002

NASIR (V.O.)

This is where Definite's story began. He has always wanted to be a Don. He was just looking for the right opportunity. But Definite wasn't alone. Bihar had become a jungle full of scavengers ... especially Dhanbad.

CUT TO:

EXT. DHANBAD STREETS - DAY

SUPER - 2002

A montage of streets of Dhanbad, people on the streets, stray animals etc.

NASIR (V.O.)

Meanwhile, a new state had been formed out of Bihar - Jharkhand. And all the mineral rich land including Dhanbad became a part of this new state. Now every greedy officer and criminal got a chance to rape the region. Everybody was part of this loot. The ones that weren't, wanted to be.

EXT. DHANBAD STREETS - DAY

SUPER - 2003

Faizal Khan's jeeps drive through Dhanbad streets. Shamshad stands in corner sipping tea and talking to someone as Faizal's jeeps go past.

SHAMSHAD

Please do something about getting a couple of my trucks in.

Shamshad turns to see Faizal Khan as the jeeps go past him.

NASIR (V.O.)

Faizal's notoriety gave birth to many small time criminals. Most significant amongst them was Shamshad Aalam.

CUT TO:

INT. CLOTH SHOP - DAY

Shamshad shows a yard of cloth to people.

NASIR (V.O.)

He started out as a cloth trader.

CUT TO:

EXT. TRANSPORT AREA - DAY

Many trucks standing in a transport area. Shamshad gets out of a truck.

NASIR (V.O.)

Then he got into the transport business. He acquired many trucks. When he lost interest in transport, he decided to trade in iron.

CUT TO:

INT. SHAMSHAD'S HOUSE - NIGHT

Shamshad and Nawab are together. Shamshad's mother pours them tea.

SHAMSHAD

We'll get into iron trade.

NAWAB

It's impossible to be in the Iron trade without giving Faizal Khan a share in the pie…

Shamshad brings the tea over. Hands one to Nawab.

SHAMSHAD

Fuck that! I hear one can't even steal without his blessings.

NAWAB

What'll you do then?

SHAMSHAD

He has one weakness … Money! He's all guts but has zero business sense. The fucker sells to anyone at any price. He sells stock worth

5 bucks at 2 bucks. If we fix the market price with him, he won't be able to resist a fat profit.

CUT TO:

INT. FAIZAL KHAN'S OFFICE - DAY

They sit across Faizal Khan finishing tea.

SHAMSHAD

The guys you sell to aren't even traders, they're middlemen. They buy from you at 2 bucks and sell at 4. You're being ripped off. Seriously! Bengalis don't care for iron anyway. The communist government over there doesn't care about industry. Lets sell the iron to Gujarat and Orissa directly and at higher rates. There's massive demand over there, and you have ample supply. What say? Even my transportation is sorted. I swear your meagre 2 bucks will turn into 3.5 with me.

Faizal gets up. He's still listening though. They all get up to leave after him. Mohsina joins Faizal on the way out. Shamshad greets her.

SHAMSHAD (CONT'D)

Salaam bhabhi *(sister in law)*. And whatever little share remains, we'll keep it. What do you say?

CUT TO:

INT/EXT. TENT. FELICITATION CEREMONY - DAY

Faizal and Mohsina walk up to a stage and applauding crowd. A big tent … the Wasseypur Youth Welfare Society banner. Shamshad felicitates Faizal.

SHAMSHAD (O.S.)

… the deputy chairman of Wasseypur Youth Welfare Society, Mr Gaffoor Khan.

Faizal and Mohsina come up on the stage.

SHAMSHAD (O.S.) (CONT'D)

And the honorable chairman of the Wasseypur Youth Welfare Society, our own, Mr Faizal Khan … Please put your hands together for him. And the chairperson of the Ladies wing, our bhabhi, Mohsina Khan.

Audience applauds. They are garlanded by Nawab and Shamshad.

NASIR (V.O.)

Making Faizal Khan the chairman of the fly-by-night institution, Wasseypur Youth Welfare Society, Shamshad Alam jumped headlong into the business…

CUT TO:

INT. BYPASS/ GODOWN - DAY

A big godown door opens out. Faizal walks in with Shamshad and Nawab.

NASIR (V.O.)

Within ten days, Faizal handed over the godown outside of the bypass to them. And in two months, everybody knew that Shamshad Alam was operating under Faizal Khan's protection…

Faizal shows the godown to Shamshad.

FAIZAL

This was my father's godown. After Danish left us, this had been lying idle.

NASIR (V.O.)

Then there was no stopping the incessant feasts, money, and excesses.

CUT TO:

INT. SOMEPLACE - NIGHT

Shamshad entertains a police officer with a *launda naach* (male-prostitute dance) and alcohol.

CUT TO:

EXT. STREET MARKET - DAY

Faizal and Mohsina are walking in the market. They're in an argument.

MOHSINA

Why do you keep calling mom, old lady? On the contrary, you don't look 30. You two look like siblings.

FAIZAL

Don't talk shit.

MOHSINA

Why, am I wrong? Have you seen those dark circles under your eyes? All because of Pot.

FAIZAL

Talk about yourself. You think you look 25?

MOHSINA

Why're you getting angry? Mom doesn't look above 40, and you don't look below 40.

Faizal's phone rings. He picks it up.

FAIZAL

Call me later, okay?

Faizal stops walking.

MOHSINA

Now let's go.

FAIZAL

If I look so old, why did you marry me?

MOHSINA

There's no reason to get angry. I'm just stating a fact.

Mohsina asks a random guy standing at a tailoring shop about Faizal's age.

MOHSINA (CONT'D)

Brother, what do you think his age is?

RANDOM GUY

Around 40?

Faizal gets upset at him. He takes out his pistol.

FAIZAL

Say it again! What's my age? 40?

Faizal goes close to him with the gun. The man re-estimates.

RANDOM GUY

35.

Faizal pushes his pistol against the man's stomach.

FAIZAL

35?

RANDOM GUY

24.

FAIZAL

24? Right, I've been born today you bastard.

RANDOM GUY

Happy Birthday!

Mohsina laughs and turns away. She starts taking interest in something at the next shop.

MOHSINA (O.S.)

Show me that one. Yeah, that one up there.

Faizal stares at the man angrily and puts his pistol back.

CUT TO:

INT. FAIZAL'S HOUSE - DAY

Nagma sees Perpendicular leave with his school bag.

NAGMA

Aye Babua, come here…

Perpendicular goes to her. Nagma is on the terrace with other women of the house. They are packing up food articles/ pickles that had been put out for sun-drying.

NAGMA (O.S.) (CONT'D)

That one … that's dry.

NAGMA'S SISTER (O.S.)

They're all turning into powder.

PERPENDICULAR

What is it?

NAGMA

Yes Babua. Go get this stuff from the market.

She gives him money and a list. Shama reminds her.

SHAMA PARVEEN

Mom, tea's over.

NAGMA

That's on the list.

CUT TO:

INT/EXT. GENERAL STORE - DAY

The owner hands over some stuff to someone. Looks out.

OWNER

Oh my God… Hide all the expensive stuff- Lux, Surf, and all. Perpendicular's coming here!

Perpendicular looking at the list comes to the shop.

PERPENDICULAR

Pack all of this stuff … Quick…

Owner takes the list and looks at it. Perpendicular picks up a box of sweets and empties it in his school bag.

OWNER
Oh, Surf is out of stock … There's Sushil washing powder. Will that do?

PERPENDICULAR
How come it's out of stock?

OWNER
Well, it just is…

PERPENDICULAR
Okay then, give me the money for it.

OWNER
Sorry?

PERPENDICULAR
Now, I'll have to buy it from another store, no?

CUT TO:

INT. SOME HOUSE - NIGHT

Few people meeting at a house. Shop owner is also present.

ONE
He took the money from you for the Surf, and took a carton from me without paying for it…

TWO
Man, these school boys broke my store's lock, and barged in. Not only did they polish off the Gulab Jamuns (a sweet), they woke me up in the middle of the night and made me fry samosas!

JEWELLER
When I told Faizal Khan about it, he just laughed it off. He said he's just a kid, let it be … He handed me a hundred rupee note as compensation.

CUT TO:

EXT. SWEET SHOP - DAY

The sweet shop owner is talking to Sultan.

MITHAIWALA

That little shit has made life hell for us.

SULTAN

My hands are tied as of now.

MITHAIWALA

You just name your price.

SULTAN

Look man, if I get implicated in this, the government won't help me out.

MITHAIWALA

We'll tell you the right place and time. This matter won't even get to the government.

SULTAN

And what about that Faizal?

MITHAIWALA

I was under the impression that you're not scared of Faizal.

Sultan looks away.

CUT TO:

EXT. CHAT SHOP - DAY

Sultan is eating chat. JP joins him and orders a plate for himself.

J.P. SINGH

You do what you want to. I'm there to take care of things.

CUT TO:

INT. SCRAP YARD - DAY

Shamshad Alam argues with the dealer.

MANGAT

The material is worth fifteen, how can I sell it at ten? My cost is fourteen, at least give me that much...

Shamshad and Nawab exchange looks.

SHAMSHAD

Mangat, so you won't come down?

Shamshad pulls his phone. Starts to dial a number.

NAWAB

Who are you calling?

SHAMSHAD

What?

NAWAB

Who are you calling?

SHAMSHAD

Faizal bhai ... we'll have to ask him, no? It's ringing.

Suddenly the dealer takes the phone from Shamshad.

NAWAB

Now hang on a minute.

SHAMSHAD

What're you doing?

The dealer disconnects the call.

MANGAT

Look.

SHAMSHAD

What?

MANGAT

Okay, tell me what's your last offer...

SHAMSHAD

Don't start again. Ten is what I've been told by the boss. Who the fuck am I to negotiate on that? I'll get you to talk directly to the man himself. Give my phone.

MANGAT

No.

Mangat is scared.

SHAMSHAD

Give my phone. Give it. Leave it.

Mangat holds on to the phone and does not give it.

MANGAT

No.

SHAMSHAD

What the hell! Give the phone. Give it!

MANGAT

No.

Shamshad is exasperated. He turns to Nawab.

SHAMSHAD

Give me your phone.

(to Mangat) You think we don't have another phone?

Nawab gives him his phone. Shamshad dials it.

Nawab

(To Shamshad, Concerned)

We'll have to first make sure his mood is alright. If in a bad mood, he might just shoot him dead.

Mangat snatches this phone too.

MANGAT

C'mon guys, you guys are completely out of your wits today.

Shamshad and Nawab get up to leave.

SHAMSHAD

Okay. I'll get him to call from where he is. For all you know, his entire family will be shot.

Mangat is really scared.

MANGAT

Hey, now don't get upset. Please have a seat.

He does not know what to say. Shamshad sits down.

MANGAT (CONT'D)

Would you like to have a *Limca* or a *Goldspot*?

CUT TO:

INT. FAIZAL'S HOUSE - DAY

Faizal looks at Guddu.

FAIZAL

Are you sure?

GUDDU

Mangat's going all around the marketplace saying that Faizal Khan picked up his stuff worth fifteen for just ten. His shop is up for auction, the day after tomorrow.

As Guddu dials the phone, Perpendicular is leaving. Faizal sees him.

FAIZAL

Hey stammerer … Where are you off to?

PERPENDICULAR

To study…

Tangent is waiting for him.

FAIZAL

Yeah right, as if you're some great scholar. Go and milk the cows, you'll become the Chief Minister straightaway…

GUDDU (O.S.)
(on the phone) Just hold on, bhaiya wants to speak with you.

Faizal is now on the phone.

FAIZAL
So asshole … How's it going?

CUT TO:

EXT. SHAMSHADS HOUSE - DAY

INTERCUT

SHAMSHAD
All good … We cracked a great deal with Mangat. Scrap worth twenty is fetching a cool seventy five…

FAIZAL
Has this Mangat fellow lost it?

SHAMSHAD
Why?

FAIZAL
Mangat's going around the whole world saying the stuff was worth fifteen…

SHAMSHAD
Really?

FAIZAL
And that you bought off at ten.

SHAMSHAD
Whom has he said this to?

BACK TO:

INT. FAIZAL'S HOUSE - DAY

FAIZAL
He's sitting right in front of me.

Guddu looks at him. Silence. Shamshad doesn't know what to say. His voice changes.

SHAMSHAD
Faizal bhai, how can you say that … Faizal bhai…

Faizal smiles. He's caught him.

FAIZAL
Why has your voice turned so feeble?

SHAMSHAD
Faizal bhai, it's not what you think. Someone's poisoning your ears.

FAIZAL
My ears are so full of wax that nothing can enter. Let's not argue. I don't want to know how much you've bought or sold it for. You're saying seventy five I believe you. Mangat says ten. I believe him too. Seventy-five minus ten equals to sixty-five. As soon as the delivery is made, entire sixty-five should reach me.

CUT TO:

INT. RAY TALKIES - DAY
Perpendicular and Tangent are watching *Munna Bhai MBBS* on screen. The title song plays. They enjoy.

CUT TO:

INT. BARBER SHOP - DAY
Tangent waits as Perpendicular get a Sanjay Dutt haircut.

CUT TO:

EXT. RAY TALKIES - EVENING
Perpendicular and Tangent drive to the theatre.

PERPENDICULAR
How do I look?

TANGENT
Good.

PERPENDICULAR

Really? Hurry up, we're late.

Ali is eating *Gol-Gappas* outside the theatre... He sees Perpendicular entering the theatre.

CUT TO:

INT. RAY TALKIES - EVENING

Perpendicular and Tangent rush in the theatre. The film has already started. The title song is on.

CUT TO:

EXT. POLICE STATION - NIGHT

Shamshad and Nawab arrive on the scooter. We can hear the police inspector's bragging voice from inside the station.

COP (O.S.)

I'll stay stationed in Dhansar. Gopal Singh is the tourist attraction in Dhansar.

All laugh at the joke. The inspector adds.

COP (O.S.) (CONT'D)

In fact I suggest that you guys also don't take promotions. Become Inspectors.

Scooter stops. They get down and enter.

SHAMSHAD

Yeah, the Inspector's there.

COP (O.S.)

Let your children also become Inspectors. Education is of no use anyway.

SHAMSHAD

You stay quiet. I'll talk.

COP (O.S.)

Everyone ultimately lands up here. Even an educated man will come to the police station sometime. Look at them...

They enter the Inspector's cabin.

SHAMSHAD
How're you Mr Singh?

COP (O.S.)
Hello, come on in. How're you?

They shake hands.

CUT TO:

INT. POLICE STATION - NIGHT
The two sit with the cop.

SHAMSHAD
We comfortably manage our business. If he goes about threatening and extorting money, how can we function!

The cop's listening. He repeats Shamshad's words, as if out of concern.

COP
How can we function?

SHAMSHAD
You know what they say about the cops?

COP
What do they say?

SHAMSHAD
That the cops scratch Faizal's balls everyday…

Cop laughs.

COP
Really!

SHAMSHAD
You find it funny?

COP
Look Shamshad bhai … You'll lodge a complaint, We'll file an FIR. We'll conduct

an enquiry. But we can take action only if we find any evidence. Do you get my point?

Shamshad stares at him.

CUT TO:

EXT. RAY TALKIES - NIGHT

Sultan's car stops outside the theatre. Ali has been waiting. Ali walks to the car and informs Sultan.

ALI

He's watching the show inside. It's about to end in ten minutes...

Sultan nods ... asks him to sit in the car.

SULTAN

Okay, get in, sit.

CUT TO:

INT. POLICE STATION - NIGHT

Cop watches as Shamshad talks on phone.

SHAMSHAD

Hello? Yes, send word to Guddu that Shamshad's delivered the goods and has reached Wasseypur. Send this message across. Just do what I tell you.

He puts the phone off and turns to the cop.

SHAMSHAD (CONT'D)

He'll call within fifteen minutes.

CUT TO:

EXT. RAY TALKIES/ WASSEYPUR ROAD - NIGHT

Film ends. They come out singing the title song of the film. Perpendicular is in high spirits. He catches the usher and pesters him.

PERPENDICULAR

Everything alright, uncle? We're coming back tomorrow morning for another show. If you don't let us in, we'll send you up there.

Perpendicular points to the sky. Tangent adds.

TANGENT

Hey brother, give him the magic hug.

Perpendicular hugs the usher, like in the film.

PERPENDICULAR

Yes, here is the magic hug.

Tangent starts the bike. Perpendicular gets on behind him.

PERPENDICULAR (CONT'D)

You're not Tangent anymore. You're Circuit. And I'll be *Munna Bhai MBBS*.

He starts singing. They leave on the bike. Sultan's car follows.

CUT TO:

EXT. STREETS - NIGHT

They're driving back home. It's late in the night. Empty streets. Sultan's car tails them at some distance.

PERPENDICULAR

I've made up my mind. I'm going to Bombay to meet Sanjay Dutt.

TANGENT

I'll also come!

PERPENDICULAR

What'll you do there?

TANGENT

Whatever you ask me to...

PERPENDICULAR

Duffer, what'll you do on meeting Sanjay Dutt?

TANGENT

I'll touch his feet...

PERPENDICULAR
Then?

TANGENT
What do you mean then?

PERPENDICULAR
What will you do after touching his feet?

TANGENT
I'll keep looking at him.

PERPENDICULAR
Till when...?

TANGENT
Till my eyes don't hurt...

PERPENDICULAR
Then?

They're now driving parallel to the railway tracks.

TANGENT
Then meaning?

PERPENDICULAR
What after looking at him?

Sultan's car overtakes the bike. The other car that was following stays behind the bike to lock them.

TANGENT
Then I'll close my eyes...

PERPENDICULAR
Then?

TANGENT
I don't know...

Sultan's car now stops in front of the bike, blocking its way. Bike stops. Perpendicular and Tangent are irritated.

TANGENT (CONT'D)

What's the rush motherfucker?

Perpendicular gets off and takes out his gun. He walks towards the car threateningly.

PERPENDICULAR

You in a hurry bastard?

Sultan and others start running towards Perpendicular. Realising he's in trouble, Perpendicular runs to save his life. He runs towards the railway tracks.

SULTAN

Fuck you bastard! Catch him.

PERPENDICULAR

(to Tangent) Run!

Tangent gets down and runs in the opposite direction.

PERPENDICULAR (CONT'D)

Tell Faizal Bhaiya that Sultan's going to kill me!

SULTAN

Catch him…

He grabs Perpendicular as two men (Ali and Qasim) run after Tangent.

CUT TO:

EXT. RAILWAY TRACKS - NIGHT

Perpendicular on railway tracks. On all fours. Tries to run away. Sultan picks up a rock and hits him. Perpendicular falls down. Sultan hits Perpendicular repeatedly with a rock. A train passes.

CUT TO:

EXT. RAILWAY TRACKS - NIGHT

Tangent runs away as a train passes. He's chased

by Ali and Qasim. Qasim fires at him. He's shot at the back by someone. He ducks. Ali goes after Tangent.

BACK TO:

EXT. RAILWAY TRACKS - NIGHT
Sultan hits Perpendicular till Perpendicular stops moving.

CUT TO:

EXT. RAILWAY TRACKS - NIGHT
A police jeep stops in front of Qasim. Qasim is caught.

CUT TO:

EXT. WASSEYPUR STREET - NIGHT
Chase through streets. As Ali chases Tangent, Tangent gets on a moving bus. Ali fires at him. Ali gets on a jeep behind the bus. Bus stops. Tangent gets off and runs back. Ali asks the jeep driver to stop.

ALI
Stop stop.

He also gets off and goes behind Tangent again...

CUT TO:

EXT. RAILWAY TRACKS - NIGHT
Perpendicular is now lying dead, alone.

CUT TO:

EXT. WASSEYPUR STREET - NIGHT
Chase continues. Tangent gets into an alley. Ali follows. Tangent notices two police guards sitting in a corner, getting warm. He goes joins him.

POLICE GUARD
Why are you panting so much? What happened?

Ali notices this and stops at a distance. He pretends to take a leak. Tangent keeps looking back towards Ali. The police guard notices this and asks.

POLICE GUARD (CONT'D)

Do you know him?

Tangent is quiet.

POLICE GUARD (CONT'D)

Will you say something?

Tangent gets up and runs away.

CUT TO:

INT. POLICE STATION - NIGHT

The Cop is waiting with Shamshad and Nawab. Phone rings. Shamshad checks it.

SHAMSHAD

It's Faizal.

Shamshad puts it on the loudspeaker. Everyone listens.

SHAMSHAD (CONT'D)

Hello.

FAIZAL (O.S.)

What's up, asshole? I hear the delivery's been made? Where's my money?

SHAMSHAD

What money?

Silence.

FAIZAL

Are you out of your mind?

SHAMSHAD

I did all the work. I bought the stuff, I sold it … Where do you figure in it?

CUT TO:

INT. FAIZAL'S HOUSE - NIGHT

Faizal's surprised.

FAIZAL

What's wrong with your voice? You haven't swallowed Ramadhir Singh's cock, have you?

CUT TO:

INT. POLICE STATION - NIGHT

SHAMSHAD

Hey mind your language.

Shamshad disconnects the call. The cops get up to leave.

CUT TO:

INT. FAIZAL'S OFFICE - NIGHT

Faizal, Guddu and other men are deliberating.

GUDDU

Let's finish him off before the night is over.

FAIZAL

No … he's up to some shit … He was not alone. He was talking on speaker phone…

There is a loud banging on the door. Faizal asks Guddu to see who's at the door.

CUT TO:

INT. FAIZAL'S OFFICE - NIGHT

Guddu opens the door as Tangent pants.

GUDDU

What's wrong?

TANGENT

He's going to kill Perpendicular!

Faizal hears that and gets up.

FAIZAL
Which bastard will kill him?

TANGENT
He's going to kill Perpendicular!

FAIZAL
Who?

Faizal is already on his way out.

TANGENT
Sultan.

They leave in anger.

CUT TO:

EXT. WASSEYPUR STREET - NIGHT
Faizal drives the jeep. Tangent, Guddu, Asgar with him. They drive and cross the police jeep going towards his house.

CUT TO:

EXT. WASSEYPUR STREET - NIGHT
The cop is in his Jeep on the phone. A constable drives.

COP
We have a report against Faizal Khan, with solid evidence. So I'm going now to arrest him. The thing is I don't have a warrant for this. So while we get him, can you arrange for the warrant? Okay, Minister Sir. Okay.

The cop disconnects the phone. He notices a Jeep crossing his own.

COP (CONT'D)
Wasn't that Faizal Khan's vehicle? Stop stop. Yes that's Faizal Khan's vehicle. Turn around.

The cop's jeep turns and goes behind Faizal's jeep.

CUT TO:

EXT. RAILWAY TRACKS - NIGHT

Jeep arrives on the spot. Faizal and everyone get down. Look around.

TANGENT

There…!

He points. Faizal looks. Perpendicular's body lying on the railway tracks. They all run.

CUT TO:

FAIZAL

Sultan motherfucker!

They all carry the body back to the jeep. Police jeep arrives. Cops get down and go up to Faizal's jeep.

COP

Hey brother … Faizal bhai. Faizal Bhai. You'll have to come to the police station with me.

FAIZAL

Watch it! This is my little brother. Somebody has murdered him.

COP

I understand Faizal bhai. You can hand the body to us. There's an arrest warrant in your name.

Cop asks his men to take the body.

COP (CONT'D)

Take the body.

CUT TO:

FADE OUT.

INTERMISSION

FADE IN:

INT. JAIL - CORRIDOR - DAY

Faizal walks in the jail corridor. He's also talking on phone.

FAIZAL

Only you've come, right? Yeah … they all think I'm an asshole … that's why I'm coming.

Faizal bums a cigarette from another prisoner who sits smoking.

FAIZAL (CONT'D)

I'm desperate to see you.

CUT TO:

INT. JAIL - MEETING ROOM - DAY

Faizal and Mohsina are in the jail meeting area. They stand in front of each other, separated by a partition. They're holding each other's hands through the small window between them. They're both very emotional.

FAIZAL

Mohsina … sing me that song…

MOHSINA

Why?

FAIZAL

Because I want to hear it.

MOHSINA

Why?

Mohsina sings.

LYRICS

Don't be frustrated my fool, don't be nervous my fool, don't upset your mood anytime, set right whatever's wrong, don't lose hope, put up a fight, put up a fight you fool.

EXT. ASH POND - DAY

Definite and Tangent get off their bike and walk towards an isolated spot. They're drinking beer.

TANGENT

Definite bhai...

DEFINITE

Yeah?

TANGENT

Shamshad is really flying high after sending Faizal bhai to jail.

DEFINITE

So let him. He has done something big like that, let him fly.

TANGENT

But how dare he do that. If we were to attack him, we'll get appreciated by Faizal bhai...

DEFINITE

But Faizal boss is in jail...

TANGENT

And you aren't.

DEFINITE

What are you trying to say?

TANGENT

Faizal's position is vacant. Before Shamshad grabs his place, eliminate him. The power will be indirectly Faizal's but directly yours. Once Wasseypur accepts you then the game's all yours.

Definite thinks. Takes a swig from the bottle.

CUT TO:

EXT. SHAMSHADS HOUSE - DAY

Definite and Tangent arrive on a bike. They park the bike outside Shamshad's place and get in. Definite screams with a gun in his hand.

DEFINITE
Shamshad … Shamshad. Hey Shamshad!

He shoots in the air.

CUT TO:

INT. SHAMSHADS HOUSE. DAY
The door is open.

DEFINITE
Shamshad … Shamshad …

Definite fires the gun in the air. They get in and look for him. An old woman (Shamshad's mother) lies down on the bed in the courtyard … Definite pulls up the charpoy and turns over the old lady on the ground.

DEFINITE (CONT'D)
Where's Shamshad? Where's he?

The woman moans.

SHAMSHAD'S MOTHER
Oh God! I'm dead. Dead.

TANGENT
Shamshad…

He asks Tangent to look in the rooms.

DEFINITE
Look in that room.

TANGENT
Where is he?

DEFINITE
Search. Find him. Dead?

TANGENT
Hey Shamshad…

DEFINITE
Check on the terrace. The terrace.

Definite's gun seems to be stuck. He's constantly trying to cock it.

DEFINITE

Where the fuck is he? Not on the terrace, no? Check on the terrace. This bloody gun also had to get jammed now. Hey Shamshad!

Tangent comes down after checking the terrace.

TANGENT

Not there.

DEFINITE

Look inside. Where can he be?

Tangent goes in the inside room again. Its dark inside but Shamshad is there.

SHAMSHAD

How did you get in? How did you get in without asking? Bastard!

Shamshad has caught Tangent by the collar, and comes out with him. Tangent gets out of his grip. Shamshad notices his mother lying on the floor with pain.

SHAMSHAD (CONT'D)

Mom … Mom … Motherfucker, why did you hurt my mom?

Tangent runs.

DEFINITE

What were you saying?

SHAMSHAD

Why are you pushing my mom around?

Definite holds the gun at him. Shamshad starts backing off.

DEFINITE

Now come on big mouth!

Just when Definite is about to fire, the gun gets jammed. Shamshad realises he's not in danger and starts attacking definite with utensils.

SHAMSHAD
Son of a whore!

Shamshad picks up a rod lying around … Definite runs … Shamshad runs after him.

CUT TO:

EXT. SHAMSHAD'S HOUSE - DAY
Shamshad runs out of the house with rod. Nawab crosses him on a scooter.

SHAMSHAD
Get the fuckers!

Nawab turns the scooter. He notices that Definite is going in the opposite direction.

NAWAB
Hey Shamshad…

DEFINITE
Fuck off!

Nawab turns the scooter back and goes after Definite. He also shouts and calls Shamshad back.

NAWAB
Shamshad.

Shamshad runs back. Nawab asks him to get on the scooter.

NAWAB (CONT'D)
Hey Shamshad, sit. You'll get tired of running, but the scooter won't. Sit.

Shamshad sits.

SHAMSHAD
Go, go, go…

CUT TO:

EXT. WASSEYPUR STREETS - DAY
Chase through the street … They get stuck in a

big traffic jam at a red light. Shamshad stands on the scooter and sees Definite stuck much ahead in the jam. He asks Nawab to turn back and take a different route.

SHAMSHAD
I think he is there. Nawab, you take a U-turn and meet me at that crossing turn.
Turn back!

He himself gets down and runs ahead. The light turns green and Definite proceeds on a bike. Shamshad gets frustrated. He tries to hail a rickshaw. Finally he manages to get into a jeep taxi. He rushes the jeep.

SHAMSHAD (CONT'D)
Drive faster...

Shamshad is irritated by his co-passenger whose chicken keeps flying into his lap. He asks him to control the chicken. Meanwhile Nawab gets into the same alley by chance as Definite. He chases definite on his scooter. Shamshad gets really irritated now with the chickens and starts throwing them in the lap of another passenger in the back seat. Definite manages to get out of the alley and come on the main street. He crosses Shamshad's jeep. Nawab is behind him. Shamshad sees this and gets off the jeep. Just when Nawab is closing onto Definite, his scooter starts giving up. Fuel is over. He drags to a petrol pump. He sees definite at the same petrol pump, getting his bike tank filled. He calls up Shamshad. Shamshad receives the call.

SHAMSHAD (CONT'D)
Yeah where are you?

NAWAB
He's at the petrol pump.

SHAMSHAD

Can't hear you, speak loudly.

NAWAB

Definite is in front of me. At the petrol pump.

SHAMSHAD

Which petrol pump?

NAWAB

The one at the new market. He's showing me the gun.

SHAMSHAD

Motherfucker, does not have gun in his bullets. Get a hold of him. Don't let him run. I'm coming.

Shamshad starts running. By now Definite has got on his bike and starts to leave. Nawab manages to catch the back handle of the bike and pulls at it. Definite still escapes. Shamshad sees him and runs behind him. Nawab also joins the chase on his scooter by now, and asks Shamshad to get on it. Definite drives on. On his way, a railway crossing gate is closed. Definite abandons his bike there and starts running at the railway tracks. Shamshad and Nawab also abandon their scooter and follow on foot. A train is passing. Definite gets on the running train and leaves Shamshad and Nawab behind. On realizing his victory, he shows the finger to Shamshad from the moving train and teases him. Gun in his hand.

DEFINITE

Come mother fucker! Come get me now.

When he's done laughing at them, he turns in style and notices. The whole train full of military men. The military men train their guns at him. Definite raises his hands in surrender.

CUT TO:

EXT. ROAD - DAY

Sultan and Shamshad together drive in a car. Shamshad is quiet.

CUT TO:

INT. RAMADHIR'S SINGH'S HOUSE - DAY

Shamshad and Sultan sit across a much older Ramadhir Singh and JP Singh (his son)… Ramadhir hands tea from a tray to all sitting there.

RAMADHIR SINGH

You should get into politics. This Wasseypur … is a jungle of savages. A guy like you with brains can't do jack-shit there. If Definite's gun was loaded, would you be having tea here with us right now?

J.P. SINGH

You might have pulled it off by yourself, but he'll think my father's behind all this. You trapped Faizal, and Sultan killed his brother.

Sultan explains.

SULTAN

Oh no, brother. The Perpendicular case was different.

RAMADHIR SINGH

Now, it's in everybody's best interests that you finish him off while he's in jail.

Shamshad looks at him. They are looking at him.

SHAMSHAD

Who, me?

RAMADHIR SINGH

No. Definite.

SHAMSHAD

That asshole?

RAMADHIR SINGH

Like only iron can cut iron, only an asshole can finish off another…

SHAMSHAD

But why will Definite kill Faizal?

RAMADHIR SINGH

Because he wants to be Faizal Khan…

Shamshad looks at him surprised. Ramadhir Singh laughs.

RAMADHIR SINGH (CONT'D)

I've been around for ages. I got Faizal Khan's grandfather killed. Got Sardar killed … And then…

He's trying to recall the name. JP reminds him.

J.P. SINGH

Danish.

RAMADHIR SINGH

Danish … But I'm still here alive. Why do you think?

SHAMSHAD

Why?

Sultan pitches in.

SULTAN

Because you're a real Godfather.

Ramadhir Singh is pleased with the comment. Ramadhir Singh asks his own son.

RAMADHIR SINGH

You say why?

J.P. SINGH

Why?

RAMADHIR SINGH

Because I don't watch movies…

SHAMSHAD
Really?

Laughs. Continues speaking…

RAMADHIR SINGH
In my younger day, all my friends watched 'Ganga Jamuna' and wanted to be Dilip Kumar … The girls liked Dev Anand. Then came a phase when women were with Rajesh Khanna, and the guys wanted to be Bachchan. And these days there's … what's his name … it's a nice name…

Ramadhir is trying to recall again. Ghanshyam reminds him.

GHANSHYAM
Salman Khan.

RAMADHIR SINGH
Yes. And that…

GHANSHYAM
Sunil Dutt and Nargis Dutt's son…

J.P. SINGH
Sanjay Dutt.

RAMADHIR SINGH
Sanjay Dutt.

Shamshad is amused.

RAMADHIR SINGH (CONT'D)
Everybody's got their own films playing inside their heads… and they all want to be the heroes of their own films. Till the time there's cinema in India, people will remain idiots.

CUT TO:

INT. FAIZAL'S HOUSE - DAY
Mohsina is singing a Hindi film song (Dil to Pagal hai).

CUT TO:

INT. JAIL - DAY

Faizal on the phone. He's hearing the song.

CUT TO:

INT. JAIL - DAY

Definite with Faizal in prison. Faizal has his arm around Definite's shoulder. They are talking something.

INT. JAIL - DAY

There is a fight going on. Faizal walks in. Definite with a gang of boys. He is fighting with someone. Qasim. Few others are trying to stop them from beating each other.

QASIM

Inside you're safe because of Faizal, asshole. Outside I'll smash your arrogance with my AK-47, bastard.

Faizal asks them to stop it.

FAIZAL (O.S.)

Stop this nonsense!

DEFINITE

Fuck off!

Faizal calls Definite out. Definite looks.

FAIZAL

Definite.

DEFINITE

What are you making these threats for? I will finish you off with a tiny country revolver. Your game will be over in flat 70 bucks.

Fight is over. Definite joins Faizal.

QASIM

I spit on you!

DEFINITE
You piece of shit … Go back to the dump!

FAIZAL
Leave it. Shamshad's withdrawn the case against you…

DEFINITE
Why? Does he plan to give his sister in marriage to me?

FAIZAL
No, he'll try to join hands with you.

They walk on.

CUT TO:

INT. PRINTING PRESS - DAY

Shamshad is in his printing press. He looks out of the window and notices Definite arriving on a bike with Tangent. He walks inside the office to Nawab and informs.

SHAMSHAD
He's here…

Definite stops the bike outside and gets off. He asks Tangent to wait outside.

DEFINITE
Wait here.

Definite walks in. Carrying a jhola. Tangent stays outside. Definite asks him to keep the bike running.

DEFINITE (CONT'D)
Keep the bike running.

Sultan and Jabbar also arrive outside the press on a bike. Sultan is surprised to see Tangent there.

SULTAN
What's he doing here?

Definite goes to Shamshad's office. Nawab is also there.

DEFINITE
Hello buddy!

SHAMSHAD
Hi!

DEFINITE
How're you?

SHAMSHAD
Did you get the cash sent for you?

DEFINITE
Ofcourse! How else would I buy these two kilos of apples?

SHAMSHAD
Two kilos of apples for two lakh rupees? That's it?

Shamshad smiles…

DEFINITE
What do you think? These are Kashmiri apples, man. Countless terrorists have grown-up on these… Want to try one?

SHAMSHAD
Okay … Have a seat.

Shamshad is smiling. Definite puts his hand inside the bag and pulls out a bomb. He pulls the pin and throws it at Shamshad and runs out. Nawab and Shamshad notice the bomb and duck to save themselves.

NAWAB
Holy shit!

CUT TO:

EXT. PRINTING PRESS - DAY
A blast inside the press. Sultan and Jabbar are

shocked. Definite gets on the bike Tangent has kept running, and they run away. Sultan fires at them. He gets back on his bike with Jabbar and chases them.

CUT TO:

EXT. WASSEYPUR ROAD - DAY

Sultan and Jabbar chase Definite and Tangent. Both parties fire at each other. Gunshots in broad daylight.

CUT TO:

INT. PRINTING PRESS - DAY

Shamshad is badly wounded and bleeding. His one leg is cut off.

NAWAB

Shamshad...

SHAMSHAD

Go fuck the bastard's happiness!

CUT TO:

EXT. FAIZAL'S HOUSE - DAY

Sultan drives in outside Faizal's house. Jabbar is surprised.

JABBAR

Why have you come here? This is Faizal Khan's house. This doesn't seem right!

SULTAN

Shut up.

Sultan stops the bike. Jabbar looks around to make sure it's safe.

SULTAN (CONT'D)

Get off. Give me the gun.

He takes the gun from Jabbar. They go in. The house appears empty.

SULTAN (CONT'D)
Is there no one here? Hello!…Faizal Khan….

JABBAR
He's in the jail.

SULTAN
Yeah, I know.

Danish's widow comes out of the kitchen.

SHAMA PARVEEN
Hey brother! Come in, sit. Will you have something?

She notices some blood on Sultan's hand.

SHAMA PARVEEN (CONT'D)
You're hurt?

Sultan points at her and shoots her in the head. Jabbar is shocked. Sultan pulls him.

CUT TO:

INT. HOSPITAL - DAY
Danish's widow in the hospital. In a coma. Nagma and people sit around.

CUT TO:

INT. JAIL - DAY
Faizal sits with his people as.

NASIR (V.O.)
Faizal had gone silent. The entire game had been turned over…

CUT TO:

INT. CENTRAL HOSPITAL - DAY
Shamshad Alam in hospital.

NASIR (V.O.)
Shamshad too was hanging on to dear life in the central hospital…

CUT TO:

INT. RAMADHIR SINGH'S HOUSE - DAY

Ramadhir Singh worried...

NASIR (V.O.)

Ramadhir Singh also knew very well that Sultan had made a fatal mistake by shooting his sister... For the first time in Wasseypur, a woman had been shot at...

CUT TO:

INT. FAIZAL'S HOUSE - DAY

Nasir is offering Namaz...

NASIR (V.O.)

And she was not just Sultan's sister. She was Danish's widow first. And no one knew this better than me. An eerie silence had descended on Wasseypur but I knew it carried a storm in its belly.

INT. RAMADHIR SINGH'S HOUSE - DAY

Ramadhir Singh looks very worried...

NASIR (V.O.)

Both Ramadhir and his son knew very well that Faizal's pride had been hurt. They also knew that all of Wasseypur was now with Faizal. Their one mistake had made Faizal so strong, that it was necessary to eliminate him before he realizes his strength.

CUT TO:

EXT. PRINTING PRESS - DAY

Shot of closed printing press ... People on the streets, pushing Nawab around.

NASIR (V.O.)

Shamshad Alam's gang had to leave Wasseypur because of this incident ... Nobody wanted to be associated with them ... And Faizal Khan's authority had been accepted by the people of Wasseypur...

Loud Music...

CUT TO:

EXT. JAIL - DAY

SUPER - 2004

Faizal comes out of jail. Brass band. People are celebrating.

CUT TO:

EXT. WASSEYPUR ROAD - DAY

It's a procession with a band playing. A band member sings filmy songs. As the procession goes through the streets it's as if a big leader is being welcomed home. Mohsina stands by his side. Definite, Guddu, Tangent and his whole family with Faizal.

CUT TO:

INT. SULTAN'S HOUSE. TERRACE - DAY

J.P. Singh at Sultan's place. Ali is also there.

J.P. SINGH

Don't even give him a chance to re-group ... He's got out of jail today ... Everyone at his place will be relaxed and at ease ... You follow, right?

Sultan listens. JP's phone rings.

J.P. SINGH (CONT'D)

One minute...

He takes the call.

J.P. SINGH (CONT'D)

Yes, father. No, I'm not planning a thing. I'm doing as you had asked, father. I'm lying really low.

Cuts it.

J.P. SINGH (CONT'D)
Father has sent a new officer from Patna...

CUT TO:

EXT. HIGHWAY - DHANBAD - DAY
A new police officer is sitting in a police jeep. The jeep is driving through an intercity highway.

INT. POLICE STATION - DAY
The new officer sits with cops.

NEW INSPECTOR
Stay on high alert. Four jeeps will do day-night surveillance. Don't be afraid. But keep your guns close. But don't make a move.

COP GOPAL SINGH
We wouldn't be able to do a thing anyway.

New inspector stares at him.

NEW INSPECTOR
You can't be sure.

COP GOPAL SINGH
No Sir, you don't understand the situation here...

NEW INSPECTOR
Go sit outside.

He shouts.

COP GOPAL SINGH
Yes Sir.

Gopal singh gets up and leaves.

CUT TO:

EXT. POLICE STATION - DAY
Gopal Singh comes out grumbling in irritation.

COP GOPAL SINGH
If you fly so high you might reach heaven!

Cop A takes out his mobile phone and looks for Ramadhir Singh's number to dial.

COP GOPAL SINGH (CONT'D)

Where's Mr Minister?

He dials and talks.

COP GOPAL SINGH (CONT'D)

My greetings to Minister Sir. Gopal Singh here … Sir, Gopal singh. Dhansar Police station incharge … Minister sir, we have a new inspector … too big for his shoes. I thought I'll update you … Sorry? … You've posted him?

CUT TO:

INT. FAIZAL'S HOUSE/ FAIZAL'S ROOM - NIGHT

Faizal with Mohsina in the room … He holds her from behind…

MOHSINA

What are you upto?

FAIZAL

My hand's exhausted from fantasizing about you.

Mohsina turns around.

MOHSINA

Not now…

FAIZAL

Why not?

MOHSINA

You've returned after such a long time. The others in the family want to spend time with you…

FAIZAL

But I want to spend time with you.

MOHSINA

You are incorrigible … doesn't look nice. Sister (in-law) is in hospital and…

FAIZAL

Why drag the Sister (in-law) between us?

Music plays in the background. The title of KSBKBT (TV Soap).

MOHSINA

Leave me please…

FAIZAL

Why?

MOHSINA

It's time…

She pushes him and goes. His phone rings … He takes a call.

FAIZAL

Yes … how's the movement on Ramadhir Singh side…?

Faizal listens.

FAIZAL (CONT'D)

And Shamshad Alam? Which hospital is he in?

Faizal listens.

CUT TO:

INT. FAIZAL'S HOUSE - NIGHT

The whole house is watching KSBKBT. Faizal sits down too.

CUT TO:

INT. FAIZAL OFFICE. NIGHT

Asgar is doing some accounting work in office. He hears gunshots.

CUT TO:

INT. FAIZAL'S HOUSE - NIGHT

Repeat opening sequence … Scene 4-21…

Faizal hears some sound. He asks Nagma to lower the TV volume.

FAIZAL
Just lower the volume.

There's another gunshot. Faizal gets up. His two men get up with guns and go out with him.

FAIZAL (CONT'D)
You all keep watching TV.

CUT TO:

INT. FAIZAL OFFICE. NIGHT
Asgar steps out to the balcony to see what's going on. He sees some gunmen hiding down the alley.

CUT TO:

INT. FAIZAL'S HOUSE - NIGHT
Faizal shuts the door and comes back in. A bomb blast rips through the door.

CUT TO:

INT. FAIZAL OFFICE. NIGHT
Asgar comes back in and shuts the door. He thinks. He then picks up his phone and calls.

CUT TO:

INT. FAIZAL'S HOUSE - NIGHT
Faizal is on the phone talking with Asgar.

FAIZAL
Uncle, where are you?

CUT TO:

INT. FAIZAL OFFICE. NIGHT
Asgar responds.

ASGAR
I'm in office. The house has been surrounded from all sides. Where are you?

CUT TO:

INT. FAIZAL'S HOUSE - NIGHT
There's another gunshot. Family panics.

NASIR
Faizal...

NAGMA
Faizal...

Faizal keeps talking on phone.

FAIZAL
Who else is there? Don't open the doors till I say. You stay there. Ok?

CUT TO:

INT. FAIZAL OFFICE - NIGHT
Asgar closes all doors.

CUT TO:

EXT. FAIZAL'S HOUSE - NIGHT
Sultan is outside Faizal's door, on the phone.

SULTAN
Yes Qasim?

CUT TO:

EXT. FAIZAL'S HOUSE - BACKDOOR - NIGHT.
Qasim on the phone. Few other gunmen.

QASIM
We've found the backdoor entry of the house. We're waiting for your orders.

CUT TO:

EXT. FAIZAL'S HOUSE. NIGHT.
Sultan on the phone.

SULTAN
What orders? Nothing should be left in one piece. Finish everyone.

CUT TO:

EXT. FAIZAL'S HOUSE - BACKDOOR - NIGHT

Qasim and his team attack. They manage to break the outside door and get in. Qasim orders his men to throw bombs in the house through windows.

QASIM

Throw it in. Put it. Bloody motherfuckers!

CUT TO:

INT. FAIZAL' HOUSE - NIGHT

Another blast, this time it's from the backside of the house. Everyone screams and takes cover. Guddu and Faizal start pushing everyone upstairs one by one.

GUDDU

Go on!

FAIZAL

Guddu, take everyone upstairs.

Chaos. Sounds.

VARIOUS PEOPLE

The kids first … oh my god … careful … where's Faizal? … Faizal call someone.

FAIZAL

Hello? Where are you Definite? … You're not yet here. Bastard I have only one life … It's either the Almighty that will take it away or the neighbourhood. But I will get those fuckers… What? … Get here fast, bastard!

Faizal walks up. Rest of the family has already been huddled into one small room. Faizal reaches them.

NAGMA

Faizal…

FAIZAL

Stay quiet everyone. No one will say anything.

Faizal begins to leave from there.

MOHSINA

But where are you going?

FAIZAL

Stay down everyone.

Guddu pleads.

GUDDU

I'll come with you brother.

FAIZAL

No one will come with me. Go inside. Stay here.

MOHSINA

But where are you going?

Faizal gives his phone to Guddu.

FAIZAL

Keep the phone. Keep the phone. If it rings, don't pick it up. Okay.

Faizal pushes them all in.

FAIZAL (CONT'D)

Go in … (to Guddu) Close the door and don't let anyone go out.

Faizal goes. More gunshots. More screams. Faizal climbs further. It's quieter upstairs. He comes up on the terrace. Washes his face. Looks down, and then jumps to the neighbors' terrace. His knee gets badly hurt. Gets up and limps. Crawls down the neighbour's house. Jumps again. More pain. His phone rings in a distance. ('Nayak Nahi Khalnayak' ringtone.) Phone stops ringing after a while. Faizal limps down the neighbour's house stairs.

CUT TO:

INT. FAIZAL'S NEIGHBOUR'S HOUSE - NIGHT.

Faizal walks past the courtyard of the neighbour's house. The neighbour's family is standing there, hiding behind pillars. They look at Faizal. They can see he's in pain. Faizal calls to one of them for help.

FAIZAL

Come here.

Boy comes. Faizal leans on to him for support and walks. He comes out of the neighbour's house towards his house. Definite and all are already there. The family also comes rushing out of the house.

FAIZAL (CONT'D)

Hey Guddu!

GUDDU

Brother, are you okay?

FAIZAL

Not okay.

Mohsina runs towards Faizal, concerned.

MOHSINA

Faizal…

NAGMA

Faizal…

Faizal goes and sits down at the porch.

FAIZAL

Bloody motherfuckers!

Definite joins with his friends.

FAIZAL (CONT'D)

Where did you run away bastard?

DEFINITE

I didn't run away … I was at the market.

FAIZAL
Motherfucker…

DEFINITE
If I had even a little clue, I would have ripped him apart out there.

Faizal asks the family to go back in.

FAIZAL
You all go inside.

Guddu supports Faizal to stand up.

GUDDU
Brother, now you won't go alone.

DEFINITE
Ladies please go inside.

MOHSINA
But where are you going? Huh?

FAIZAL
Close the doors.

NAGMA
Be careful Faizal.

FAIZAL
You all go in.

They all leave. The family watches.

CUT TO:

INT. FAIZAL OFFICE - NIGHT
Asgar cautiously steps out of the office.

CUT TO:

EXT. FAIZAL OFFICE - NIGHT
Faizal walks down the alley with his men. He asks one of the men to go back to guard the house.

FAIZAL
You go back and stand guard outside the house. Don't let anyone get in. Understood?

Asgar is out of the office by now. He notices Faizal passing.

ASGAR

Hey Faizal, what happened?

FAIZAL

Go home, uncle. It was that fucking Sultan! Just guard the house, uncle.

ASGAR

Okay.

Asgar turns towards the house. They all get into the jeep. Faizal asks Guddu to go back.

CUT TO:

EXT. CHECK NAKA - NIGHT

Sultan notices a cop coming towards the car.

SULTAN

They're here for us! Jabbar, bastards, they are coming, a police officer is coming here.

Fire between police and Sultan's men … Sultan's windshield breaks. Sultan asks his driver to turn the car and get away.

SULTAN

Move it … take the car back…

They back the car. More fire from police's side.

SULTAN (CONT'D)

Now turn…

A police jeep comes behind them.

JABBAR

Go fast … hurry.

Sultan turns back to check the police jeep.

SULTAN

Just check, are they near us…?

The car stops. They all get down. Sultan asks the

driver to drive away from there to mislead the jeep.

SULTAN (CONT'D)

You take the car and run!

Sultan and men escape in the gully as the cops chase the car…

CUT TO:

INT. HOSPITAL - NIGHT

Faizal getting plaster done his leg. Definite is on the phone.

DEFINITE

Yeah, go on. One minute … Brother, there's police at home…

FAIZAL

Why?

DEFINITE

They say they'll provide protection…

FAIZAL

Give me the phone…

Faizal takes the phone.

FAIZAL (CONT'D)

Who's the officer, put him on the phone … I don't need protection.

INTERCUT

INT. FAIZAL'S HOUSE - NIGHT

New Inspector is listening on the phone. Rest of Faizal's family is standing around shocked.

CUT TO:

INT. HOSPITAL - NIGHT

FAIZAL

Faizal can protect himself. Now you listen to me. It's Ramadhir Singh who needs protection.

And not some ordinary protection… Call the whole fucking army because I'm going to shred that bloody codger to bits!

CUT TO:

INT. RAMADHIR SINGH'S HOUSE - NIGHT.
J.P. Singh is talking to someone on phone.

J.P. SINGH
We can't give him time to get back on his feet. Kill anyone you find from his family, his servant, launderer, pet…

CUT TO:

INT. FAIZAL'S HOUSE - NIGHT
A doctor enters. Definite stops him. Faizal is sitting with his plastered feet up. Other gunmen stand around. Definite frisks him for any dangerous weapon and finds a pair of scissors.

DEFINITE (CONT'D)
What's this?

DOCTOR
It's a scissor for cutting the plaster.

Doctor begins cutting the plaster while Faizal looks on, serious.

CUT TO:

EXT. MARKET - DAY
Moharram processions are on. Lots of people on streets. In the middle of the crowd, we see Nagma, her sister and Asgar walking in the market. Nagma asks Asgar and heads for some shop.

NAGMA
I'll be back in a minute.

Asgar is unhappy.

ASGAR
But, you don't get Haleem here.

NAGMA

Just a minute.

Both Nagma and her sister go into a jewellery shop. Drums and festivities on streets. Nagma and her sister are sitting at the jewellery shop waiting to be shown something. Nagma explains.

NAGMA (CONT'D)

I'm checking it out for Mohsina.

Asgar gets distracted … goes to a clothes shop. One dark man behind, watches him. He's on the phone.

ASGAR

Brother, do you sell Pathanis in your shop?

SHOPKEEPER

Yeah I can show you pathani shirts.

The dark man comes up to Asgar and hands him a visiting card, expecting to be guided to the address.

ASGAR

Okay, and any other kurtas…

Asgar stops talking to the shopkeeper as notices something in the address.

ASGAR (CONT'D)

Brother, this is Dhanbad. The address is for Varanasi. Get it? Varanasi.

The dark man just nods, but hasn't understood a thing. He's doesn't say anything but continues to ask Asgar the address in signals. Asgar is irritated.

ASGAR (CONT'D)

Varanasi … this is Dhanbad. The address written in it is Varanasi. You don't get it? Okay do one thing…

He's still haggling with the dark man, when Qasim arrives on a bike and shoots at Asgar. Nagma notices. She stands calmly, as if she has accepted her end.

NAGMA

Run, lil sister

She's also shot at. Her sister runs. Qasim goes after her and shoots her dead too.

CUT TO:

EXT. MARKET - EVENING

Faizal Khan fires in the air in the market. He's angry. Definite, Tangent, Guddu and others are busy interrogating people and getting the market shut.

FAIZAL

Shut every shop. Shut the whole motherfucking city down. Son of a bitch murdered my mother in the middle of the street.

The men start creating a riot. Guddu grabs someone.

GUDDU

You fucking rat…

DEFINITE

Close it.

Definite turns. Guddu holds a boy.

GUDDU

Definite, This rat lives with the fucker who killed mother.

CUT TO:

INT. QASIM'S HOUSE - NIGHT

The gunman Qasim … Sits watching TV … Definite enters with his men and attacks Qasim. Qasim runs into the inside room. Definite chases him and shoots at him thrice.

CUT TO:

EXT. MARKET - EVENING

Faizal is angrily giving instructions to his men.

FAIZAL

I want Sultan, dead or alive.
I know that bastard's behind this.

CUT TO:

INT. SULTAN'S HOUSE - NIGHT

They start breaking things … Definite and Tangent try to break open the door of Sultan's house…

TANGENT

Open up, bastards…!

Sultan's family members come out. Badoor is also with them. They talk with Definite through the door.

DEFINITE

Where is Sultan?

BADOOR

He doesn't live here anymore.

DEFINITE

Where does he stay?

BADOOR

He moved out the day his sister got married to Danish.

DEFINITE

Where did he go?

CUT TO:

INT/EXT. PASSENGER TRAIN - DAY

Four people in a train. Definite, Guddu and two other men.

CUT TO:

EXT. BHAGALPUR RAILWAY STATION - NIGHT

Train stops at Bhagalpur station. They get down.

CUT TO:

INT. BHAGALPUR HOTEL - DAY

Shot of hotel.

CUT TO:

Guddu talks to Definite, Aakash and Azeem.

GUDDU

Sultan goes to the mosque for his afternoon prayers.

EXT. MASJID - DAY

Sultan exits Masjid.

INT. SULTAN'S CAR - DAY

GUDDU (V.O.)

He parks outside the vegetable market but leaves his gun behind. So as soon as he enters the mosque you empty his gun.

Sultan puts his gun in the glove compartment and exits from the car. Aakash opens his car through and empties bullets out of his gun.

INT/EXT. MEAT SHOP - DAY

GUDDU (V.O.)

After that he goes to the meat market.

Sultan buying meat at a shop.

EXT. BHAGALPUR STREET-1 DAY

GUDDU (V.O.)

He then goes home via the bazaar. That's where we should catch him.

Sultan driving through the street.

CUT TO:

EXT. BHAGALPUR DHABA - DAY
Azeem enters a dhaba and sits.

AZEEM
Some bread and stew, please.

From behind him a man gets up. He is Sultan. Sultan walks to the counter.

AZEEM
(on the phone) Hello.

Pays money and walks out.

CUT TO:

INT. BHAGALPUR HOTEL - DAY
Guddu gets a call.

GUDDU
Hello.

CUT TO:

EXT. BHAGALPUR DHABA - DAY

AZEEM
Sultan was behind me.

Azeem is scared.

CUT TO:

INT. BHAGALPUR HOTEL - DAY

GUDDU
He'll go to the meat market now. Stay with him, and stay on line.

CUT TO:

EXT. BHAGALPUR DHABA - DAY
As he gets up his food comes. He looks at the food. Almost hungry. But walks out.

CUT TO:

EXT. BHAGALPUR STREET 1 - DAY
Definite is standing in the middle of the street with a helmet on. He receives a call.

DEFINITE
Yeah!

INT. BHAGALPUR HOTEL - DAY

GUDDU
Where are you?

CUT TO:

EXT. BHAGALPUR STREET 1 - DAY

DEFINITE
I'm at the bazaar.

He stands holding a scooter holding it down, half way to the ground.

CUT TO:

INT. BHAGALPUR HOTEL - DAY

GUDDU
He's headed towards you.

CUT TO:

EXT. BHAGALPUR STREET 1 - DAY

DEFINITE
So?

CUT TO:

INT. BHAGALPUR HOTEL - DAY

GUDDU
Keep hitting the kick-shaft.

CUT TO:

EXT. BHAGALPUR STREET 1 - DAY

DEFINITE
But then my scooter will start.

CUT TO:

INT. BHAGALPUR HOTEL - DAY

GUDDU
So first remove the spark plug and then keep kicking.

CUT TO:

EXT. BHAGALPUR STREET 1 - DAY

Definite takes out the spark plug.

CUT TO:

INT. BHAGALPUR HOTEL - DAY FROM THE PHONE.

GUDDU (CONT'D)

Azeem, What's the status?

INTERCUT

EXT. BHAGALPUR STREET 2 - DAY

AZEEM

He's buying fruits.

CUT TO:

INT. BHAGALPUR HOTEL - DAY

GUDDU

Why the fuck isn't he buying meat? Which fruit is he buying?

CUT TO:

EXT. BHAGALPUR STREET 2 - DAY

AZEEM (looks)

Banana.

CUT TO:

INT. BHAGALPUR HOTEL - DAY

GUDDU

Oh!! Then he's got the loosies. What else?

CUT TO:

EXT. BHAGALPUR STREET 2 - DAY

AZEEM

I can't tell. Shall I go closer?

CUT TO:

INT. BHAGALPUR HOTEL - DAY

GUDDU

Let it be.

CUT TO:

EXT. BHAGALPUR STREET 2 - DAY

AZEEM

Poor guy doesn't know we'll eat his fruits.

Laughs.

AZEEM (CONT'D)

Shall I ask him to get lychees?

CUT TO:

INT. BHAGALPUR HOTEL - DAY

GUDDU

Shut up, asshole! It's not lychee season yet.

CUT TO:

EXT. BHAGALPUR STREET 1 - DAY

DEFINITE

What's up?

INT. BHAGALPUR HOTEL - DAY

GUDDU

Fucker's buying bananas.

CUT TO:

EXT. BHAGALPUR STREET 1 - DAY

DEFINITE

For whose ass?

CUT TO:

INT. BHAGALPUR HOTEL - DAY

GUDDU

Yours! Just keep kicking the shaft!

CUT TO:

EXT. BHAGALPUR STREET 1 - DAY

DEFINITE

I don't want to break it.
I'll kick it once he's done shopping.

CUT TO:

EXT. BHAGALPUR STREET 2 - DAY

AZEEM

Brother… he's moving.

CUT TO:

EXT. BHAGALPUR STREET 2 - DAY

Azeem follows Sultan.

AZEEM

Guddu he's going into the vegetable market.

CUT TO:

INT. BHAGALPUR HOTEL - DAY

GUDDU

Why's he going to the vegetable market?

Second phone in other hand.

CUT TO:

EXT. BHAGALPUR STREET 1 - DAY

DEFINITE

But I'm not going anywhere.

CUT TO:

INT. BHAGALPUR HOTEL - DAY

GUDDU

I'm not talking to you.

CUT TO:

EXT. BHAGALPUR STREET 2 - DAY

AZEEM

He went into the market.

CUT TO:

INT. BHAGALPUR HOTEL - DAY

GUDDU

Fucking Dumb and Dumber!! I was talking to Definite.

CUT TO:

EXT. BHAGALPUR STREET 1 - DAY

DEFINITE

So talk to one of us at a time. Hello? Bastard disconnected me.

CUT TO:

INT. BHAGALPUR HOTEL - DAY

GUDDU

So what fruit do you get in a vegetable market?

CUT TO:

EXT. BHAGALPUR STREET 2 - DAY

AZEEM

Custard apple?

CUT TO:

INT. BHAGALPUR HOTEL - DAY

GUDDU

Isn't that sugar-apple?

CUT TO:

EXT. BHAGALPUR STREET 2 - DAY | 2004 |

AZEEM

Well … some call it pumpkin.

CUT TO:

EXT. BHAGALPUR STREET 4 - DAY

Third one watches as Sultan buys vegetables…

CUT TO:

INT. BHAGALPUR HOTEL - DAY

Guddu picks up the third phone.

GUDDU

Yes.

CUT TO:

EXT. BHAGALPUR STREET 4 - DAY

THIRD
He's buying jackfruit.

CUT TO:

INT. BHAGALPUR HOTEL - DAY

GUDDU
Jackfruit?

CUT TO:

EXT. BHAGALPUR STREET 4 - DAY

THIRD
Yes, brother.

INT. BHAGALPUR HOTEL - DAY

GUDDU
Now why would he want to buy jackfruit??

CUT TO:

EXT. BHAGALPUR STREET 4 - DAY

THIRD
I feel … he wants to pickle it.

CUT TO:

INT. BHAGALPUR HOTEL - DAY

GUDDU
Can't one make a curry out of it?

CUT TO:

EXT. BHAGALPUR STREET 4 - DAY

THIRD
Sure. My mother makes mean jackfruit balls!

CUT TO:

INT. BHAGALPUR HOTEL - DAY

GUDDU
My granny used to fry finely chopped jackfruit and serve it with rice.

CUT TO:

EXT. BHAGALPUR STREET 4 - DAY

THIRD
Don't Brahmins consider it their 'meat'?

CUT TO:

INT. BHAGALPUR HOTEL - DAY

Guddu's phone rings...

GUDDU
What's up?

CUT TO:

EXT. BHAGALPUR STREET 1 - DAY

DEFINITE
I've been calling you for eons, you deaf fuck!

CUT TO:

INT. BHAGALPUR HOTEL - DAY

GUDDU
But you asked me to speak to only one.

CUT TO:

EXT. BHAGALPUR STREET 1 - DAY

DEFINITE
So talk to me, fuckwit. I'm suffering in this heat...

CUT TO:

EXT. BHAGALPUR STREET 1 - DAY

Third sees SULTAN leave...

THIRD
Sultan's moving.

CUT TO:

INT. BHAGALPUR HOTEL - DAY

GUDDU
But this was your idea...

CUT TO:

EXT. BHAGALPUR STREET 1 - DAY

THIRD

Hello

CUT TO:

EXT. BHAGALPUR STREET 1 - DAY

DEFINITE

There's an aquarium inside my fucking helmet.

CUT TO:

INT. BHAGALPUR HOTEL - DAY

GUDDU

Don't threaten me.

EXT. BHAGALPUR STREET 1 - DAY

Third follows Sultan. Sultan throws stuff in a Maruti and starts it.

THIRD

Sultan's in the car!

Cuts the phone … Dials again…

CUT TO:

INT. BHAGALPUR HOTEL - DAY

GUDDU

Then chuck the helmet. Show that pretty face to the world… come on!

CUT TO:

EXT. BHAGALPUR STREET 1 - DAY

Definite take off his helmet. Behind him in a maruti…

CUT TO:

INT. BHAGALPUR HOTEL - DAY

Guddu's phone rings…

CUT TO:

EXT. BHAGALPUR STREET 4 - DAY

THIRD
He's right behind Definite.

CUT TO:

EXT. BHAGALPUR STREET 1 - DAY
Maruti honks…

DEFINITE
Shut up!

He turns…

CUT TO:

INT. BHAGALPUR HOTEL - DAY

GUDDU
He's behind you.

CUT TO:

EXT. BHAGALPUR STREET 1 - DAY

DEFINITE
No, he's in front of me.

They stare at each other. Definite goes for the gun. Definite firing… Third boy comes firing at him… Definite keeps shooting. Shakes Sultan to check if he's dead. They leave.

CUT TO:

EXT. POLICE STATION - DAY
Definite walks into the police station and surrenders.

NASIR (V.O.)
After Sultan's death Faizal had no threats in Wasseypur. Danish, his widow, Nagma, Asgar … Definite had avenged them all. To cement Definite's lethal reputation, Faizal asked him to surrender. Ramadhir was also watching this keenly.

CUT TO:

EXT. RAMADHIR'S HOUSE 2 - DAY

NASIR (V.O.)
Ever since Definite was a child, Ramadhir had hoped to make him his weapon. But Definite was untamable. He had no masters. And Sultan's death had made him even more fierce. So Ramadhir used his trump card...Durga!

Durga comes to Ramadhir's rest house.

CUT TO:

INT. RAMADHIR'S HOUSE 2 - DAY

RAMADHIR SINGH
Who took care of you and your son after Sardar's death?

Durga is quiet.

RAMADHIR SINGH (CONT'D)
I'd also given you my word that ... Definite will get what is rightfully his.

DURGA
Don't worry! He'll take it himself.

RAMADHIR SINGH
It's not easy. Definite's not only in jail ... he's also accepted all of Faizal's crimes. Sometimes I feel like he is ... not your son ... as much as Sardar's.

She is quiet.

NASIR (V.O.)
Ramadhir wanted to drive a wedge between Faizal and Definite. All he needed was Faizal's one weakness. And Ramadhir knew which one ... Money ... black money! Whatever the source or amount. Faizal had no business sense. People came to him only out of fear.

Ramadhir took advantage of this. So he first shifted Definite to the state capital prison.

CUT TO:

EXT. ROAD/ POLICE JEEP - DAY
Definite being transferred to Patna jail.

CUT TO:

EXT. ROAD/ CAR - DAY
Durga travels in an ambassador car. The car enters Patna jail.

CUT TO:

INT. JAIL - DAY
Definite sitting in a jail … Durga comes to visit him. Definite looks at her and doesn't speak.

DURGA
Prison is in your blood, isn't it?

DEFINITE
Please leave. I'm fine … without you.

DURGA
I raised a killer, not a coward.

CUT TO:

INT. FAIZAL'S OFFICE - DAY
Faizal is in a discussion with Nasir. Guddu is attending to someone at the door.

FAIZAL
Shamshad's still in hospital and Ramadhir is unarmed.

NASIR
But he's in the capital where you can't touch him.

FAIZAL
He has to return … someday.

Guddu walks in.

NASIR

They've shifted Definite to the capital prison.

FAIZAL

Who told you that?

NASIR

He had called.

FAIZAL

Why didn't he call me?

NASIR

You don't pick up your calls.

FAIZAL

Get me the police station in-charge.

NASIR dials the phone. Guddu intervenes.

GUDDU

Brother...?

FAIZAL

Yes?

GUDDU

Someone's here to see you.

SUPER - 2005

FAIZAL

Let him in.

(On the phone)

Hello! This is Faizal Khan. Why has Definite been shifted to the capital? Definite! I mean the name.

(Keeps hand on phone ... to Nasir)

What's the meaning of 'Definite'?

NASIR

Definite.

FAIZAL

What's his real name?

NASIR
Definite.

FAIZAL
Yeah, but what's his real name?

NASIR
Definite's real name is Definite.

FAIZAL
Guddu, what is Definite's real name?

GUDDU
It is Definite.

FAIZAL
What had dad named him before 'Definite'? You know, like Perpendicular's real name was Babua.

GUDDU
I've always known him as Definite.

FAIZAL
So what's the meaning of the word 'Definite'?

GUDDU
'Definite' is … what is definite?

FAIZAL
So What - is - Definite?

GUDDU
See, 'Def' means deaf…

NASIR
And 'nite' means net!

The guy who's just arrived (Iqlakh) speaks up.

IQLAKH
Definite is that which is certain.

Everyone looks at Iqlakh. Faizal smiles.

NASIR (V.O.)
Neither Faizal nor his gang spoke English.

But Iqlakh did. And Faizal liked that. However, Iqlakh was Ramadhir's mole. He was going to make Faizal pots of money and make him forget about Definite.

CUT TO:

INT. FAIZAL'S OFFICE - DAY

Iqlakh and Faizal eat together as Mohsina serves.

IQLAKH

Indian trains often get de-railed. Ever wondered where these trains go? The government auctions these trains but at rates that are 40 years old. Now an old compartment is valueless. But if one breaks it down to its components, its value multiplies. The tyres, springs and sheets sell separately and the rest can be melted down to make pipes. And that's how a whole train gets auctioned. From the Internet to any government commodity, it's all auctioned. Bidders come from all over the country for this…and it all takes place right here in Dhanbad.

NASIR (V.O.)

But Iqlakh also had a past.

CUT TO:

FLASHBACK FROM PART 1-

SUPER - 1985

Shot of girl being kidnapped from the street by 4 men.

Shot of wedding between the girl and the kidnapper while Sardar and Asgar watch.

JP hands over a briefcase of money to Sardar.

NASIR (V.O.)

20 years ago, his father had abducted and raped a Wasseypur girl. Sardar had forced him

to divorce his first wife to marry this girl. Iqlakh was Mohsin's son from the abandoned first wife.

CUT TO:

INT. FAIZAL'S OFFICE - NIGHT

Guddu and Faizal are walking down the stairs.

FAIZAL

How can Iqlakh be Ramadhir's guy? He's an educated city-slicker.

GUDDU

Thing is, Iqlakh was left fatherless because of your dad … while Ramadhir supported and educated him.

Faizal thinks.

CUT TO:

INT. AUCTION ROOM - DAY

An auction officer is conducting the auction of railway scrap.

AUCTION OFFICER

And here is the result for the tender issued on…

Iqlakh and Ashfaque walk in with Guddu.

NASIR (V.O.)

But Faizal had bought into Iqlakh's vision. Auction officer continues announcing result of the auction

NASIR (V.O.)

His ambition now included all of Dhanbad.

Iqlakh and Guddu take centre stage. The auction officer stops announcement. Iqlakh takes the mike.

NASIR (V.O.)

And so he chose to overlook Iqlakh's past.

IQHLAKH

I've been sent by Faizal Khan. And from now we will run a syndicate here. All bids will go through Faizal Khan. And only he will approve who gets the tender.

Someone objects from the audience. Guddu slaps him.

SOMEONE 1

What the hell?

SOMEONE 2

This is hooliganism!

GUDDU

Sit…!!

IQHLAKH

Any other issues?

SOMEONE 3

You can't bully us like this!

Guddu takes out his gun. Loads it and fires in the air.

Silence.

IQHLAKH

You may now leave your quotations here and go.

Guddu starts collecting their bids.

CUT TO:

INT. FAIZAL KHAN'S OFFICE - DAY

MONTAGE.

NASIR (V.O.)

Iqlakh first made Faizal a fearful figure amongst the traders. He then took control of the Auction Room.

CUT TO:

EXT. RAIL YARD - DAY

Faizal pays off railway officers.

NASIR (V.O.)

And before the next auctions Faizal himself bribed railway officials.

CUT TO:

EXT. SKYLARK HOTEL - CORRIDOR. DAY

Shot of Skylark hotel. Faizal walks through the corridor with Iqlakh and Guddu.

IQLAKH

All you need to do is tell them I'm your guy.

CUT TO:

EXT. SKYLARK HOTEL - CONFERENCE ROOM. DAY

Faizal in room full of people…

FAIZAL

The auction will be led by Iqlakh. And his word will be the final one. And all of you will submit to him. Cool?

CUT TO:

EXT. SKYLARK HOTEL - CORRIDOR. DAY

Faizal walks back with Iqlakh and Guddu after the meeting.

IQLAKH

You said 'submit' instead of 'stand by'.

FAIZAL

What is 'stand by'?

IQLAKH

Total support.

FAIZAL

So what's 'submit'?

IQLAKH

Total surrender.

FAIZAL
So I was right.

CUT TO:

INT. INTERNET CAFE - DAY

Iqlakh and Ashfaque are participating in an auction on a computer.

NASIR (V.O.)
To break this syndicate, the government started auctioning on the Internet.

CUT TO:

INT. MUMBAI INTERNET CAFÉ - DAY

Some men are trading on the Internet. Someone amongst them wins an auction.

NASIR (V.O.)
So the bids became faceless and the bidders didn't fear the syndicate.

CUT TO:

INT. IQLAKH OFFICE - DAY

Auctioneer 1 comes in…

AUCTIONEER 1
The Auction's done.

IQLAKH
When?

AUCTIONEER 1
The bastards did it on the internet.

Phone rings…

CUT TO:

AUCTIONEER 2 (on phone)
The auction is over, brother. Some guy from Gujarat got the tender.

IQLAKH
Well, guess where he'll have to come to collect the goods?

CUT TO:

EXT. RANCHI AIRPORT. DAY

A man comes out, gets into a taxi. Guddu follows his taxi in another car.

CUT TO:

EXT. RANCHI ROAD. DAY

Taxi stops...driver gets out to take a leak ... Guddu gets out from the following car under the pretence of wanting to take a leak too.

GUDDU

Salaam!

Guddu then takes out his gun and kidnaps the business man at gunpoint.

CUT TO:

INT. SKYLARK HOTEL - DAY

Man tied and tortured...

BUSINESS MAN

What do you want?

Iqlakh walks in with some documents.

IQLAKH

Sign here please.

NASIR (V.O.)

And thus things stayed in Faizal's control.

CUT TO:

INT. BOAT - NIGHT

Faizal is entertaining some officer with wine women and money.

NASIR (V.O.)

... and he made pots of money. His power over the auctions and railways opened a goldmine of wealth.

CUT TO:

INT. FAIZAL'S OFFICE - DAY

Iqlakh puts money in front of Faizal.

NASIR (V.O.)

Eventually Faizal became blind with power and black money.

CUT TO:

INT. PATNA JAIL - DAY

Shot of Definite in jail.

NASIR (V.O.)

Just like Ramadhir had wanted. Definite was left rotting in jail.

CUT TO:

EXT. PATNA JAIL - DAY

Definite is trying to make a phone call.

CUT TO:

INT. FAIZAL'S OFFICE - DAY

Iqlakh talks to Faizal.

IQLAKH

It's all about people's power! Everyone respects you here since you've opened a school.

Faizal looks at him.

IQLAKH (CONT'D)

If you represent Wasseypur in these elections you will surely win. No one can touch you then.

Faizal listens to him.

IQLAKH (CONT'D)

In fact, stand as an independent candidate and win. Then any party will want an alliance with you. Once that happens you can openly dictate!

FAIZAL

What if I contest against Ramadhir from Dhanbad, and not Wasseypur?

Iqlakh looks at him.

CUT TO:

INT. RAMADHIR'S OFFICE - DAY

Ramadhir Singh sits talking to Iqlakh… He smiles.

RAMADHIR SINGH

He'll contest from Dhanbad? Against me?

Silence. He looks at JP.

RAMADHIR SINGH (CONT'D)

Find out what his plans are.

J.P. SINGH

Yes Father.

CUT TO:

EXT. RAMADHIR'S OFFICE - DAY

Iqlakh and Ashfaque exit the building … Get into a maruti …

Drive off.

CUT TO:

INT. RAMADHIR'S OFFICE - DAY

Ramadhir Singh sits with JP and Ghanshyam. He looks concerned. He signals JP to go for some errand. JP nods and leaves.

J.P. SINGH

Get the car.

CUT TO:

EXT. PATNA JAIL - DAY

Definite is brought out of the jail by some policemen. A jeep waits outside the jail … Definite sits in it … Jeep drives off.

NASIR (V.O.)
Now Ramadhir got Definite released from jail and sent JP to meet him.

CUT TO:

EXT. STREETS - DAY

J.P. Singh travels in a car through the streets.

NASIR (V.O.)
But JP's agenda was not so much Faizal as much as his own father. He knew that only one man could remove Ramadhir out of his way.

Music stops.

CUT TO:

INT. RAMADHIR'S CIRCUIT HOUSE - NIGHT

Definite eats non-vegetarian food. J.P. Singh watches him. Two girls sitting opposite Definite ... White women.

J.P. SINGH
Faizal Khan!

DEFINITE
How will you get him to do that?

J.P. SINGH
If you do as I say, it will all fall into place.

DEFINITE
And what do I get?

J.P. SINGH
You get Wasseypur!

DEFINITE
And you get?

Music starts again. JP does not respond. Just smiles. He leaves from there and also ushers one of the women to leave with him.

CUT TO:

INT. RAMADHIR'S CIRCUIT HOUSE - BEDROOM – NIGHT

Definite gets up from the bed in his shorts. A woman is sleeping on the bed. He walks up to the mirror and puts on his trousers. He poses in front of the mirror … looks pleased with himself … and evil.

CUT TO:

EXT. STREETS- DAY

Ramadhir is campaigning for election with JP and others. He is distributing blankets to people. Celebration.

CUT TO:

INT. NOMINATION OFFICE- DAY

Faizal walks in the nomination office with Mohsina, Iqlakh and Guddu. Faizal files his nomination.

CUT TO:

EXT. STREETS- DAY

Posters of Faizal Khan are being pasted over Ramadhir posters. Music stops.

CUT TO:

EXT- WASSEYPUR ROAD / JEEP – DAY

Faizal, Definite and Guddu driving somewhere in a jeep.

DEFINITE

Ramadhir has promised me your land and Wasseypur if I kill you. He's given mom 10 lacs as advance.

FAIZAL

What'd you do?

DEFINITE

I kept the advance.

Faizal laughs.

DEFINITE (CONT'D)

He's asked me to watch you 24 hours and report to him.

FAIZAL

So when's the D-day?

DEFINITE

On the Election day. Iqlakh will kill you. I'm the back-up!

Faizal laughs again. The jeep moves on.

CUT TO:

EXT- WASSEYPUR ROAD- DAY

Caravan of Ramadhir's Ambassador cars are moving on the streets.

CUT TO:

INT. FAIZAL'S HOUSE/ KITCHEN - DAY

Mohsina pukes.

CUT TO:

INT. FAIZAL'S HOUSE - NIGHT

Nasir finishing his Namaaz. Faizal sits alone ... Mohsina comes from behind.

MOHSINA

Faizal? What happened? Tell me...

FAIZAL

Mohsina, You know, I never wanted to get into father's business.

Nasir has now finished his Namaaz. He asks the maid for tea.

NASIR

May I get some tea?

FAIZAL

In fact, I didn't want anything. How did all of this happen?

MOHSINA

It's okay! But you're also getting out of this trap now… aren't you?

FAIZAL

Not if I win these elections - 'cos then I will sink deeper. Father had a chance to not return to Wasseypur. But he came back … and everyone got caught in the quicksand.

MOHSINA

Enough … hey…!

FAIZAL

Ramadhir's story could have ended long back…

MOHSINA

Enough.

FAIZAL

… with Shahid Khan. But that blood bath is still continuing! I don't want any part of this.

Mohsina sings to calm him down.

MOHSINA

Whatever's wrong … Set right whatever's wrong … Don't lose hope, and fight some more, my dear fool.

CUT TO:

EXT. OPEN GROUND - DAY | 2004

Definite sits with large group of young boys, giving them instructions.

DEFINITE

12 of the total 26 polling booths are strongly in our favour. The remaining 14 will be a worry and our main targets. The voting here will be against us and the booths will be full of armed cops.

CUT TO:

EXT. POLLING BOOTH -DAY

A polling booth with a lot of policemen with arms.

DEFINITE (V.O.)

So first, 6 of our shortest guys will enter the booth in burqas.

Boys wearing burqa enter a polling booth, join the voting queue. People are busy casting votes in this booth.

CUT TO:

EXT. MARKET PLACE- DAY

Definite with some boys walk around in the market with guns. They blank fire and blast small bombs.

DEFINITE (V.O.)

Meanwhile, we will open fire in the market

CUT TO:

EXT. POLLING BOOTH 1-DAY

Policemen hear bombing sound and leave from the polling booth.

DEFINITE (V.O.)

… and distract the cops.

Some other boys get into the polling booth in cars.

DEFINITE (V.O.)

You guys attack and capture the booth.

Tangent leads the group…they fire in the air, threaten the voters in queue. Start sending them back. They also push away the media people stationed at the booth.

DEFINITE (V.O.)

Grab the ballot boxes and run, but only if there aren't too many civilians Or pour ink and shake the box… or just burn it.

Boys in burqua get inside the booth and pour ink in a ballot box and shake it.

DEFINITE (V.O.)
Or just burn it.

Tangent and boys pour kerosene in the ballot boxes and light them on fire.

CUT TO:

EXT.STREET 1 -DAY

Definite and his boys threaten and torture people. Bombing and firing all over.

DEFINITE (V.O.)
The rest of you will spread out and riot all day with guns and bombs. Terrorise all the neighbouring areas of the polling booths......so people get scared to even step out.

A family comes out of their house, and Definite and the boys threaten them and send them back in and lock the house.

CUT TO:

EXT.STREET 2-DAY

A polling officer is on an inspection round in his jeep.

DEFINITE (V.O.)
A few of you will only keep an eye on the Polling Officer. When he heads towards us, one of you will inform him:

A man comes running towards his jeep.

BOY 1
Sir, they're firing in the market area booth.

Officer leaves in that direction.

DEFINITE (V.O.)
The officer will rush to that booth through bad roads.

CUT TO:

EXT. STREET 3 -DAY

Officer reaches Pandarpara polling booth and notices everything is under control. He asks the police officer in charge.

POLLING OFFICER

Was there any gun fire her?

POLICE OFFICER INCHARGE

No sir, its peaceful here.

DEFINITE (V.O.)

Just as he realises he's been misinformed, an 'injured' guy will tell him:

A wounded man runs towards him.

WOUNDED MAN

I was at the booth in the college area, they shot us and cast our votes by force.

DEFINITE (V.O.)

And like this, we will keep setting up decoys and capture all 14 booths.

Police and officer leave from there. Tangent and other boys come in cars and burn more ballot boxes forcefully.

TANGENT

Everyone get the fuck out of here.

CUT TO:

EXT. OPEN GROUND - DAY

Definite finishes instructing the boys.

DEFINITE (V.O.)

Make sure Faizal Khan doesn't win!

CUT TO:

EXT- ROAD - DAY

Faizal and Guddu in a jeep with Iqlakh…

FAIZAL (TO GUDDU)
Where's Definite? Call him.

Guddu's phone rings. He picks it up…

GUDDU
Talk of the devil! Hello … We've just stepped out for inspection. Get there fast. Okay.

(He hangs up).

GUDDU
He'll meet us at the booth.

IQLAKH
Brother … how about a quick visit to the shrine first? They say all prayers get answered there.

Faizal looks at Guddu … Guddu is unsure.

FAIZAL
Alright.

CUT TO:

EXT- ROAD- DAY

Jeep turns towards the shrine, followed by other jeeps.

IQLAKH
Does everyone need to come?

GUDDU
I'm sure everyone would like to pray.

IQLAKH
I think more people will mean more time. It's a tiny lane. We'll quickly go and come back.

FAIZAL
Guddu, ask the others to stay back.

Guddu calls Azeem in the following Jeep.

GUDDU
You guys wait at the gate. We'll be back soon.

The other two jeeps stop at the gate.

CUT TO:

EXT- BYLANE - DAY

They stop outside a lane. They get off and walk. Iqlakh is nervous.

FAIZAL

Is this the shrine?

IQLAKH

This one's for the tourists. The real one's ahead.

FAIZAL

Why are you sweating so much?

IQLAKH

It's just … this heat, brother.

As they walk ahead, suddenly Guddu is shot in the shoulder. He falls off.

FAIZAL

Guddu…! Who the fuck shot him?

Iqlakh takes out a gun and points at Faizal.

FAIZAL

What the…?

Guddu points the gun at Iqlakh. He shoots but misses him. Iqlakh hides on the other side of the wall. Guddu's bullet almost hits Faizal. Faizal scolds him.

FAIZAL

Guddu, you're shooting me…

Faizal is angry at Iqlakh and shoots at him. Iqlakh doesn't get hit.

FAIZAL

Iqlakh, motherfucker!

Iqlakh shoots back. Faizal hides.

FAIZAL
Want to kill me, (smiles) motherfucker?

IQLAKH
Oh, I won't.

FAIZAL
Then who will?

Definite runs closer to Iqlakh.

FAIZAL
So who'll kill me. Tell me, motherfucker…

Definite joins Iqlakh from behind.

DEFINITE
Where is he?

IQLAKH
They're behind the wall.

Definite shoots Iqlakh. He falls.

DEFINITE
Come out, brother. Nobody will kill you now.

He walks to Iqlakh and puts more bullets in him. Faizal comes out.

FAIZAL
Where the fuck were you, asshole? Someone shot Guddu.

DEFINITE
That was my mistake, brother. Their shirts were so similar, I shot Guddu mistaking him for Iqlakh. This was the best time to kill him.

FAIZAL
But who changed the plan?

DEFINITE
Ramadhir, who else!

FAIZAL
Let's go.

DEFINITE

He will be at the hospital.

FAIZAL

Let's go to the hospital.

DEFINITE

But he's scheduled to come to the circuit house at...

FAIZAL

Fuck his schedule!

Faizal walks. Definite picks Guddu and they go.

GUDDU

Watch before you shoot, bugger!

CUT TO:

FAIZAL'S HOUSE - DAY

Faizal and his men take out weapons from the office and load them on an ambulance. Mohsina and Nasir run up to him. Nasir watches.

MOHSINA

Faizal, what the hell is this?

He is quiet.

MOHSINA

You said you were going to quit!

FAIZAL

Let me go today ... I promise I'll quit tomorrow.

MOHSINA

You need to be alive to quit.

FAIZAL

I swear on you, I'll come back alive.

MOHSINA

(starts to cry)

Faizal, please don't go.

He pushes her.

MOHSINA

I am pregnant.

Faizal takes in the news.

FAIZAL

Tell the baby his father says 'hello'!

Faizal sits on the in the ambulance. Definite gets in the driver seat. Starts the ambulance. They leave. She cries. Nasir holds her.

CUT TO:

EXT. FAIZAL'S HOUSE /ROAD - DAY

Faizal, Definite, Tangent and Guddu are in the ambulance. Guddu is bandaged crudely and is sitting behind. Two jeeps follow. Faizal sees them.

FAIZAL

Why are our guys following us? Hey, Guddu … Tell them we don't need them.

GUDDU

But we might, brother.

FAIZAL

Faizal Khan doesn't need anyone's protection.

Guddu calls Azeem.

GUDDU

You guys don't have to cover us. 'Cos brother says so, fucker.

The other jeeps turn back. Faizal asks Definite for his phone and dials a number.

FAIZAL

No one will shoot. Every single bullet in Ramadhir's body will be mine.

I/C

INT. HOSPITAL- WARD - DAY

Ramadhir with Shamshad at the hospital.

SHAMSHAD

They're saying another 15 days here.

Ramadhir's phone rings...

RAMADHIR SINGH

Hello.

I/C

INT. AMBULANCE - DAY

DEFINITE

Greetings, sir. Faizal Khan is history. But in the process Guddu killed Iqlakh. So I had to kill Guddu too.

I/C

INT. HOSPITAL. WARD - DAY

Ramadhir gets up. Ramadhir walks to the window and looks out.

RAMADHIR SINGH

Where's his dead body?

DEFINITE

I'm on my way to the hospital. The bodies are with me in an ambulance.

He nods at Faizal to indicate the call is over. Faizal removes the phone from his ear.

CUT TO:

EXT. WASSEYPUR ROAD - DAY

Ambulance moves on the road.

CUT TO:

EXT. HOSPITAL - DAY

Ambulance comes to the hospital. Ghanshyam is waiting downstairs. He's on the phone. As soon as he sees the ambulance, he informs on the phone.

GHANSHYAM

Yes, he's here.

Definite gets down and sees Ghanshyam.

DEFINITE

They're in there.

Definite loads his gun. Ghanshyam comes to the ambulance, stiil on the phone, and opens it. He gets fired at. Ramadhir hears gunshots on the phone, doesn't understand. Faizal and others come out of the ambulance. Ramadhir's men lock the main door of the hospital from inside. Faizal starts shooting. He shoots the door open. The public runs away scared.

I/C

INT. HOSPITAL. WARD - DAY

Ramadhir is still listening on the phone. He also overhears gunfire and scared people in the hospital.

RAMADHIR SINGH

Hello?

Someone shouts.

SOMEONE

They're firing outside!

Ramadhir calls his men on the phone.

RAMADHIR SINGH

Stay alert! Keep your guns handy.

CUT TO:

EXT/ INT. HOSPITAL - DAY

Faizal breaks open the door. Hands a gun to Definite.

FAIZAL

Hold this.

Faizal enters the hospital and checks in all rooms. He signals to Definite not to fire. Some of Ramadhir's men fire at him. Definite counter fires. Faizal gets angry at this and slaps him.

FAIZAL

Definite...!

Shoot out continues. Faizal finds Shamshad lying in one of the rooms. He shoots at Shamshad. He scares off all other patients and staff from the rooms. Shoot out continues till he finds to Ramadhir. Police arrive outside. Tangent and Guddu shoot at the police to hold them back. Eventually Tangent and Guddu both lose their lives. Faizal shoots Ramadhir. Definite keeps supplying him with more and more guns. Faizal keeps pumping him with bullets. Till police arrests him and Definite.

CUT TO:

EXT. HIGHWAY - DAY

Three police jeeps travel through the highway. Both Faizal and Definite in the jeep... Arrested.

CUT TO:

EXT. SOMEPLACE - DAY

The caravan of police vehicle stops.

COP

Want some tea?

DEFINITE

I'll have some.

COP

Bring him outside.

A constable gets down ... open Definite's cuffs and lets him out. They take Definite out, cuffed in one hand ... We stay with Faizal ... Focus stays on Faizal. We see the rest of them blurred behind him ... we see a blur walk back. Faizal gets shot. He looks ... Definite pointing the gun at him. Definite shoots him ... Faizal dies ... He falls back. In the background we see J.P. Singh thanking the cop. Durga is also there. Definite walks up to Durga.

CUT TO:

MUMBAI - HOUSE NEXT TO RAILWAY TRACKS - DAY

SUPER - MUMBAI 2009

Mohsina is drying clothes on a clothesline, on the terrace of a house. A small boy is playing around her. Nasir comes up and picks up the boy.

NASIR (V.O.)

We left Wasseypur. Mohsina wanted us to shift to Bombay. Wasseypur was not affected by either Faizal or Ramadhir's deaths. It was a battlefield then, like it is today … and will perhaps always remain one.

THE END

Acknowledgements

It took all of half an hour for Shantanu Ray Chaudhuri to say 'yes' to our idea. Thank you, Shantanu.

For the building blocks of the book and going back and forth through their memories, we thank Anubhuti Kashyap (associate director), Neeraj Ghaywan (second AD), Shlok Sharma (second unit director), Vicky Kaushal (AD), Zeishan Quadri (story and script) and Akhilesh Jaiswal (story and script), Shweta Venkat (editor), Sneha Khanvilkar (music director), Varun Grover (lyricist), Mukesh Chhabra (casting director) and Kunal Sharma (sound design).

The actors who broke open their characters for us: we thank Richa Chadda, Manoj Bajpai, Piyush Mishra, Tigmanshu Dhulia, Pankaj Tripathi, Nawazuddin Siddiqui.

For getting our messages to Anurag, thank you Murari Kumar and Abhinav.

For the images used in the book, thank you Ketan Mehta, Soumyajit Nandy and Vasan Bala.

Special thanks to Hansal Mehta and Vikramaditya Motwane for their special appearances in the book.

Thanks to our in-house beta readers K. Bala and Priyanka Kothari.

and

Anurag Kashyap, thank you for letting us tell this story…